CW01337801

FISHERMAN'S GUIDE
FISHES OF
THE SOUTHEASTERN
UNITED STATES

FISHERMAN'S GUIDE

FISHES OF THE SOUTHEASTERN UNITED STATES

BY CHARLES S. MANOOCH, III

ILLUSTRATED BY DUANE RAVER, JR.

FIRST PUBLISHED BY THE NORTH CAROLINA STATE MUSEUM OF NATURAL HISTORY IN 1984

FISHERMAN'S GUIDE TO THE FISHES OF THE SOUTHEASTERN UNITED STATES is published by the Raver and Manooch Partnership

Fourth Printing 2007
Copyright © 1984 Charles S. Manooch, III and Duane Raver, Jr.
Designed by Ellen Kirven Johnson
All Rights Reserved
Library of Congress Catalog Card Number: 84-60641
ISBN: 978-0-917134-07-4
Published by Raver and Manooch Partnership

Printed in the United States

Some of the scientific names of fish featured in this book have changed since the first printing in 1984. The current scientific names are listed below in order as featured in the text:

Rainbow Trout	*Oncorhynchus mykiss*
Walleye	*Sander vitreus*
White Catfish	*Ameiurus catus*
Yellow Bullhead	*Ameiurus natalis*
Brown Bullhead	*Ameiurus nebulosus*
Spottail Pinfish	*Diplodus holbrookii*
Skipjack Tuna	*Katsuwonus pelamis*

To Order Book

Raver and Manooch
2900 Dogwood Lane
Morehead City, NC 28557
252-726-4711
cmanooch@starfishnet.com
-or-
50 Beech Trail
Garner, NC 27529
919-550-9873

This book is lovingly dedicated to those
who have made my memories pleasant, and who give me
hope and happy anticipation for the future.
To
Rebecca, Sam, and Alexandra

**In Memory of
Genevieve Jeffreys Manooch
and
Ann Bowman Manooch**

PREFACE

Fishery scientist Dr. Charles Manooch, III, and artist Duane Raver, Jr., have teamed up to create what is sure to become the Bible of fresh- and saltwater angling and commercial fishing in southeastern Atlantic coastal states. The book is remarkable for its breadth of coverage and clarity of prose. Anglers, commercial fishermen, nature lovers, and devotees to wildlife art are sure to find hours of enjoyment between the book's covers. For the tactical angler, Charles Manooch provides tips on how, when, and where to catch fish. For those who enjoy cooking what they catch, the book contains a number of tasty recipes.

Relatively few authors of natural history books have depicted the southeastern Atlantic salt- and freshwater fishes. None have addressed a broad audience in such understandable terms. Yet it is the southeastern fishes, especially marine species, that are understood least by anglers. Even scientists readily admit a lack of knowledge on the ecology and management of these economically and recreationally important species.

In 1982, commercial landings of fish in the Chesapeake Bay and South Atlantic region were valued at nearly $3 million, and the catch totaled 1.2 billion pounds. The region accounted for 19% of the total U.S. harvest and 13% of the total value of the catch. Landings at the port of Beaufort-Morehead City, North Carolina, ranked seventh in the nation. On the average, each American consumes about 35 pounds of fish annually. For the Southeast that means a tremendous market for a commercial harvest of species such as Striped Bass, King and Spanish Mackerel, shrimp, crabs, and Red Snapper.

Recreational fishing in the Southeast provides enormous economic benefits but in addition it offers tremendous sport. In the states covered by Manooch and Raver, an estimated 8.5 million anglers fish both salt and fresh water. For anglers over 15 years of age, over 100 million days are spent freshwater fishing and 50 million days are spent fishing salt water. Because anglers spend about $20 (1980 currency) per day on fishing, the economy of the Southeast receives an over $1 billion boost each year as a result of the recreational fisheries.

Commercial and recreational fishing also means jobs in the Southeast. Over one thousand fish processors and wholesalers employ an average 14,460 workers throughout the southeastern region.

The great value of southeastern fisheries to anglers, commercial fishermen, and local economies, is tied directly to the quantity and quality of fishery habitat. For example, in Glynn County, Georgia, where 95,000 acres of estuarine habitat support an annual catch of 100 million pounds of fish, wetlands are valued at between $2,500 and $4,000 per acre for fishery production alone.

Notwithstanding the value of coastal and inland habitat to fisheries production, major losses of habitat are threatening fisheries throughout our nation and the Southeast is certainly no exception. Over one million acres of coastal wetlands have been lost nationwide in the last 20 years, with present losses estimated at just under a half-million acres yearly. A third of North Carolina's 2.3 million acres of pocosin wetlands were converted to non-wetland uses between 1962 and 1979, and another third is now being drained, cleared, or planned for development. By 1973, about 70% of southern Florida's wetlands had been lost. In Delaware over the last 30 years at least 7,500 marshland acres have been lost to residential and commercial development, and pollution continues to poison fish habitat throughout much of the Delaware Bay. Vast areas in the southeastern states are highly susceptible to the devastating effects of acid rain. And, the potential for habitat damage continues to grow as paper mills, oil refineries, beachfront communities, etc., continue to multiply.

Many readers will discover new knowledge and some may find greater enjoyment in the pastime of fishing. I hope, too, that you gain a new respect for our great southeastern fishery resources. Perhaps you will feel a sense of awe over the magnitude, and yet fragility, of these resources. But whatever your feelings after reading this book, please enjoy our magnificent fisheries, and also please remember we hold our fisheries and their habitats under our control — and our control can be for better or it can be for worse.

Washington, D.C.

Jay D. Hair
Executive Vice President
National Wildlife Federation

CONTENTS

INTRODUCTION

Most of us at one time or another have wanted to know more about fish. Whether we fish for fun, profit, or just enjoy studying nature's creations, we have an urge to recognize a species of fish by name and to share with others our knowledge of its natural history.

To catch fish regularly, we must know when and where different fishes occur, and certain basic facts about their life histories, such as what they eat, their spawning behavior, and their migrations. Many books provide some of this information. For the average fisherman, most of them are too highly technical, lack vivid color illustrations and descriptive discussions, or are too restricted in the fishes they cover. This book, although limited to the southeastern United States, includes freshwater and saltwater species that are most important to fishermen. Thus it is not a complete taxonomic presentation of all the fishes inhabiting the region, but rather a compendium of those that are most frequently caught. Each species is depicted by an artist's full-color painting and is accompanied by an up-to-date commentary and range map. For many, this book offers the first species account written for the general public. The Vermilion Snapper, for example, is very important to fishermen, yet in no other book may one find a color plate of the species, read about its life history, and learn how to catch it.

The geographic coverage is from Delaware to Cape Canaveral, Florida, including Delaware, Maryland, Virginia, North Carolina, South Carolina, Georgia, and northern Florida. This region contains a broad spectrum of fishes ranging from those found in cold mountain streams to those inhabiting offshore ocean waters. Fish illustrations and discussions are presented by a fishing situation basis: cold fresh water, cool fresh water, warm fresh water, anadromous-upper estuarine, coastal ground, coastal pelagic, offshore reefs, and oceanic pelagic. In other words, if one is fishing in warm fresh water such as in a lake, pond or river, one will find all the species likely to be caught in that environment discussed consecutively in familial phylogenetic order, or by evolutionary development, from the most primitive to the most recent.

Unfortunately, fish do not recognize these proposed fishing zones, and are not content to stay put as though they were fenced in. You may catch a species in an area totally unlike that described as its usual habitat. The White Perch is a good example. Throughout much of the country it is found in large lakes and reservoirs. However, in the southeastern United States most are caught in low-salinity sounds and coastal rivers. Thus, for readers of this book, we place it in the anadromous- upper estuarine category.

Preceding the discussion and color plate is the accepted common name of the fish, its scientific name, and localized common names. Unlike most fisheries-related publications, this book capitalizes the accepted common name. This enables the reader to identify a particular fish quickly and to distinguish easily between species names and generic terms, such as gar or bass, that refer to several closely related species. The text is divided into three major headings: **Habits**, **Fishing**, and **Preparation**.

The **Habits** section contains a physical description of the fish and explains how it differs from those it most closely resembles; states its geographical range and habitat; and summarizes knowledge of reproduction (e.g. age at maturity, spawning season, spawning behavior, number of eggs produced, incubation time), age and growth, longevity, and feeding habits. When foods of the various fishes are discussed, the reader should understand that the dietary items listed were identified in scientific studies, and the foods listed are not necessarily the only ones the fish eat. Fish lengths are always given as total lengths, measured from the tip of the snout to the tip of the tail, unless otherwise stated. Under the **Fishing** heading, the reader will learn the importance of the species to sport and commercial fishermen, and how, when, and where the fish is usually caught. The **Preparation** section details the edibility of the fish and suggests some basic methods of preparing it for the table, particularly as they apply to the region.

Because the color plates in this book are a significant contribution to ichthyology as well as esthetically pleasing renditions of the fish, it is appropriate briefly to discuss fish colors and how the illustrations were prepared. Readers should remember that most fish change color radically very shortly after they are dead. The various hues that one sees in living fishes are displayed for a short period of time after landing and we may actually remember only the relatively faded shades seen long after the fish has been removed from the water. Even in life, a single fish may show many different color patterns at different times due to clarity of the water, color and type of bottom, or spawning intensity. Color may reflect the mood of the fish. Dolphin, for example, frequently change from a pale silver-green when quiet and undisturbed, to a vivid neon green or blue when hooked or feeding. Color patterns may change while the fish is being landed. In addition, regional and time of day differences in coloration occur. Fluctuations in color present the fish illustrator with problems that are virtually impossible to overcome. The color plates in this book represent each fish as it usually appears either in the water or just after it has been caught. Thus great care was taken by the artist to select hues most often seen by fishermen.

As an assistance to the reader, a distribution map is provided for each species. The objective is to identify areas where a particular fish is most likely to be caught. Therefore, the range map is applicable to fishing and does not attempt to pinpoint every location where the species has been collected. This approach somewhat reduces the problem of constant changes in distribution that results from introductions, dwindling habitat, and species being recorded from unusual or inadequately studied areas.

It is difficult to write a book such as this without using terms that may be unfamiliar to the general reader. To compensate for this, each such term is defined in a Glossary, and some are presented graphically on an anatomical drawing of a hypothetical fish. To encourage further reading on fish and fishing, a Bibliography is included which lists the references used to compile the text. Each is numbered for your convenience, and may be identified by its number under **Suggested Readings** following each species account. In addition to those cited, information on sport fishing was obtained from many excellent articles in *Outdoor Life*, *Field and Stream*, and *Salt Water Sportsman* magazines.

It has been said that the quality of life is reflected by the quality of fishing. There is a great deal of truth in this. We are fortunate to live in a country where fish are thought of not only as a source of food, but also as a source of recreation. Sport fishing, an attractive leisure pastime for millions of Americans each year, is an unaffordable privilege in many parts of the world. We have been told that of all the groups of vertebrate animals on earth, we know the least about fish. For those who study fish as a profession or just for fun, something new and exciting is waiting to be discovered in every lake, stream, estuary, or sea. I trust that this book will offer an informative, beautiful display of those fish most frequently encountered as inhabitants of their watery world or as delicious and nutritious food on our dining-room tables.

The production of this book was aided by the dedicated efforts of many people to whom gratitude is expressed. John Funderburg, David Lee, Eloise Potter, and Cathy Wood of the North Carolina State Museum of Natural History, Raleigh, assisted us with preliminary drafts of the manuscript. John Reintjes, Morehead City, North Carolina, offered technical suggestions, and Diane L. Mason, Beaufort, North Carolina, supplied many of the reference materials. Special appreciation is extended to Carter Gilbert, University of Florida, Gainesville, who provided a very thorough, technical review of the book, and to Frank J. Schwartz, University of North Carolina Institute of Marine Sciences, Morehead City, who offered suggestions on marine fish distributions. The efforts of Ann Bowman Hall, Morehead City, who spent many hours proofing various editions of the manuscript, and who made numerous helpful suggestions instrumental in the publication of the book are greatly appreciated.

Charles S. Manooch, III

COLD
FRESHWATER FISHES

SEA LAMPREY
Petromyzon marinus

Lamprey

Habits. The Sea Lamprey is a grotesque, eel-shaped fish that is parasitic on other fishes as an adult. It uses its suctorial mouth and rasping teeth to attach to prey, suck their blood, and cause large ulcerous sores, which may lead to death. The Sea Lamprey is the most common of eight species of lampreys found in the region and is by far the largest, attaining a maximum length of 4 feet. The other species, only 5 to 12 inches long, belong to two genera: *Ichthyomyzon* (Ohio Lamprey, Chestnut Lamprey, Southern Brook Lamprey, and Allegheny Brook Lamprey), and *Lampetra* (Least Brook Lamprey, American Brook Lamprey, and Gulf Brook Lamprey).

Lampreys are among the most primitive of all living fishes and have skeletons consisting of cartilaginous material instead of bone. Sea Lamprey were originally anadromous, distributed in coastal rivers and streams on both sides of the northern Atlantic. In North America today, the species ranges from Labrador to northeastern Florida and westward through New York and the Great Lakes, where it has become landlocked. Color varies with size and sexual development, and between anadromous and landlocked populations. Generally, the young (ammocoetes) and small adults are pale gray-blue above and lighter on the undersides. Larger, nonspawning adults are marbled dark brown to black, whereas those in spawning condition are mottled rusty brown.

In the early spring when waters are approximately 40°F, anadromous Sea Lamprey begin to ascend coastal rivers and streams to locate suitable spawning grounds, sometimes as far inland as 200 miles. Landlocked Sea Lamprey also migrate, but over much shorter distances. The species is able to negotiate almost vertical barriers, up to 6 feet high, by using their sucker-like mouths to pull them slowly upward. Once on the spawning grounds, males select rubble-strewn areas to build nests where the water has a moderate current and is 1 to 2 feet deep. Egg laying begins when the water temperature is 52° to 53°F and peaks at 58° to 60°F. Between 34 and 240 thousand adhesive eggs are deposited in batches of 20 to 40 each.

Spawning completed, the exhausted, emaciated adults drop downstream and die. Meanwhile, the eggs hatch in about 2 weeks and the ammocoetes, as the young are called, drift downstream to seek refuge in the silty sediments of backwater pools and eddies. During this 4- to 7-year period of their lives, Sea Lamprey are not parasitic, but filter-feed on small plants and animals. Growth for the ammocoete stage is

2

slow—attaining only 1.5 inches the first year and about 5 inches at the end of the fifth—compared with rapid growth once the fish become parasitic. Adults are aided in their feeding by a secretion, lamphredin, which prevents the victim's blood from clotting and also renders muscle tissue into a more digestible form.

Fishing. The Sea Lamprey is considered a delicacy food item in Europe, where it is harvested commercially, but is usually despised in North America as a destroyer of populations of commercial and recreational fishes. In the Great Lakes, Sea Lamprey developed large populations in short periods during the 1940s and caused the decline of important stocks such as Lake Trout and whitefishes.

Electrical weirs were successfully employed to block upstream migrations, and selective poisons were used to kill the young. Today, Sea Lamprey populations are smaller and therefore not as destructive as in the past. The ammocoetes are often sold as live bait.

Preparation. Sea Lamprey are eaten fresh, salted, and canned in Europe. The flesh is usually prepared by frying or smoking.

Suggested Readings. 78, 133.

RAINBOW TROUT
Salmo gairdneri

Steelhead, Rainbow

Habits. Trout fishermen in the southeastern United States are thankful for the Rainbow Trout, for without this species, trout fishing in the South would be much reduced. Rainbow were originally native only to the west of the Rocky Mountains, but have been stocked throughout the United States, including cold waters of the Atlantic Coast States. As early as the 1870s introductions were made on all the major continents.

There are two major groups of American *Salmo gairdneri*: the large silvery Steelhead anadromous along the Pacific Coast; and the smaller, vividly colored, heavily spotted fish found in rivers and streams east of the Rockies. Rainbow prefer waters that are less than 70°F. They are a deep olive-green on the back with bluish-silver sides and white underparts. The back, upper sides, and dorsal and tail fins are flecked with many small black spots. Rainbow Trout derive their common name from the broad pink to red band extending along the side from cheek to tail.

Rainbow Trout spawn in riffles and pools of moderate-gradient streams from February through June, and as late as August at higher elevations. Age at sexual maturity ranges from 1 to 5 years, with males maturing earlier than females, some at age 1 or 2. Nonanadromous fish spawn at age 3; Steelhead mature at 3 to 5 years. During the spawning season, Steelhead may migrate hundreds of miles, but nonanadromous fish move upstream for distances less than 30 miles. Females select nesting sites and dig redds several inches to more than a foot in depth by turning on their sides and dislodging gravel with tail movements. Rainbow spawn one time each year, laying from 0.2 to 9 thousand eggs. The eggs, covered with gravel and left unattended, hatch in 80 days at 40°F, in 31 days at 50°F, and in about 19 days at 60°F.

Like other fishes, Rainbow Trout grow at different rates depending on water temperature, food availability, and genetic characteristics. Average lengths for nonanadromous Rainbow Trout aged 1 to 7 years are 3.5, 8.1, 11.8, 15.1, 17.5, 17.8, and 18.2 inches. A 10-inch Rainbow weighs about half a pound; a 20-inch fish 3 to 4 pounds; and a 30-inch fish 9 to 12 pounds. The largest Rainbow caught on hook and line weighed 42 pounds; the largest caught commercially was 52 pounds. The diet consists of insects, crayfish, fishes, and fish eggs. Short duration, heavy intensity feeding is usually initiated by the emergence of aquatic insects.

Fishing. Rainbow are excellent game fish on fly rods and light spinning tackle. They are more wary than Brook Trout and successful angling requires skill. When feeding, Rainbows will rise to expertly presented flies as well as to larger artificials such as spoons and spinners. Proven flies are Pale Evening Dunn, Light Cahill, Adams, and Greenwall's Glory. On spinning tackle, Mepps spinners, Rooster Tails, and Colorado spinners with Woolly Worms are good baits. A fly-fishing outfit might include a 7- to 9-foot rod, single action reel with a 3-inch diameter spool, 30- to 40-inch 6× tippet, 3- to 5-weight floating line attached to a 100-foot, 20-pound test flat monofilament shooting line with 100 yards of 18-pound test Dacron or nylon backing. Rainbow are also caught on natural baits. Worms, crickets, crayfish, and nymphs may be rigged on a single hook with a small split shot and drifted through riffles and pools.

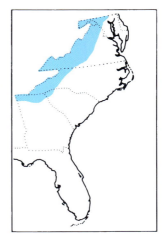

Preparation. Rainbow Trout are excellent broiled, poached, baked, fried, or cooked over an open fire.

Suggested Readings. 24, 108.

BROWN TROUT
Salmo trutta

Habits. To the fly fisherman, the Brown Trout is the most challenging, best-loved trout of all. Once found only in Europe, the species now occurs on every continent except Antarctica. It was introduced into the southern section of the United States during the early 1900s. Brown Trout thrive in cold-water streams, rivers, lakes, reservoirs, and tailraces where water temperatures vary from around 33° to 75°F. The species can tolerate warmer, more turbid waters than the Rainbow Trout. The color of the fish is spectacular. The top half of the body has a background with hues of olive, bronze, and yellow to give a brownish tint highlighted with red and black spots, often haloed in blue. Unlike some trout, the Brown Trout tail and paired fins are not spotted.

Perhaps the most interesting aspect of the behavior of this species, one that affects fishing, is that the Brown Trout is phototrophic negative—it shuns light. Browns become active during low light-intensity hours, late in the afternoon and early in the morning. During the day they hide under logs, behind boulders, and under the banks of streams.

Courtship takes place from September through December and is initiated by rising water, falling temperatures, and diminishing light. The female builds a nest approximately 6 inches deep and 12 inches in diameter, which is guarded by both parents. Fertilized eggs are buried in the nest under a couple of inches of sand and rubble and develop slowly, taking up to 5 months to hatch during cold winters. Males are sexually mature by the end of the second year, and females by the third year. A few Brown Trout live to 5 years, most only 3. A 1-year-old fish is about 4 inches long, and may reach 19.5 inches by age 5. While Brown Trout feed on almost anything that flies, crawls, jumps, or swims, they favor mayflies, which may compose 80 percent of the diet. Other foods are insects, worms, crayfish, salamanders, and fishes.

Fishing. Dry fly fishing is the traditional, and preferred, method of taking Brown Trout. Fly fishermen center their sport on the emergence of aquatic insects, such as mayflies. Late on April and May afternoons, fishermen stalk the stream banks looking for signs of the "evening rise." Care is taken to "match the hatch"—to select a fly that is a replica of the species of insect that is swarming, at least to match the color and shape. A wide variety of fly rods is used, some as short as 6 feet, others as long as 12. The weight of the rod varies from about 2 to 4 ounces. Some fishermen prefer bamboo, others like fiber glass. Care is taken to

select both the appropriate weight of tapered line and assortment of flies. Some of the preferred dry flies are Quill Gordon, Henderson, Red Quill, Light Cahill, Royal Coachman, White Wulff, Pale Evening Dunn, and the Rat Faced McDougall. Besides fly fishing, anglers drift Woolly Worms over the bottom; cast with Mepps, Rooster Tails, and other spinners; and fish with live minnows, crayfish, and earthworms. However, these techniques are viewed with disdain by the purists.

Preparation. Fresh trout are excellent cooked over an open fire. Wrap the fish, potatoes, onions, white wine, butter, and seasonings in foil and roast in the coals. Trout may also be poached in water, wine, or vinegar.

Suggested Readings. 63.

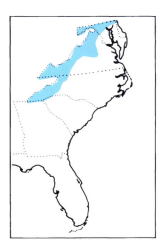

BROOK TROUT
Salvelinus fontinalis

Speckled Trout

Habits. The Brook Trout is an important sport fish found in many lakes and small cold-water streams in North America. It is popular for its eating quality and willingness to take artificial and natural baits. Preferred habitats are high-altitude streams, headwater sections of rivers, and beaver ponds where water temperatures seldom exceed 68°F. The species is native to eastern North America from Labrador and the Saskatchewan Valley southward along the Allegheny Mountains to the headwaters of the Chattahoochee River. Brook Trout have been widely introduced elsewhere in the United States (and throughout the world) where cold, clean waters are found.

Brook Trout are beautifully colored. The back and upper sides are olive-green to gray, mottled with dark green wavy markings that extend onto the dorsal and caudal fins. The lower sides are lighter, with small, distinct red spots surrounded by blue. The belly is buff-orange and becomes brilliantly colored during the spawning season. A key color character is the bright, creamy white strip that borders the edge of all fins except the dorsal and adipose.

Spawning takes place from August through January when water temperatures range from 40° to 50°F. In the southeastern United States, most of the spawning occurs in September and October in moderate to fast-flowing streams with gravel bottoms. Although some fish are capable of spawning when they are a year old, most attain sexual maturity as 2- or 3-year-olds. In some streams Trout as small as 3.5 to 4 inches may form part of the spawning population. Brook Trout display sexual dimorphism, and males are easily identified by their hooked lower jaws, deep bodies, and bright spawning colors. The female locates a suitable nesting site, usually in sand or gravel, and prepares a nest by working the bottom sediments to a depth of several inches over an area of 2 to 3 square feet. As she readies the nest, the male courts her constantly with gentle nudges, and chases away intruding males. The mating pair finally settles in the redd and the milt and ova are released simultaneously. The number of eggs spawned varies with fish size. A 6-inch fish may lay 100 eggs, and a 22-inch Trout about 5 thousand. The eggs are covered by sand and gravel and hatch in 100 days at 41°F, 75 days at 43°F, and 50 days at 50°F.

Brook Trout seldom live longer than 5 years in the wild. Hatchery reared Trout are known to live much longer, perhaps as long as 15 years. Average lengths for fish aged 1 to 6 years are 6, 10, 13, 16, 18, and 21

inches. Brook Trout have a tendency to overpopulate, and many streams in the southeast have adult trout that are all less than 8 inches long. Like other trouts, Brook Trout feed extensively on aquatic and terrestrial insects. They also eat spiders, clams, snails, fish eggs, frogs, salamanders, and small fishes.

Fishing. Brook Trout are caught almost exclusively by sport fishermen using fly rods and light spinning tackle. This is one of the most eagerly sought of all trouts, perhaps because it has the reputation of being easily caught. When Brook Trout are in the mood to strike, they are not at all picky about what they take. Small streams, headwater sections of rivers, beaver ponds, and gravel areas of lakes, all with water temperatures less than 68°F, are prime fishing spots. Angling techniques described for Rainbow and Brown Trouts apply equally well for Brook Trout.

Preparation. The flesh is considered by some to be superior to that of any other freshwater fish. It is excellent poached, broiled, or wrapped in foil with spices and wine and cooked over an open fire.

Suggested Readings. 24, 133.

FALLFISH
Semotilus corporalis

Silver Chub, Creek Chub

Habits. The largest native cyprinid (member of the minnow family) east of the Rockies, the Fallfish inhabits cold, clear, gravel-strewn streams and lakes along the Atlantic slope from Canada to the James River, Virginia. Reaching a maximum length of about 20 inches and a weight of 2 pounds, Fallfish are frequently caught by trout fishermen using wet or dry flies. It is a slender, green-silver to silver-gold fish with a single dorsal fin and a bluntly pointed head. The body is olive to black along the back, the sides are silvery, and the undersides are whitish. Scales of adults present a characteristic pattern of a series of dark, triangular black bars at the base of each scale. Unlike the Creek Chub, *Semotilus atromaculatus*, Fallfish lack a black spot at the base of the dorsal fin.

Spawning takes place in the spring and summer, from April through June, over gravel bottom in flowing water. When the water warms to approximately 54°F, adult males (3 years old and older) begin to build nests by carrying rocks in their mouths and gathering them in conical piles. A single nest may contain over 200 pounds of small rocks. The nests, 3 to 6 feet in diameter and 1 to 2 feet in height, are placed either in midstream or near the stream's edge under overhanging vegetation. Females older than 3 years gather at the nesting sites to lay their eggs when water temperatures reach 60° to 63°F. The eggs are nonadhesive at first, but after fertilization they become adhesive and are covered with gravel by the parent fish. The eggs hatch in 138 to 144 hours at 63°F. A female 9 inches long may lay approximately 3 thousand eggs in an season, an 11-inch fish 6 thousand, and a 13-inch fish 11 thousand.

Fallfish grow slowly, some living for at least 10 years. Approximate average lengths for fish aged 1 to 10 years are 1.8, 2.8, 5.6, 7.4, 9.6, 11.7, 13.7, 16, 17.7, and 18.2 inches. Young Fallfish feed on zooplankton and phytoplankton. Larger fish eat aquatic and terrestrial insects such as mayflies, stoneflies, beetles, wasps, and ants, as well as crayfish, fishes, and algae.

Fishing. Fallfish often are caught by anglers fly fishing for trout and are considered nuisances if they occur in large numbers. However, because they readily strike artificial flies and small spinners, and attain weights in excess of a pound, they can provide exciting sport on light tackle. Many times the largest fish the average trout fisherman catches is a Fallfish. The species is found in quiet, open stretches between riffles, easily accessible by wading or from a drifting boat.

Preparation. Although the flesh is reported to be firm, white, and sweet, Fallfish are seldom eaten by man. They probably would be best prepared like a trout or deep fried.

Suggested Readings. 123, 129, 133.

GOLDEN REDHORSE
Moxostoma erythrurum

Horsefish, Sucker

Habits. Redhorses are a group of large suckers so closely resembling one another that only an expert can distinguish the various species. They have long slender bodies, short spineless dorsal fins, and large protractile mouths with thick lips. There is also a well developed lateral line with 50 or fewer scales along its length.

The Golden Redhorse is one of the most widely distributed redhorse suckers in the southeastern United States. The native range extends from Minnesota to southern Ontario and south to Texas and Georgia. The species usually inhabits riffle areas and pools of small to large streams and rivers. It is only occasionally found in lakes and reservoirs.

The upper sides and back of the Golden Redhorse are gray or bronze-olive with a bronze luster overall. The lower sides are pale gold and the belly is milky white. In life, the dorsal, caudal, and anal fins are slate-gray. Fins of spawning fish are orange to red.

The species spawns in April and May when adult fish, those 3 years old and older, migrate upstream and concentrate on gravel shoals as water temperatures rise slightly above 60°F. Little information is available on details of the spawning behavior of the Golden Redhorse; therefore, the following description is based on that of the River Redhorse, *Moxostoma carinatum*, a closely related species. Males usually arrive on the spawning grounds several days prior to the females. Redds, or nests, are excavated in the gravel by fish using a sweeping motion of their tails and by pushing gravel away with their heads and mouths. The redds are found in water 6 inches to 4 feet deep and range in size from 4 to 8 feet in diameter and from 8 to 12 inches in depth. Redhorses are communal nesters, and many nests are generally found together. After the redd is prepared, a male moves over it and faces upstream. When a female approaches, the male begins a courtship behavior of darting back and forth across the nest. Usually a second male joins the first and together they mate with the female. Anywhere from 6 to 25 thousand eggs are released by a Golden Redhorse. The eggs are fertilized and covered with gravel. Incubation probably lasts from 4 to 10 days at 65°F.

Golden Redhorses are capable of attaining a length of 26 inches and a weight of 7 or 8 pounds. Average lengths for fish aged 1 to 7 years are approximately 4.9, 7.4, 10.4, 11.4, 12.8, 18.6, and 19.2 inches. These data are representative of northerly populations; therefore, fish in the southeastern United States probably reach a larger average size for a

given age. Like other suckers, redhorses use their protractile mouths to gather food from the bottom. Bivalve mollusks are important in the diet. Strong pharyngeal teeth enable the redhorse to crush hard-shelled animals. Other foods are aquatic larval insects such as mayflies, caddisflies, and midges.

Fishing. Although redhorses are generally reluctant to take natural or artificial baits, this does not keep fishermen from catching Golden Redhorse by other methods. In some rural areas, people flock to the riverbanks in the spring to capture suckers as they migrate to the spawning grounds. Suckers are caught by netting, trapping, gigging, snagging with treble hooks, shooting with arrows, and by snaring with wire loops attached to stout poles.

Preparation. The white flesh is very flavorful but bony. It may be made into fish cakes; stewed with potatoes, onions, and tomatoes; or fried, smoked, baked, or broiled.

Suggested Readings. 60, 156.

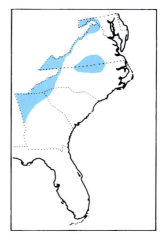

WHITE SUCKER
Catostomus commersoni
Sucker, Bugle-mouth Bass

Habits. Like other members of the family Catostomidae, the White Sucker is a bottom-foraging fish with a large protractile mouth and thick lips. It is found primarily in the cooler waters of the southeastern United States from Delaware to Georgia. The species is very common east of the Rockies from Canada south to Colorado, Missouri, and Georgia, where it inhabits flowing waters and lakes, usually at depths of 20 to 30 feet, but occasionally as deep as 150 feet.

As a rule, suckers are not easily identified to species. The White Sucker is perhaps best characterized as a robust fish that attains a length of 24 inches, has 55 to 75 scales in the lateral line, and 8 to 12 dorsal fin rays. Adults vary from gray, coppery-brown to almost black on the back and upper sides with creamy white lower sides and belly. Young fish, 2 to 6 inches long, usually have three prominent black spots on the sides of the body. During the spawning season, coloration is more intense and most fish are bright golden.

Spawning occurs at dusk and dawn in the spring from April through early June. Mature fish, or those 5 to 8 years old, migrate to gravel-bottom areas of lakes and streams when the water temperature approaches 50°F. The spawning act generally involves two to four males and one female, lasts 2 to 4 seconds, and may be repeated 30 times in one hour. The fertilized eggs are not deposited in a bed, but are scattered over the bottom where they adhere to the substrate. Fecundity ranges from approximately 36 thousand eggs for a 7-inch female to more than 140 thousand for a fish 20 inches long. The adults return to their resident habitats 10 to 14 days after spawning begins. Hatching takes place in about 2 weeks in waters 50° to 59°F, and the young remain in the gravel for a couple of weeks before migrating to deeper waters.

Young White Suckers feed near the surface on plankton. Adults are bottom feeders and consume aquatic insects and mollusks, which they dislodge from the substrate with their sucking mouths. Growth is variable although females appear to grow faster than males, attain larger sizes, and live longer. Average fork lengths for fish collected from Ontario and aged 1 to 15 years are 7, 10.8, 13.2, 15.2, 16.7, 17.8, 18.6, 19.1, 19.6, 20, 20.3, 20.6, 20.8, 21, and 21.1 inches. Suckers in the southeastern United States may be larger at a given age.

Fishing. White Suckers are caught commercially in seines, gill nets, traps, and weirs. The species is also caught by anglers and provides

good sport on light tackle. It readily takes artificial lures such as small spinners and flies as well as a variety of natural baits. A small hook baited with a worm or doughball is probably the most effective method of catching suckers. Young fish are marketed as live bait for bass, pickerel, and Walleye.

Preparation. The flesh is edible, even highly palatable if it is prepared properly. It is white and flaky, although very bony. Suckers caught in cold waters are reported to be delicious pan fried in butter. Other methods of preparing are to smoke, make into fish cakes, or use in fish chowders.

Suggested Readings. 133.

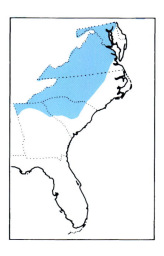

COOL
FRESHWATER FISHES

MUSKELLUNGE
Esox masquinongy

Muskie

Habits. Muskellunge, Northern Pike, Chain Pickerel, and Redfin Pickerel are known as pikes and belong to the family Esocidae. All but the Redfin, which does not reach a large size, are considered to be excellent game fish. Pikes have long, round bodies and prominent jaws that resemble a duck's bill equipped with numerous sharp teeth. There is only one dorsal fin, which is near the tail. The Muskellunge is the largest of the pikes and reaches a length of 60 inches and a weight of nearly 70 pounds. It is distinguished from the other native species by having scales on only the upper half of the cheeks and operculum, by having six or more pores along the ventral surface of the lower jaw, and by the presence of dark spots on a light background. The spots separate this species from the Northern Pike, *Esox lucius*.

Muskie are olive brown with pale silver bellies. The sides are usually marked with vertical bars or spots; occasionally they are plain. Muskie prefer swift streams and rivers, but also inhabit lakes and reservoirs where water temperatures range from 41° to 68°F. East of the Appalachian Mountains they are distributed from Canada south to eastern Tennessee and the French Broad River of North Carolina. Muskie have been successfully stocked elsewhere.

Spawning takes place in the spring from March through May when waters have warmed to 50°F for 4 to 10 consecutive days. Males mature when they are 3 or 4 years old (24 to 25 inches long), females a year later when they are 26 to 28 inches long. Favorite spawning areas in lakes are sand- and mud-bottomed shallows near aquatic vegetation. In rivers and streams spawning often occurs along upper and lower edges of pools in slack water in the vicinity of riffles. No parental care is given to the 200 thousand to 300 thousand scattered eggs, which hatch in 10 to 19 days.

Adult fish tend to be solitary and to establish territories or home ranges, which they defend from intruders. Muskie are reported to live at least 8 years, and are capable of attaining a size unmatched by most freshwater fish. Average lengths for ages 1 to 8 years are 11.5, 19, 24, 27.6, 30.1, 31.8, 34.6, and 37 inches. The species adopts piscivorous feeding habits at a very small size. Muskellunge usually hang motionless near the water's surface waiting for their prey—any consumable-sized fish.

Fishing. Large bodies of water produce the biggest Muskie. When fishing lakes or reservoirs, one should search for shallow bays with logs and submerged vegetation adjacent to a ledge with a dropoff to deeper water. Being quiet is a key to success. A natural drift, paddling, or use of an electric trolling motor will allow the angler to fish the shallows before moving to deep water.

When fishing flowing waters, fishermen should concentrate their efforts where tributaries enter. Favorite lures are shallow-running models of fish such as Rapalas or Rebels. Use gold or fluorescent red lures in turbid waters, and blue and silver where the visibility is good. Spoons and other deep-running lures as well as live minnows produce good results. Rods 5½ to 6 feet long and bait-casting or spinning reels with 12- to 17-pound test monofilament line are standard. Weather and time of day are important. Select overcast, misty, warm days with a slight breeze. Just before a low-pressure system enters the area is an ideal time to catch Muskie. Best fishing is early in the morning, late in the afternoon, and at night.

Preparation. The white and flaky flesh may be fried, baked, or broiled. Be prepared to deal with a lot of bones.

Suggested Readings. 44, 75, 77.

WHITE BASS
Morone chrysops

Stripe

Habits. Known as White Lightning in the southern part of its range, the White Bass is a hard hitting, fierce fighting fish that resembles the White Perch and Striped Bass. It is readily distinguished from the former by the comparative size of the anal spines. The second spine of the White Perch is as long as the third; that of the White Bass is much shorter. White Bass differ from Striped Bass by having humped backs, deeper bodies, less distance between the two dorsal fins, and a single, rather than double, patch of teeth near the base of the tongue.

The species inhabits cool water lakes, reservoirs, and rivers from Canada to the Gulf of Mexico. It is found in rivers of the Mississippi and Ohio Valleys and the Great Lakes. General boundaries are the St. Lawrence River in the east; Lake Winnipeg in the north; the Rio Grande in the west; and northwest Florida and Louisiana in the south. It has been stocked within and outside its natural range. The White Bass is silvery overall, with a dark gray-green back shading to silver-white below. There are five to eight horizontal dusky stripes along the sides.

The species is potamodromous, migrating 40 miles or less in fresh water to spawn. Males, sexually mature as 2-year-olds, arrive on the spawning grounds about a month prior to the females, when the water temperature is higher than 45°F, February or March in the Southeast. Spawning may extend 1 to 2 months as temperatures range from 50° to 65°F. Spawning is similar to that of Striped Bass, as males concentrate around a female and bump her to the surface. Eggs (62 thousand for a small female to 1 million for a large fish) are released and fertilized in seconds. The demersal, adhesive eggs settle to the bottom in shallows and stick to rocks, gravel, and vegetation. Their survival depends on encountering a silt-free substrate, where they hatch in 45 hours at 60°F.

The young grow rapidly and follow the adults into deep, open water. Females grow faster and probably live longer than males. Longevity for the species is at least 10 years. Average lengths for ages 1 to 6 years are 8.4, 14.4, 15.8, 16.7, 17.4, and 17.7 inches.

White Bass are primarily piscivorous. Schools may be seen chasing minnows that frantically skip across the surface to escape the Bass. Foods are Gizzard and Threadfin Shads, silversides, Yellow Perch, sunfishes, insects, and crayfish.

Fishing. White Bass are caught by anglers fishing with live minnows or artificial lures. Spoons, spinners, small lead-headed jigs, Bucktails,

Cordell Hot Spots, and streamer flies are fished slowly near the bottom by rocks and ledges in lakes and reservoirs. In rivers, lures are cast across riffles below pools. Light spinning tackle with 4- to 8-pound test line is standard. Most White Bass are caught in the spring during the spawning season, but larger fish are landed in the summer and fall. The species occurs in schools and good catches may be made in a short time. Many fishermen hoping to catch Largemouth Bass or Walleye have had a poor day salvaged by a string of White Bass.

Preparation. The flesh is similar to that of the Striped Bass and may be prepared by frying, baking, broiling, or stewing.

Suggested Readings. 24, 108, 133.

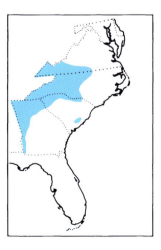

ROCK BASS
Ambloplites rupestris

Redeye

Habits. There are three species of *Ambloplites* in the Southeast: the Rock Bass, *A. rupestris*, the Roanoke Bass, *A. cavifrons*, and the Shadow Bass, *A. ariommus*. The Rock Bass is more widely distributed than the other species, occurring in western sections of Maryland, Virginia, and North Carolina and parts of northern Alabama and Georgia. The Roanoke Bass is native to the Roanoke, Chowan, Neuse, and Tar River drainages of North Carolina and Virginia, and the Shadow Bass occurs in the Tennessee River drainage of northern Alabama.

All resemble the Warmouth because they are dark olive-brown and have short, robust bodies with relatively large mouths. They differ, however, by having five or six anal spines, whereas the Warmouth has only three. The sides of the Rock Bass are covered with dark spots, which tend to form 8 to 10 horizontal rows. The underside may be deeply pigmented, and the iris is red. Roanoke Bass resemble Rock Bass in coloration, but may be recognized by their scaleless cheeks, a concave curvature of the head, and 10 to 12 rows of scales above the lateral line.

These sunfishes inhabit cool streams and rivers with rocky bottoms where they compete with each other and with Smallmouth Bass for food and space. They often aggregate in deep pools near boulders, ledges, logs, and other cover. Aspects of the life histories of the three species are almost identical; therefore only those for the Rock Bass will be discussed.

Fish are first capable of reproducing when they are 2 years old, or 3 to 5 inches long. Spawning occurs in May and June when water temperatures range from 60° to 70°F. The adhesive eggs, which number 3 to 11 thousand, are released and fertilized in short intervals over a period of about 1 hour. The eggs hatch in 3 or 4 days at 69° to 70°F. As is customary with the sunfishes, the male constructs the bed and then guards the eggs and subsequent fry until they swim from the nest.

A **medium-sized centrarchid,** the Rock Bass reaches a maximum length of 12 to 14 inches and a weight of 1½ to 2 pounds. Although fish in aquaria have lived for 18 years, those in the wild live for only 10 to 12. Average lengths for fish aged 1 to 10 years are 3.3, 4.7, 5.8, 6.6, 7.5, 8.2, 8.9, 9.5, 9.9, and 10.5 inches. Major foods in the diet are crayfish, aquatic and terrestrial insects, and fishes. Even at small sizes, Rock Bass, Roanoke Bass, and Shadow Bass are able to consume relatively large food items because of their large mouths.

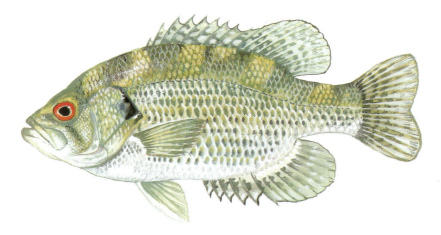

Fishing. All three species provide excellent sport fishing on fly rods and light spinning tackle. They deserve the rank of first-class game fish, for they fight hard and are easily caught on small spinners, streamer flies, wet and dry flies, and small top-water plugs. They are also caught with natural baits such as crayfish, salamanders, worms, hellgrammites (dobsons), and minnows. A favorite method of fishing is to drift through pools below riffles and cast in the vicinity of boulders and rock ledges with small slow-sinking lures.

Preparation. Like other sunfishes, the Rock Bass and its close relatives are good to eat, and may be prepared by deep frying, broiling, or baking.

Suggested Readings. 24, 81, 133, 146, 147.

REDBREAST SUNFISH
Lepomis auritus

Robin, Redbelly

Habits. The Redbreast, or Robin, is the most abundant sunfish in Atlantic coastal-plain streams. Adults are readily identified by the very long, uniformly black opercular flap. Other key characteristics are the short, stiff gill rakers, and the 43 to 49 scales along the lateral line. The original distribution is the Atlantic slope of North America from New Brunswick, Canada, to central Florida, and westward to the Appalachian Mountains, the Apalachicola River, and eastern Alabama. The present range includes parts of Texas, Oklahoma, Arkansas, and Kentucky.

Redbreasts are olivaceous on the back and upper sides, blending into blue-tinged bronze on the lower sides with orange or red underneath. Several light blue streaks radiate from the mouth. During the spawning season, males have bright orange-red bellies, whereas the undersides of females are pale orange. Redbreasts inhabit rocky areas of coastal-plain streams, rivers, and lakes. In streams with rapids, they prefer the deeper stretches that have gravel or rocky bottoms, and frequently concentrate around boulders, limestone outcroppings, logs, or aquatic vegetation. In the southeastern United States, Redbreasts have been reported in waters at elevations up to 3,500 feet.

Spawning is during the spring and summer, as early as April in the South. Peak spawning in the region occurs in May and June when water temperatures range from 68° to 82°F. Fish as small as 4 inches may be sexually mature, or when they are 2 to 3 years old. Males build nests in sheltered areas—near stumps, logs, or rocks—with sand or gravel substrates. The nests, 30 to 36 inches in diameter and 6 to 8 inches deep, are generally located in water 1 to 2 feet deep. Redbreasts often occupy beds that have been abandoned by other sunfishes. The number of eggs laid in a season ranges from about 1 to 10 thousand, varying with the age and size of the female. Estimated fecundities for fish aged 2 and 7 years are 963 and 10 thousand.

Robins grow at a slow rate and attain a medium size. Average lengths for fish aged 1 to 7 years are 2.5, 4.5, 5.5, 6.5, 7.6, 8.6, and 9 inches. The species feeds at the water's surface and on the bottom on a variety of insects and small fishes. Predominant foods are aquatic insects, including caddisflies, dragonflies, beetles, midges, and mayflies, and terrestrial insects. Robins also eat detritus, snails, crayfish, and fishes.

Fishing. Redbreasts are prized game fish and are caught on natural baits and artificial lures. Of the genus *Lepomis*, they are exceeded in size only by the Bluegill and the Redear (Shellcracker). Redbreasts seem to take small artificials more readily than do other lepomids. The best time to fish is late in the afternoon or early in the morning, in the spring and early summer. Good fishing spots in streams are limestone outcroppings and around boulders and logs in areas with moderate currents. In lakes one should fish rocky or vegetated areas. Fishing from a drifting or slowly powered boat is the best way to catch Robins, although angling from the bank can be productive. Two methods are recommended. The first is to fish from a slowly moving boat with light (2- to 4-pound test line) spinning tackle or fly rod. Effective lures are Beetle Spins, Colorado spinners positioned in front of Woolly Worms, Panther Martins, and wet flies, such as a black ant. The second method is to locate a diversion in the current and fish in the backwater using a cane or fiber glass pole rigged with a tiny split shot and a small hook baited with worms or crickets.

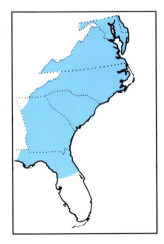

Preparation. The sweet, flaky, white flesh is excellent eating. Redbreasts are most often fried after dipping them in seasoned corn-meal or pancake batter.

Suggested Readings. 44, 130, 133.

SMALLMOUTH BASS
Micropterus dolomieui

Smallmouth

Habits. The Smallmouth Bass, a member of the sunfish family, closely resembles the Largemouth Bass. There are, however, distinct differences in the habitats of the two species, and the coloration and several anatomical characters also differ. Smallmouth Bass prefer cool waters, usually streams and large lakes in the northern part of the range and rocky, fast-flowing streams and rivers in the southern part. The species is often found between cold-water trout habitat and warm waters that contain bream, Largemouth Bass, and other centrarchids.

The coloration is brownish-green with an overlay of dark bronze vertical bands on the sides. In adults several dark streaks radiate from the eyes. The upper jaw in adults is shorter than that of the Largemouth Bass, extending only to the middle of the eye when it is closed. Smallmouth Bass have 12 or more rows of scales on the cheeks, whereas the Largemouth Bass has fewer than 12. Largemouth Bass have almost completely separated spiny and soft dorsal fins, and a much longer first dorsal spine. The range of the Smallmouth extends from northern Minnesota to Quebec south to the Tennessee River drainage of Alabama and west to eastern Oklahoma.

Spawning occurs in the spring when water temperatures range from 40° to 70°F. Peak spawning activity takes place at 50° to 65°F. Although some fish are capable of spawning when they are only 2 years old, most spawn for the first time when they are aged 3 or 4. The male fans out a nest, which is 2 to 4 feet in diameter, in sand or gravel, or between large rocks, in water 10 inches to 12 feet deep. One male may mate with several females. Each female is capable of laying 2 to 21 thousand eggs, which are demersal and adhesive. The eggs hatch 9 to 10 days after they are fertilized. The preferred habitat of adults in lakes and reservoirs is limestone ledges and rocky areas where waters are 3 to 20 feet deep. In flowing water systems, Smallmouth prefer streams with gradients of 4 to 25 feet per mile, characterized by riffles, pools, large rocks, and borders of aquatic vegetation. Temperatures usually range from 70° to 80°F during the summer. While Smallmouth Bass are reported to live as long as 12 years, most of the fish caught are 3 to 7 years old. Average lengths for fish aged 1 to 12 years are 3.7, 7.2, 10.3, 12.5, 14.4, 15.7, 16, 16.6, 17.4, 17.8, 18.3, and 18.7 inches. Smallmouth feed on a variety of fishes and invertebrates. Foods in the diet include Chain Pickerel, Yellow Perch, sunfish, shiners, suckers, tadpoles, crayfish, and nymphs of dragonflies, damselflies, stoneflies, and mayflies.

Fishing. Smallmouth Bass are excellent fighters when caught on fly rod or light spinning tackle. There is much debate among freshwater fishermen about whether the species is pound for pound the gamest of all centrarchids. Most would admit, however, that the fishing experience is usually in very scenic surroundings, and is different from fishing for most other sunfish in the South. One of the most enjoyable ways to fish for Smallmouth Bass is to drift down a quiet stream in a canoe and use a fly rod or spinning rod to cast behind boulders, in riffles, and in pools. Preferred artificial baits are black-and-white streamers, Beetle Spins, Rebels, Rapalas, small jigs with deer hair, Rooster Tails, and Mepps spinners. Large fish are caught on live minnows, crayfish, or spring lizards (salamanders). Fishing is best in May and June, in the early morning or late afternoon, and when streams are clear.

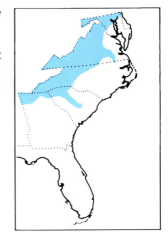

Preparation. Smallmouth Bass are excellent to eat and may be fried, baked, or broiled. The flesh is white, flaky, and easily filleted.

Suggested Readings. 2, 24, 108.

WALLEYE
Stizostedion vitreum
Pike, Walleyed Pike

Habits. Like the Yellow Perch, the Walleye is a member of the family Percidae. The two species are similar in that both have long, slender bodies, separated dorsal fins, and only two anal spines. Walleye, however, have strongly toothed jaws; lack dark vertical bands on the sides of the body; have marble-like eyes; and are much larger than Yellow Perch, reaching a weight of about 25 pounds. The habitat requirements of Walleye are more specific than for Yellow Perch. They prefer cool waters that are deep, rock bottomed and clear. The Sauger, *Stizostedion canadense*, looks like the Walleye, but is caught less often in the region, has spots on the spinous dorsal fin, and is smaller. It also differs from the Walleye by lacking a whitish lower lobe of the tail fin and by having a black spot at the base of the pectoral fin.

Walleye exist in waters with temperature extremes of 32° to 90°F, but they usually prefer waters with a maximum of about 77°F. The species was originally distributed from Canada southward through the Mississippi River basin, eastward to North Carolina, and westward to Georgia, Alabama, Arkansas, and Nebraska. In recent years, Walleye have been stocked in cool waters throughout the United States. They are olivaceous along the back and upper sides and white ventrally. Six to eight obscure saddle markings are more or less evident on the back; the sides are mottled; the soft-rayed dorsal fin and caudal fin are spotted.

Spawning takes place in the spring in shallow water over rocky bottom when water temperatures range from 37° to 61°F. Males mature when they are 4 years old, and females when they are 5. Spawning females race along the shore rolling and twisting as the eggs are released. Males follow, scattering milt over the deposited eggs. The number of eggs spawned increases with fish size. A 16- to 17-inch female is capable of laying 44 thousand eggs, and a 28- to 31-inch fish 495 thousand.

Growth rates vary from one area to another due to climate, food, competition, and other environmental and population-related factors. Average lengths for fish aged 1 to 9 years compiled from throughout the southeast are 9.3, 15, 18.7, 21.3, 24.8, 27.2, 28.7, 29.7, and 31 inches. Most conservation agencies place a minimum-size regulation on Walleye so that only mature fish may be caught. Although young Walleye feed on small planktonic crustaceans and insects, fish larger than about 3 inches are piscivorous. Sticklebacks, sculpins, suckers, herrings, shiners, smelts, and other small fishes form the bulk of the diet.

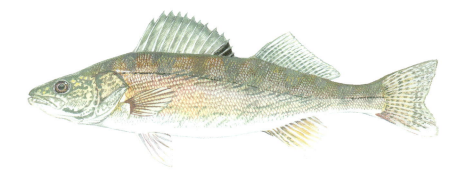

Fishing. Pound for pound the Walleye ranks among the best of all freshwater game fish. Because they fight hard, are excellent to eat, and inhabit scenic waters, the species is highly regarded by sport fishermen. Walleye are caught by trolling and casting artificial lures, by float fishing, and fishing through ice with natural baits. Walleye occur deep, among rocks and boulders, like to look at their prey before striking, are primarily piscivorous, and feed at sundown and at night. Therefore one should fish deep, rocky areas, retrieve the bait slowly, use fish or models of fish for bait, and fish at dusk or after dark for best results. Because Walleye bring top market prices, commercial fishermen also catch the species. To avoid conflicts with anglers, commercial fishermen restrict gill netting to large secluded lakes in Canada and in the northern United States.

Preparation. The species is best fried or roasted fresh over a campfire. Walleye are also excellent baked or broiled.

Suggested Readings. 24, 61, 75, 77, 108.

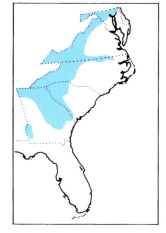

29

WARM
FRESHWATER FISHES

LONGNOSE GAR
Lepisosteus osseus

Gar, Garfish

Habits. Gars are members of the family Lepisosteidae and are the only living representatives of a group of primitive fish known mostly from fossil records, formerly found in the Old World, but now confined to eastern North America. Gars are distinguishable by their ganoid scales—small, diamond-shaped enamel plates—unlike the thin, flexible scales of most fish.

There are five species in the United States: Longnose, Shortnose, *Lepisosteus platostomus*, Alligator, *L. spatula*, Spotted, *L. oculatus*, and Florida, *L. platyrhincus*. The Longnose Gar is the most widely distributed in the southeastern United States and is recognized by its very long, narrow snout. The Shortnose Gar does not occur in the region. The Alligator Gar has a short, wide snout and reaches a size of 10 to 12 feet. Spotted and Florida Gars are similar in color, shape, and size. Adult Florida Gar have bony plates on the throat; Spotted Gar do not.

Longnose Gar are olive-brown or deep green along the back and upper sides, with silver-white bellies. There are numerous irregular black spots on the body, and on the dorsal, anal, and caudal fins. Fish inhabiting clear waters are more green overall; those in turbid environments are brownish.

Groups of adults often lie motionless at the surface in fresh and brackish, sometimes poorly oxygenated, water. In summer, they will rise with a soft rolling motion to gulp supplementary atmospheric air and expel gases from their air bladders.

Males become mature when they are 3 or 4 years old (25 to 29 inches long), and females reach first maturity as 6-year-olds (32 inches). They spawn in spring and early summer from April through June. The large, green eggs are strewn in shallow water, where they adhere to vegetation and rocks. A female may produce from 4 to 77 thousand eggs which hatch in 6 to 8 days. The young use sucking disks located at the front of their blunt snouts to attach to submerged objects. As the snouts lengthen the attachment organs are lost.

Females grow faster, bigger, and live longer than males (22 years compared with 17 for males). Gars may grow to 6 feet. Average lengths for fish aged 1, 2, 5, 10, 20, and 22 years are 18.8, 23.9, 27.8, 30.4, 47.2, and 49.5 inches. Gars feed primarily on fishes: shiners, sunfish, Gizzard Shad, catfish, and bullheads. They may follow their prey in a slow, continuous stalk, or lie in wait for it to come within striking

distance. Foods of secondary importance are mayflies, freshwater shrimps, crayfish, and frogs.

Fishing. Gars are not important to commercial fisheries, although they are caught in trawls and nets. Sport fishermen take them using live minnows and artificial lures, and by spearing and snagging them with treble hooks. The most effective tackle is a piece of stainless steel wire threaded through the eye of a short-shanked hook to form a loop. The hook is baited with a live minnow and is set when the Gar strikes, tightening the noose around the upper jaw. Another effective bait is an unravelled piece of nylon rope, which entangle a Gar's teeth in the loose strands when it strikes. Fishermen consider Gars nuisances because they damage commercial fishing nets and are accused of preying on the young of species important to fisheries, an accusation that has not yet been proven.

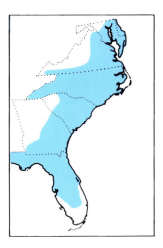

Preparation. There are few reports on the use of Gars as food for man. Longnose Gar were one of the principal food fishes marketed at New Bern, North Carolina in 1880. Seminole Indians in Florida reportedly preferred Gars over other fish and roasted them whole in the coals of open fires. The roe is considered poisonous.

Suggested Readings. 15, 133.

BOWFIN
Amia calva

Blackfish, Mudfish, Grindle, Cypress Bass

Habits. Bowfin are the only living representatives of the family Amiidae. Scientists believe them to be primitive compared with most freshwater fish because of the abundance of cartilage in the skeleton, the bony plates that sheath the head, and the simple fins.

Bowfin are identified by their cylindrical bodies, long dorsal fins, and large naked heads. Two short, tube-like barbels are located near the nostrils. The body is olive-green above, shading to pale yellow or cream on the belly. Several dark brown, horizontal bars are often evident on the cheeks. Males have an ocellus, a dark spot haloed in bright orange, on the upper part of the caudal fin base. The spot is absent or inconspicuous on females. During the spawning season the ventral fins may be green or aqua. Along the east coast, Bowfin are distributed from Connecticut to Florida, where they inhabit sluggish, swampy rivers and shallow lakes. The ability to rise to the surface and gulp air enables Bowfin to live in hot, poorly oxygenated waters that are uninhabitable to most fishes.

Spawning occurs from April through June when water temperatures range from 60° to 66°F. Sexual maturity is first attained when fish are 3 to 5 years old (18 inches for males, 24 inches for females). Males move into shallow, vegetated backwaters to build bowl-shaped nests. The nests, 15 to 24 inches in diameter, are lined with sticks and cut vegetation, and are located under logs, stumps, or brush in water 1 to 2 feet deep. A courted female moves into the nest and is encouraged by the male to release her eggs. A 21-inch fish is capable of laying 64 thousand eggs in short-duration spurts, as many as four or five in a 90-minute period. The eggs hatch in 8 to 10 days and the fry are guarded by the male, who herds the young and stirs up a cloud of silt to hide them from danger. Young Bowfin have adhesive organs on their snouts that enable them to attach to submerged objects.

Although reported to live for 25 to 30 years in captivity, Bowfin seldom live longer than 9 years in the wild. The maximum size is about 3 feet with a weight of 15 pounds. Average lengths for fish aged 1 to 9 years are 9, 15.3, 17.6, 20, 22.6, 22.8, 26.4, 26.7, and 27 inches. Bowfin stalk their prey using their senses of smell and sight. Foods include water beetles, dragonfly nymphs, freshwater shrimps, fishes, frogs, and crayfish. One researcher discovered the leg bone of a bird in a stomach, but did not know if it came from a wild bird or was a fried chicken drumstick.

Fishing. Bowfin are caught by sport and commercial fishermen, but are considered nuisances. Many a bass fisherman has been unpleasantly surprised to find that a Blackfish has taken his lure. While the species will strike topwater and deep-running artificials, it is most often caught in the spring and early summer on minnows, worms, frogs, crayfish, or cut bait. Fresh herring gills and cut suckers are excellent baits. Unlike catfish and Striped Bass which eagerly grab the bait, Bowfin nibble like eels and are difficult to hook. Commercial fishermen working in rivers and low-salinity estuaries catch Bowfin with nets, traps, and trotlines. Blackfish can cause damage to commercial fishing gear, and are difficult to remove from gill nets. In the South, Bowfin are occasionally sold fresh as food fish at small, local markets. Live fish are transported and stocked in ponds where anglers pay to fish.

Preparation. The flesh is reputed to be soft and jelly-like, but it is good to eat if prepared properly. Three methods of serving are suggested: smoked, fried as patties after dipping in egg and bread crumbs, and stewed.

Suggested Readings. 78, 108, 133.

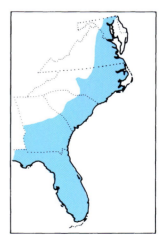

AMERICAN EEL
Anguilla rostrata

Eel, Freshwater Eel

Habits. The American Eel is a complex subject of study to scientists and the source of folklore to fishermen. Eels have been thought to possess aphrodisiac qualities, and tales have been told among river folk about romantic encounters between male Eels and female catfish. While there is no basis for these folk stories, the Eel does look more like a snake than a fish and its life history is complicated, particularly in regard to spawning.

The fish is long and cylindrical with the dorsal, caudal, and anal fins united. It is brown to yellowish-brown with paler undersides. Other identifying characters are the presence of pectoral fins, tongue, thick lips, small shiny eyes, and the secretion of heavy white mucous when it is distressed. American Eels are found in most warm seas, except the eastern Pacific. In the Western Hemisphere, they occur from Canada to Brazil including the Gulf of Mexico and West Indies. While males only inhabit salt or brackish water, females ascend rivers and streams and enter lakes and reservoirs that range from warm habitats to cold trout waters.

The species is catadromous, and fish migrate from fresh water to salt water to spawn. In late summer, females that are approximately 7 years old migrate to the sea, where they are joined by mature males 4 to 7 years old. Together they travel to the Sargasso Sea where spawning takes place. Eggs hatch in February and the larvae undergo several changes in body shape, a process that takes about a year. During this time, young Eels are carried northward and inshore by currents and winds to the coastal waters, from which they will begin their upstream migration. At this time they are 2 to 5 inches long and are called elvers. The upstream trek is one of Nature's miracles. Elvers have been observed climbing the wet walls of dams and squirming through moist grass to bypass physical barriers. Some females remain in fresh water for 15 to 20 years before returning to the sea, where they may lay 10 to 20 million eggs in one season. The age and growth of the species is not well understood, although females as old as 35 to 40 years are known to have lived in landlocked lakes in the United States. In a Swedish museum, an Eel lived for 88 years. American Eels eat many different kinds of animals including fishes, insects, worms, snails, clams, and crabs. They will also feed on carrion.

Fishing. Although sport fishermen catch American Eels on hook and line using cut bait, most Eel are harvested by commercial fishermen using trotlines, eelpots, traps, seines, pound nets, and fyke nets. The best time to catch Eels is late summer and early fall when adults are migrating downstream and through the estuaries. Eels are a delicacy in Europe and Asia, and in recent years the international market has resulted in a growing Eel fishery in the United States. In 1984, the price of live elvers air shipped to Japan was $400 to $500 per pound.

Preparation. Salted Eels are used in this country as catfish bait. Most Americans do not eat them, but skinned Eels are good fried or smoked.

Suggested Readings. 45.

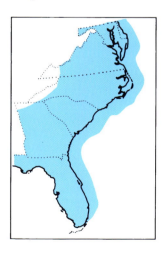

GIZZARD SHAD
Dorosoma cepedianum

Nanny Shad

Habits. The Gizzard Shad is one of two species of freshwater clupeids (herring family) that has the last ray of the dorsal fin elongated into a slender filament. The other species, the Threadfin Shad, *Dorosoma petenense*, has a similar body shape, but is much smaller and has 20 to 25 anal rays, whereas the Gizzard Shad has 29 to 35. The Gizzard Shad also has a distinctively clear, bulbous snout with a V-shaped notch on the ventral surface of the upper jaw. The common name comes from the heavy muscular stomach that resembles a chicken gizzard.

The species occurs in schools and prefers productive, calm waters, although it is also found in rivers, streams, and even tailraces below dams where currents are strong. Gizzard Shad are distributed from southern Canada south through the central drainages of the United States to Mexico and eastward throughout the Southeast and north along the Atlantic Coast to New York.

They are silvery overall, with bluish-gray on the back and sides fading to a creamy white belly. Fish often have a lustrous appearance stemming from brassy gold reflections on the scales. Occasionally six to eight horizontal dark stripes occur along the upper sides, originating behind a large black shoulder spot.

Individuals are first able to spawn when they are 2 to 3 years old (7 to 13 inches long). Spawning is in the spring and summer from March through August when water temperatures range from 50° to 70°F. The number of eggs per female varies from 3 thousand to more than 380 thousand. The yellowish, adhesive eggs are scattered in open water or along the shoreline. They are left unattended by the parents and sink to the bottom, where they adhere to rocks, sticks, roots, and other submerged objects. Hatching occurs in 36 hours at 80°F and in 95 hours at 62°F. Young Gizzard Shad school in open water and are often observed at the surface with their snouts protruding as they strain plankton. Although the species is known to live for 10 years and reach a length of 21 inches, most fish die before they are 7 years old. Average lengths for fish aged 1 to 5 years are 6.3, 10.6, 12.6, 14.4, and 15.7 inches. Gizzard Shad are filter feeders and use their gill rakers to strain microscopic plants and animals from the water. They also pick through mud and detritus on the bottom for small foods.

Fishing. Gizzard Shad are labeled as forage, trash, and nuisance fish by fishermen and biologists. They are of little direct value to fisheries. Small

sport fisheries have developed at tailraces below dams, at warm-water outfalls of electropower plants, and at other concentration points, where anglers use treble hooks to snag the fish. The species is caught incidentally to other finfish by commercial fishermen using nets. Gizzard Shad bring a low price on the market and are sold for swine and poultry feed, fertilizer, and bait for fish traps. The greatest value of the species is as forage for large fish that are important to commercial and recreational fisheries. Striped Bass, Largemouth Bass, catfish, and pikes are a few of the many species that eat Gizzard and Threadfin Shads. However, Gizzard Shad grow rapidly and soon exceed a consumable size for most predators. The species is not hardy and is very susceptible to drastic changes in temperature and low concentrations of dissolved oxygen. Large die-offs are common, and result in outcries from lakeside residents, boaters, and fishermen who are confronted with large numbers of rotting fish.

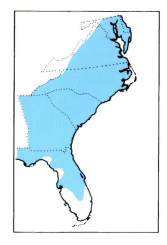

Preparation. Not many people have eaten Gizzard Shad. Those who have report mixed reactions to the taste. If deprived of something better to eat, one might prepare the bony fish by frying it.

Suggested Readings. 15, 34, 64.

REDFIN PICKEREL
Esox americanus

Jack, Pike, Redfin, Banded Pickerel, Grass Pickerel

Habits. The Redfin Pickerel is the smallest member of the pike family in the southeastern United States. Because it seldom exceeds 10 inches, the fish is of little importance to adult anglers. Like other members of the family Esocidae, Redfin have slender cylindrical bodies with prominent jaws shaped like a duck's bill and armed with numerous fang-like teeth. Redfin Pickerel are found in the same waters as Chain Pickerel, but may be distinguished from the latter by their broader, shorter snouts; fewer scales in the lateral line; 20 to 36 dark, wavy, vertical streaks on the sides of the body; and a teardrop-shaped bar that points downward and to the rear across the cheek. The general coloration is olive to black on the back and upper sides with a white belly. All of the fins except the dorsal are tipped with red.

The distribution is from the St. Lawrence River, Canada, along the Eastern Seaboard from Connecticut to Lake Okeechobee, Florida, and westward along the Gulf of Mexico through Texas. There are two subspecies: *Esox americanus americanus* and *E. a. vermiculatus*, the Grass Pickerel. The Grass Pickerel is found in the Gulf and Mississippi drainages, and intergrades of the two subspecies occur in Florida, Georgia, Alabama, and Louisiana. The preferred habitat of Redfin Pickerel is quiet, small, heavily vegetated fresh waters such as mill ponds, drainage canals, streams, and small lakes. The waters are usually dark stained and slightly acidic. The species also has been reported from brackish waters in New York, New Jersey, and Chesapeake Bay.

Redfin reach sexual maturity when they are 2 years old, and as small as 5 inches long. Spawning takes place in heavily vegetated areas on flood plains, on inundated grassy banks, and in overflow ponds in early spring when water temperatures approach 50°F. The water is usually shallow, and backs of spawning fish may be partially out of the water. No nests are constructed, and the eggs, scattered in small batches over vegetation, hatch in 12 to 14 days without being guarded by the parents. The eggs are golden-yellow and number about 4 thousand for fish in the 7- to 9-inch class. Only a small fraction of the eggs may be spawned in a season; the remainder may be reabsorbed.

Although some Redfin may live as long as 8 years, most of the fish caught in the Southeast are 2 to 4 years old. Females live longer and grow faster than males. Average lengths for males and females combined for ages 1 to 6 years are 4.6, 5.8, 7.4, 8.7, 10.1, and 11.8 inches. Like other members of the pike family, adult Redfin Pickerel are piscivorous

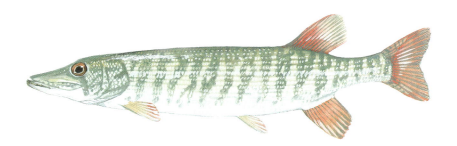

and almost always have fish in their guts. Fish less than 2 inches long feed on invertebrates such as cladocerans, amphipods, and aquatic insects. Larger fish eat suckers, shiners, and sunfish.

Fishing. The Redfin Pickerel is an excellent little game fish, although it is certainly not regarded as such by most fishermen. It readily takes live bait, small plugs, spinners, and flies. Because of its size, nonschooling habits, and insignificant market value, the species is not sought by commercial fishermen. Redfin occasionally are caught in traps, gill nets, and fyke and hoop nets. Most fish are caught in the late winter and early spring in coastal streams, canals, and ponds.

Preparation. Although bony, the white, sweet flesh has an excellent flavor when it is fried or baked.

Suggested Readings. 35, 78, 133.

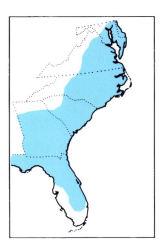

CHAIN PICKEREL
Esox niger

Jack, Pike

Habits. The most widely distributed and frequently caught pike in the southeastern United States is the Chain Pickerel. The species may be distinguished from the Muskellunge, *Esox masquinongy*, because it is generally much smaller and has completely scaled cheeks. It differs from the Redfin Pickerel by having more lateral line scales (122 to 126; Redfin have about 105), and 13 or 14 dorsal fin rays (Redfin have 11 or 12). Chain Pickerel, or Jack, are greenish with lustrous golden scales above, and are silver-white on the lower sides and belly. The common name is derived from the chainlike pattern of dark bands occurring on the sides of larger fish from the operculum to the caudal fin. There is a dark vertical bar under the eye.

Jacks typically inhabit weedy, log-choked streams and rivers as well as shallow bays and coves of large lakes and reservoirs. They are occasionally found in low-salinity estuaries. Their range extends from Nova Scotia south through northeastern West Virginia to the Everglades and Lake Okeechobee, Florida. To the west, the species occurs to the Louisiana-Texas border and north through eastern Arkansas, southeastern Mississippi, and southwestern Kentucky.

Spawning takes place in the early spring when water temperatures reach about 45°F, usually in March and April. Each female lays from 20 to 50 thousand yellow-white eggs in long glutinous strands. The eggs tangle in aquatic vegetation, brush, and limbs of fallen trees and hatch in 7 to 10 days. It does not take long for the young Chain Pickerel to adopt the hiding behavior of adults, as they remain motionless in patches of vegetation waiting for small fish to venture too close. Jacks feed almost exclusively on fish—sunfish, Gizzard Shad, and shiners —and are capable of eating fish almost as long as they are. Chain Pickerel may reach a weight of about 9 pounds, however, individuals larger than 5 pounds are rare, and the average fish caught is around 2 to 3 pounds. Growth is more rapid in the southern part of the range.

Fishing. A good rule of thumb when fishing for Chain Pickerel is to locate the worst tangles of weeds and brush and fish them. Many Pickerel are bypassed by anglers who wish to make life a little more simple by avoiding tangles. A small, easy-to-handle boat with an electric motor is essential for fishing in and around prime Jack habitat. Several techniques are used to catch Chain Pickerel. Live baits such as minnows

and frogs are preferred in the winter and early spring in open waters and through ice.

When fishing with artificials, one may select streamers such as white and black Marabou or the Mickey Finn, weedless rubber worms, or surface and deep-running lures. Surface plugs with propellers fore and aft, such as the Devil's Horse, are reported to be good baits, particularly when fished in shallow water in the early morning. In the spring, before the aquatic vegetation gets too thick, deep-running lures and spoons are very effective. Pickerel strike swift and hard. Remember that a Jack's mouth is very bony; don't be afraid to set the hook. A 6- or 6½-foot spinning rod with 4- to 6-pound test line will provide plenty of action.

Most Chain Pickerel are caught from October through April. Although Chain Pickerel may not legally be taken with commercial fishing gear in most states, they are susceptible to being taken in traps, gill nets, and fyke nets.

Preparation. The flesh is white and flaky, but has an unusual arrangement of bones. When eating Pickerel, one should be especially wary of bones in unexpected places. The meat may be fried, broiled, baked, or roasted over charcoal.

Suggested Readings. 24, 61, 75, 108.

CARP
Cyprinus carpio

Habits. Most of the nearly 300 species of North American fishes known as minnows (family Cyprinidae) are small and slender-bodied. The large, robust Carp with its protractile, sucker-like mouth is an exception. The species was introduced from Europe in 1831 because of its suitability for pond culture and its popularity as a food fish. Carp are found in all of the southeastern states except Florida at elevations below 2,000 feet in rivers, streams, lakes, reservoirs, swamps, and low-salinity estuaries where water temperatures range from 34° to 96°F.

Besides their large size, they have the following features: two pairs of barbels at the corners of the mouth, 35 to 39 large scales along the lateral line, molar-like pharyngeal teeth, and a heavy, serrated spine in front of the dorsal and anal fins. The Smallmouth Buffalo, *Ictiobus bubalus*, a member of the sucker family, may be confused with the Carp because of its size and shape, but is seldom caught in the region, is duller in color, and has no serrated spines. Carp are olive to brassy on the back and upper sides, and golden on the lower sides and belly.

Spawning occurs in spring and early summer. A great commotion caused by fish splashing in the shallows aids in distributing the eggs, which adhere to aquatic vegetation and brush. Courtship rituals begin when the water warms to about 63°F and may last several weeks, until the water temperature reaches 82°F. Spawning aggregations of 1 to 3 females and 2 to 15 males may include fish aged 2 to 16 years. Males may reproduce by their second year; females are 3 years or older. A 15½-inch fish may lay 36 thousand eggs and one 33½-inches long more than 2 million. Eggs are broadcast in batches of about 500 and hatch unattended in 3 to 10 days.

The maximum age for Carp is at least 47 years, but the normal life span seldom exceeds 20 years. Limited information on age and growth indicates the average lengths for fish aged 1 to 7 years are 6.3, 12.8, 18.5, 22.8, 25.5, 27, and 28 inches. More data are needed to describe the growth of older fish. The world-record 82-pound Carp was caught in South Africa; the North American angling record is 58 pounds. Carp are omnivorous throughout life and feed on the bottom using their protractile mouths to suck up mud and detritus. Edible materials are swallowed; the rest is expelled. Important foods are organic detritus, plants, small crustaceans, and worms. Contrary to popular belief, few Carp feed on fishes or fish eggs.

Fishing. Each year thousands of pounds of Carp are harvested commercially by nets and fish traps, and are marketed at low prices. Anglers catch them on cane poles using doughballs, bread, corn, or worms as bait.

Carp occasionally feed at the water's surface with loud gulping or kissing sounds when insects such as cicadas emerge. Fishermen then may find fly rods and popping bugs very effective. Archery fishing and gigging are popular recreation during the spawning season. Although the young serve as prey for important food and sport fishes, Carp are considered nuisances because their feeding activity increases the turbidity of the water, destroying aquatic vegetation that serves as food, cover, and nesting sites for other fish and for waterfowl.

Preparation. Most Southerners will not eat Carp, but they are consumed throughout much of the world. The meat may be used to make fish cakes, following the recipe used for salmon, but one should not expect the same results.

Suggested Readings. 24, 108, 133.

GOLDEN SHINER
Notemigonus crysoleucas

Roach, Shad Roach, Shiner

Habits. The Golden Shiner is the most widely used bait fish in North America. The species is excellent bait for medium- to large-sized piscivorous fishes such as Largemouth Bass, Walleye, Striped Bass, pike, and catfish. The Golden Shiner is raised commercially in ponds and concrete tanks throughout the region. It is easily propagated artificially because it has a long spawning season, lays a large number of eggs, and is tolerant to handling and low levels of dissolved oxygen. With supplemental feeding, up to 420 pounds have been raised in a 1-acre pond in one season, a considerable yield for a fish whose average size is less than an ounce.

The species is easily recognized by the lateral line, which curves downward, and by the golden-brassy coloration. The back is olive-green to dark brown, and the sides are brassy-gold. The lower fins are yellow or red tinged, being particularly conspicuous during the spawning season. The preferred habitat is clear, quiet, vegetated areas of lakes, ponds, and sluggish stretches of rivers and streams from Manitoba and Quebec south to Florida and Mexico. The Golden Shiner has been introduced west of the Rocky Mountains.

Fish reach sexual maturity during their second year, when they are as small as 2.5 to 3.5 inches long. Spawning occurs in the spring and summer from April through August depending on latitude, when water temperatures range from about 60° to 80°F. The eggs are adhesive and stick to aquatic vegetation and brush, and hatch in approximately 4 days. Fish culturists often use synthetic egg mats to catch the ova once they are fertilized. A large female may lay more than 200 thousand eggs during a spawning season. Although a few fish may live for 10 years and attain a length of 10.5 inches (weight 12 ounces), most are much younger and smaller. Average lengths for fish aged 1 to 6 years are 3, 4, 4.5, 5, 6, and 6.5 inches. Golden Shiner generally feed at the surface. Favorite foods are cladocerans, midges, flying insects, algae, dragonfly nymphs, and mollusks.

Fishing. Anglers fishing for bream with small hooks baited with worms frequently catch Golden Shiner. Other baits such as doughballs and tiny artificial flies are also used to catch the species, usually in shallow, vegetated areas near the surface. Larger individuals may make spectacular runs and provide sport on fly rods and ultra-light spinning tackle. However, it is rare indeed when a fisherman in the United States returns

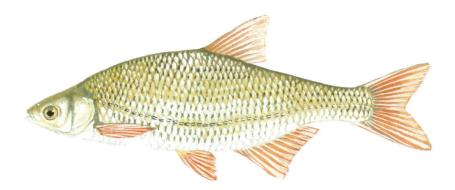

home from the stream to brag about a string of Golden Shiner. Commercial fishermen seldom catch Shiners because of their small size.

Preparation. The flesh is edible, but hardly delectable.

Suggested Readings. 24, 108, 133.

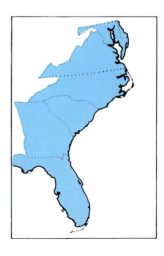

LAKE CHUBSUCKER
Erimyzon sucetta

Sucker, Mullet

Habits. Suckers are soft-rayed freshwater fishes that have protruding, sucker-like mouths with thick, fleshy lips. There are over 50 North American species, including approximately 28 that occur in the southeastern United States. Three genera are most frequently encountered by fishermen in the region: *Erimyzon* (chubsuckers), *Moxostoma* (redhorse suckers), and *Catostomus* (represented by the White Sucker, *C. commersoni*).

Chubsuckers are found primarily in warm, still, or slow-flowing waters; but the last two genera usually inhabit cooler waters with moderate to swift currents. There are two species of chubsuckers: the Lake, *E. sucetta*, and the Creek, *E. oblongus*. Both have similarly shaped bodies, lack lateral lines, and have young that possess a distinct longitudinal stripe. The species may be differentiated by the number of scales in the lateral series. The Lake Chubsucker has 36 to 38 and the Creek Chubsucker has 39 to 41.

The Lake Chubsucker is widely distributed in the South. Its overall range in the United States is southern New York to south Florida, west into Texas, and north through Arkansas, Missouri, Illinois, and northwestern Minnesota. Preferred habitats are sluggish rivers and streams, as well as lakes, oxbows, and quarry pits, all of which usually have submerged vegetation. The fish is bronze to deep olive-green dorsally, with a golden-silvery luster on the lower sides. The caudal fin is often reddish, and the anterior edge of the dorsal fin is black. Young fish have a wide, dark band that extends from the eye to the tail.

Spawning takes place in the spring and early summer, depending on the latitude, when adults migrate up small tributary streams. Eggs are broadcast randomly over sand, gravel, or vegetated bottom, and are left unattended to hatch. Lake Chubsuckers may live as long as 8 years and reach a length of about 18 inches. Average lengths for fish aged 1 to 6 years are 2.5, 5, 8, 10, 11, and 12 inches. As indicated by the shape and location of the mouth, suckers feed on or near the bottom. Small fish eat copepods, cladocerans, and midges, while larger fish feed on aquatic insects, fish eggs, worms, and vegetation. The life history of the Creek Chubsucker is very similar to that outlined above.

Fishing. Compared with most other freshwater fish of a similar size, suckers are of little importance to fisheries in the Southeast. Although they are susceptible to being caught by some commercial fishing

gear—wire traps, gill nets, and seines—markets for the flesh are at best local. Some anglers manage to catch a few fish on live worms and small wet flies.

Preparation. When taken from cold water, chubsuckers have good-flavored, firm flesh. It may be stewed, made into fish cakes, fried, baked, or broiled.

Suggested Readings. 78, 133.

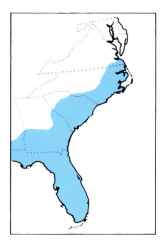

WHITE CATFISH
Ictalurus catus

Catfish

Habits. To some fishermen all catfishes look alike. This is particularly true with large fish of different species that are of similar shape and color, and occur together in the same body of water. The White Catfish is a good example because in the Southeast it is found with Channel Catfish, Yellow and Brown Bullheads, and occasionally with Blue Catfish. The true identities of these species are not too difficult to determine, however, with a closer look. First, White, Channel, and Blue Catfishes have forked tails; bullheads do not. Second, the number of anal rays is different for the species. White Catfish have 19 to 23, Blue Catfish have more than 30, and Channel Catfish have 24 to 29. The two bullheads may be separated to species by the color of their barbels. The barbels of Yellow Bullheads are usually white-yellowish, whereas those of Brown Bullheads are much darker. White Catfish are bluish-gray on the back and sides, olive-gray on the head, and white underneath. The species inhabits fresh and slightly brackish coastal waters from New York to Florida. The preferred habitat is silty bottom areas of slow-flowing streams, rivers, ponds, lakes, and low-salinity estuaries.

Spawning occurs in the early summer when waters warm to about 70°F. Both the male and the female of a mated pair prepare a nest by fanning the bottom with their sides and fins. Large objects such as sticks and rocks that are in the nest area are carried away in their mouths. The nests are much larger than those of most freshwater fish. They are saucer-shaped and may be 30 to 36 inches in diameter and 12 to 18 inches deep. Fish are able to reproduce when they are 3 or 4 years old, or about 7 to 9 inches long. A 12-inch female lays approximately 4 thousand adhesive eggs that stick to the bottom of the nest and hatch in 6 to 7 days at 80°F.

Most of the White Catfish caught in the southeast are about 13 inches long and weigh 1 to 1½ pounds. The species has been aged as old as 11 years but probably lives longer. Average lengths for fish aged 1 to 11 years are 3.2, 5.4, 8.1, 10.7, 12.8, 14.4, 15.7, 17.2, 18.5, 18.6, and 20.9 inches. A White Catfish that is 10 inches long weighs about ½ pound, a 13-inch fish 1 pound, and a 14.5-inch fish about 2 pounds. White Catfish are omnivorous, and usually feed at dusk or at night on fishes, insects, and aquatic plants. Major foods in the diet of White Catfish studied in South Carolina were Gizzard and Threadfin Shads, herring, bream, catfish, mayfly larvae, and pondweed. The last may have been consumed incidentally.

Fishing. The species is caught by both sport and commercial fishermen. Commercial fishermen working in bays and sounds catch the species with pound nets, trotlines, traps, gill nets, and trawls, whereas those fishing in streams and rivers harvest catfish with hoop and fyke nets, gill nets, traps, and trotlines. The meat is sold fresh and frozen, generally bringing prices that are intermediate between those of Channel Catfish and bullheads. Sport fishermen use cane poles and spinning and bait-casting outfits to catch the species. Most catfish are caught bottom fishing with natural baits such as cheese, minnows, shrimp, cut fish, and worms. In some southern states White Catfish are stocked in ponds to be caught by paying anglers or to be bulk harvested for commercial markets.

Preparation. Like other catfish, this species must be skinned before it is eaten. This is easiest accomplished with specialized pliers. The meat is usually fried or stewed. A good catfish stew served on a camping trip is hard to beat.

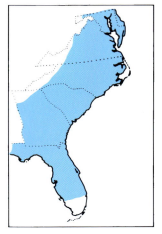

Suggested Readings. 24.

BLUE CATFISH
Ictalurus furcatus
Catfish

Habits. The Blue Catfish is one of the largest freshwater fishes in North America. Individuals in the 200- to 400-pound range have been reported in old popular articles and newspapers of the last century, and a 150-pound fish caught in the Mississippi River was sent to the United States National Museum in 1879. Today, fish larger than 50 pounds are rare.

Blue Catfish inhabit the major rivers of the Mississippi, Missouri, and Ohio basins of the central and eastern United States, south to Mexico and east into Georgia and western North Carolina. They have been introduced into some southern reservoirs. This distribution makes the species only marginally important to fisheries in the Southeast. Adults have stout bodies with prominently humped backs in front of the dorsal fin. They resemble Channel Catfish by having deeply forked tails, but are dissimilar because they are unspotted as juveniles and have more anal rays, 30 to 35. The back and upper sides are dusky gray to blue and the lower sides and belly are white.

Spawning occurs in late spring and summer, May through July, at temperatures of 70° to 75°F. Egg masses are deposited in nests that have been constructed under logs, brush, or the riverbank. Blue Catfish have been aged as old as 14 years, but they undoubtedly live much longer. Average lengths for fish aged 1 to 14 years are 5.9, 10.6, 14.4, 18.1, 21.5, 24.8, 26, 27.3, 32.3, 34.9, 37.9, 38.8, 41, and 42 inches. Foods include fishes, crayfish, aquatic insects, and miscellaneous other animals unfortunate enough to get in the way of these nocturnally foraging predators.

Fishing. Because of its size and palatability, the Blue Catfish is important to commercial and recreational fisheries. Commercial fishermen working large, deep, fast-flowing rivers catch the species with traps, seines, trotlines, bush lines, and jug lines. The meat, sold fresh and frozen, brings a good price on local and export markets. Sport fishermen catch Blue Catfish with cane poles, spinning tackle, and bait-casting outfits. Most of the fish are caught while bottom fishing with cut meat rigged on large hooks weighted down by lead sinkers. Favorite fishing sites in rivers are deep holes in moderate to fast current. Methods of fishing described for Channel Catfish also apply for Blue Catfish.

An interesting technique used to catch large catfish, including Blue, Channel, and Flathead, is by tickling and noodling, or grabbling. The

fish are caught by sticking the hand in the fish's mouth or gill cover. Experienced noodlers wade the edges of creeks and streams feeling for catfish under logs and banks. Once located, the fish are enticed to open their mouths, either forceably or by tickling the belly, and the hand and lower arm are thrust inside. Scarred hands can attest to successful fishing.

Preparation. A suggested method of preparing is by deep fat frying. Cut 1 pound of fillets, steaks, or pan dressed fish into serving-sized portions. Sprinkle both sides with salt and pepper. Beat one egg slightly and blend in 2 teaspoons of milk or water. Dip the fish in the egg and roll in ½ cup of bread crumbs, cracker crumbs, cornmeal, or flour that has been seasoned with salt and pepper. Use a deep kettle with a frying basket and enough fat to cover the fish, but do not have the container more than half full of fat, preferably vegetable shortening with a high smoke point. Heat the fat to about 350°F. Place a layer of fish in the frying basket and cook to an even golden brown, about 3 to 5 minutes. Raise the basket, remove the fish, and drain on a paper towel. Serve immediately on a hot platter, plain or with a sauce. Serves 3 or 4.

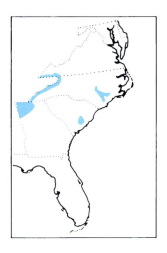

Suggested Readings. 34, 72, 73, 78.

YELLOW BULLHEAD
Ictalurus natalis

Yellow Cat, Creek Cat

Habits. A medium-sized member of the catfish family, the Yellow Bullhead is distributed throughout most of central and eastern North America. In the United States, the species ranges from the Connecticut River southward along the East Coast to Florida, westward through the Gulf States to southern Texas, and north to Minnesota. The habitat is variable and includes vegetated areas of shallow, clear lakes, reservoirs, ponds, slow-flowing streams, and polluted waters. The species is more tolerant of polluted environments than most other ictalurids.

The Yellow Bullhead closely resembles the Brown Bullhead. The body is squat, ugly, and the tail is square. Uncharacteristic of the Brown, the Yellow usually has white chin barbels and more rays in the anal fin, between 24 and 27. In addition to the Yellow and Brown Bullheads, four other species are locally important in the region: Black Bullhead, *Ictalurus melas*, Flat Bullhead, *I. platycephalus*, Snail Bullhead, *I. brunneus*, and Spotted Bullhead, *I. serracanthus*. The Black is very similar to the Brown but lacks strong serrations on the pectoral fins. The Flat Bullhead is separated from the Black by having fewer anal rays and a broader, flatter head. The Snail Bullhead resembles the Flat but has fewer anal rays and more gill rakers. The Spotted Bullhead is recognized by the many small, pale gray-white spots on the sides. The body of the Yellow Bullhead varies from light olive to dark brown above, shading through yellow on the sides to a creamy white belly.

Spawning occurs in May and June as the water temperature rises. Sexually mature fish, those 3 years old and older, move into shallow water to locate a suitable nesting site. The nest may be merely a shallow depression in an open area, or a burrow 2 feet deep in the bank. Some nests are hidden under logs or in patches of vegetation. Batches of 300 to 700 cream-colored, glutinous eggs are released and fertilized at a time. The eggs, which may number about 2 to 4 thousand, hatch in 5 to 10 days. After hatching, the young are herded by the male in a tight school until they are capable of caring for themselves.

Little information is available on age and growth. Approximate lengths for fish age 1 to 5 years are 4.8, 7.1, 8.6, 10.7, and 13.6 inches. Like many species of freshwater fish, the Yellow Bullhead becomes stunted when too many fish are confined in a given area. The Yellow Bullhead is a scavenger that feeds extensively at night by smell and taste. Foods identified in the diet include small fishes, dragonfly nymphs, crayfish, mollusks, and fragments of aquatic vegetation.

54

Fishing. The Yellow Bullhead is the least prized of the catfishes, although it often provides a fishery in waters that do not support other edible fishes. It is one of those species that occurs only sparingly in the fisherman's creel and very seldom in large numbers. Bullheads are caught by fishermen using cane poles or light spinning tackle fishing on the bottom with cut bait, worms, crickets, or doughballs. Commercial fishermen land bullheads in baited fish traps and nets.

Preparation. The flesh of the Yellow Bullhead is considered inferior to that of the Channel, White, and Blue Catfishes, and brings a lower price on the market. This species, as well as other catfishes, bream, and bass, supplements the diets of some rural residents in the South. Whole fish and fillets are usually prepared by frying after rolling them in seasoned cornmeal.

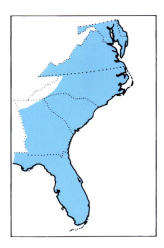

Suggested Readings. 24, 108, 133.

BROWN BULLHEAD
Ictalurus nebulosus

Creek Cat

Habits. Brown Bullheads generally inhabit still or slowly-flowing warm waters—ponds, lakes, and sluggish streams—in the eastern half of the United States from Maine to Florida and from the Great Lakes to Texas. Brown Bullheads are medium-sized ictalurids. They have the typical catfish shape and are easily recognizable by the 20 to 24 anal rays, serrated pectoral spines, dark lower chin barbels, and square tails. The brown body is dark on the back and lighter on the sides, which are often mottled. The extent of mottling varies with the latitude. The belly is creamy white.

Spawning occurs in the spring, from April through June, when water temperatures range from about 70° to 80°F. Sexually mature fish, or those 3 years old or older, move into the shallows to build nests. Both sexes help to construct the circular nests, which are several inches deep and have diameters slightly larger than the parents' lengths. The nests may be situated over open sand or mud bottom, or under logs, brush, or banks. While spawning, the paired fish are positioned side by side in the nest, facing in opposite directions. The eggs are released in masses at intervals and are immediately fertilized by the male. Fish may reproduce several times during a spawning season. The number of eggs produced is fairly low. An 8-inch female may lay 2 thousand eggs, and a 13-inch fish about 13 thousand. The eggs hatch in approximately 7 days in water that is 69°F, and in 5 days at 77°F. Both parents guard the eggs during the incubation period. Young Bullhead are teardrop shaped and resemble tiny tadpoles. Because Bullheads do not have scales, cross sections of their dorsal and pectoral spines are used for determining age. Average lengths for fish aged 1 to 6 years are 3.2, 8.4, 10.3, 10.8, 11.1, and 11.6 inches. These lengths do not accurately reflect the age-size relationship for larger fish, for Brown Bullheads may attain a length of at least 25 inches and are probably older than 10 years. Although fish as large as 5 pounds are occasionally caught, most weigh about 1 pound. Bullheads feed on the bottom, usually at night or late in the afternoon, and use their barbels to help locate food. Favorite foods are mollusks, insects, fishes, fish eggs (even their own), crayfish, algae, scuds, and midges.

Fishing. Fishing for Brown Bullheads is like fishing for catfish. Live and cut baits fished on the bottom with cane poles or spinning outfits are very effective. Shrimp, worms, chicken innards, and minnows are good

baits. The best time to fish is in late winter or early spring—just before crappies start to spawn. Most of the fish are caught from February to April, although the species may be taken all year. Commercial fishermen catch Brown Bullheads with baited wire or wood traps, trotlines, fyke and hoop nets, gill nets, seines, and pound nets.

Preparation. The meat is excellent to eat, but usually brings a much lower price on the market than that of Channel, White, and Blue Catfishes. The flesh is best fried, particularly that of smaller fish, or stewed with onions, potatoes, and bacon.

Suggested Readings. 24, 108, 133.

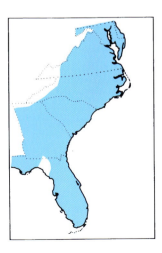

CHANNEL CATFISH
Ictalurus punctatus

Blue Channel Catfish, River Catfish

Habits. Anyone who has read *Tom Sawyer* or *Huckleberry Finn*, or has fished the warm fresh waters of the South, is familiar with catfishes —those whiskered members of the family Ictaluridae who probe the bottom constantly in search of food. The Channel is the most important catfish because of its wide distribution, unique sporting qualities, and because it is an excellent food fish.

Channel Catfish are distinguished from the White and Blue Catfishes by the deeply forked tails and 24 to 29 anal rays. Young fish have numerous black spots on the sides, which are lacking on other species. The scientific name *punctatus* comes from the Latin word meaning "point" (spot). The body is gray to greenish-gray above, silver-gray on the sides, and white underneath. The native range extends from southern Canada through the Great Lakes and central drainage of the United States south to Mexico including parts of the Atlantic Coast and all of the Gulf States. The species has been widely introduced elsewhere. Channel Catfish inhabit rivers, streams, reservoirs, and ponds.

Spawning occurs from May to July when waters warm to 70° to 85°F. Females are sexually mature when they are 10 to 11 inches long (3 to 4 years old), whereas males reproduce for the first time when they are about 12 inches long (4 years old). Age and size at maturity varies with latitude. Younger (smaller) fish develop faster in the southern part of the range; farther north fish mature at larger sizes. Eggs are deposited in nests secluded under banks or logs or over open bottom. The male selects the site, clears the nest, and guards the gelatinous egg mass. Females spawn once each year; males may mate several times. Fecundity ranges from 2 thousand eggs for a 10-inch female to 21 thousand for a fish 36 inches long. The eggs hatch in 6 or 7 days at 80°F.

Age and growth studies indicate 14 years as the maximum age but some fish probably live for 15 to 20 years. Average lengths for Channel Catfish aged 1 to 14 years are 3.6, 7.3, 10.3, 12.6, 14.8, 16.7, 18.8, 20.7, 24, 25.7, 26, 27.7, 28.6, and 31.1 inches. Although Channel Catfish normally feed on the bottom, they also feed at the surface and at mid depths. Major foods are insects, crayfish, amphipods, fish eggs, and fishes such as darters, sunfish, shiners, and Gizzard Shad. Small Channel Catfish eat invertebrates, but larger ones eat fishes.

58

Fishing. Commercial fishermen catch Channel Catfish with traps, bush hooks, and trotlines. Millions of pounds are harvested annually from ponds where fish are raised in suspended cages or in open water. Sport fishermen catch the species on natural and artificial baits. Cane poles with corks, split shot, and small hooks baited with worms, minnows, or cut bait probably catch most of the fish. Avid anglers, using bait-casting outfits, spinning rods and reels, or fly rods catch their share. Shrimp, squid, cut fish, and chicken innards are preferred baits for bottom fishing, while small spinners, spoons, and dry flies are good artificials. A good choice of fishing methods would be to use a spinning outfit with 8-to 10-pound test line, 4/0 hook, and sliding 1-ounce sinker and fish on the bottom at night with saltwater shrimp.

Preparation. Channel Catfish are excellent to eat and may be prepared in a variety of ways. Small fish, called sharpies, are best deep fried whole; larger fish may be cut into steaks and fried, or cooked in a stew. Catfish have sharp, serrated dorsal and pectoral spines that can cause injury if the fish are not handled properly.

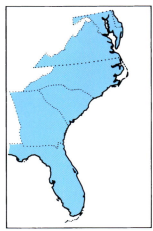

Suggested Readings. 24, 108.

FLATHEAD CATFISH
Pylodictis olivaris

Shovelhead Catfish

Habits. The Flathead, together with the Blue and Channel, are the three largest species of catfishes found in the United States. Flathead are distinguishable from the other two species by their very broad flat heads, only slightly notched caudal fins, large adipose fins, and 14 to 17 anal fin rays. Although the young are black with a white blotch on the upper lobe of the tail, adults are mottled yellow-brown above with pale gray on the undersides.

The species was originally native to the large rivers of the Mississippi, Missouri, and Ohio basins, extending southward to the Gulf of Mexico. It has been introduced into some rivers and reservoirs in the Carolinas and Georgia. The preferred habitat is deep holes scoured by currents, such as those in eddies and adjacent to bridge pilings, and in tailraces below dams. These depressions often contain driftwood and cut timber.

Spawning occurs from June through August in shallow waters that range from about 72° to 84°F. Nests are made in secluded spots such as hollow logs, holes in riverbanks, crevices in rock outcroppings, and among submerged timber in waters 6 to 15 feet deep. Sexually mature females, those older than 4 years, lay their eggs in large adhesive masses. Males guard the eggs and newly hatched fry, chasing away intruders. The number of eggs spawned by a female in a season varies from approximately 4 thousand for a fish weighing 2 pounds to more than 93 thousand for an 80-pound female.

Although individuals have been aged by scientists to 13 years, the species is probably capable of living much longer, based on the maximum size of about 56 inches and 100 pounds. Average lengths for fish aged 1 to 13 years are 2.4, 4.6, 7.8, 12.2, 17.7, 21.7, 24.2, 25.9, 27.3, 28.7, 30.3, 32, and 32.3 inches. The species is more piscivorous than either the Blue or Channel Catfishes. Adults feed on live fish including Gizzard Shad, Freshwater Drum, Carp, Channel Catfish, bullheads, Bluegill, and occasionally crayfish. Juveniles rely more extensively on insects and crayfish than do the adults.

Fishing. Flathead Catfish are caught by commercial and recreational fishermen. Commercially, the species is taken by baited traps, hoop nets, and trotlines, and also by gill nets and trammel nets. Recreational fishermen catch Flatheads by fishing on the bottom using heavy tackle with live or freshly cut fish. The species often feeds at the surface or in shallow water at night, and then returns to its residence in a hole or

brush pile to rest during the day. In reservoirs, Flathead Catfish usually concentrate in old riverbeds or at the headwaters. Unlike Blue and Channel Catfishes, Flathead are reluctant to take old, decaying bait. They prefer live fish such as Gizzard Shad, bream, catfish, and crappie, fishes that are illegal baits in some southern states.

Preparation. The species is regarded as a food fish, and the meat is excellent fried or stewed. Since some fillets may be large, they should be cut into slices before they are deep fried. Meat to be used in fish stews may be chunked.

Suggested Readings. 61, 100, 157, 158.

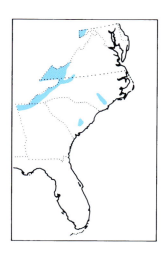

FLIER
Centrarchus macropterus
Round Sunfish, Millpond Flier

Habits. The Flier is a small sunfish that inhabits dark, slightly acidic waters of coastal swamps, creeks, ponds, and canals from eastern Virginia to central Florida. The species also occurs throughout much of the Gulf coastal plain and up the Mississippi Valley as far north as southern Illinois. It is a short, deep-bodied, almost round fish with very spiny dorsal and anal fins. The coloration is yellow-green to brown overall, with a brown dot on each scale giving the appearance of numerous rows of spots. A dark vertical streak is present below the eye and extends to the lower edge of the operculum. Fliers are often confused with Black Crappies, but may be easily distinguished by counting the number of dorsal spines. Fliers have 11 to 13, whereas Black Crappies have 7 to 8.

Seemingly typical of many species of freshwater fish that inhabit coastal-plain waters, Fliers spawn in the early spring. As the water temperature approaches 55°F, males start to build nests and defend small territories. Spawning may last from mid-February through May when temperatures range from 60° to 65°F. Average fecundities for females 3, 5.5, and 7 inches long are 2, 17, and 36 thousand eggs. Laboratory studies indicate that the eggs hatch in 51 hours at 72°F. Under normal incubation temperatures, the hatching times are presumably much longer. Males continuously guard the eggs and recently hatched young.

The Flier is a relatively slow-growing centrarchid that may attain a length of about 10 inches and a weight of 1 pound, but most of the fish caught in the Southeast are much smaller. There is no apparent difference in size or rate of growth between males and females. Average lengths for Fliers aged 1 to 7 years are 2, 3, 4.4, 5.3, 6, 6.3, and 7 inches. Fliers feed throughout the water column on cladocerans, midges, beetles, worms, and fishes. The diet and feeding behavior are similar to other sunfishes.

Fishing. The Flier is more popular with sport fishermen than most of the small sunfishes. One reason for this popularity is its willingness to take both artificial and natural baits. It rises to take dry and wet flies almost as readily as the Bluegill, and like the Black Crappie, is easily caught on small minnows. Most Fliers are probably caught by anglers who are fishing for crappies in the early spring. Light spinning tackle or cane or fiber glass poles rigged with a tiny split shot, cork, and small hook

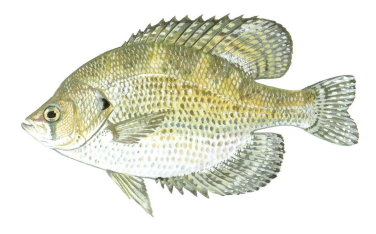

baited with a minnow or worm are ideal for catching the species. Fliers do not seem to school as densely as crappies, but several fish often are caught in the same spot. Good fishing locations are around cypress trees and stumps, near brush piles, and at the mouths of small creeks and canals. There is no commercial fishery for the species in the Southeast.

Preparation. The flesh is sweet and excellent to eat. The same methods of cooking bream apply for Fliers.

Suggested Readings. 26, 27, 77.

GREEN SUNFISH
Lepomis cyanellus

Habits. The Green Sunfish is a small centrarchid found in creeks and streams in the eastern and central portions of the United States. It can successfully survive periods of drought by inhabiting residual pools in streams characterized by having seasonal, temporary flows. The species is known to establish territories near the water's edge under brush, rocks, or exposed roots. Green Sunfish are easily identified by their large mouths, short rounded pectoral fins, stiff black opercular flaps, and 45 to 50 scales along the lateral line. Adults are dark olivaceous on the back and sides. The belly is yellow-orange, and the cheeks have bright iridescent emerald flecks or wavy lines that radiate from the mouth toward the operculum. Dark vertical bars may be evident on fish that are excited or stressed.

Both males and females are sexually mature when they are 2 years old, when they may be as small as 2 to 3 inches long. Multiple spawning occurs at 8- to 9-day intervals from April through August when water temperatures range from 68° to 84°F. The yellow, adhesive eggs are deposited in shallow saucer-shaped nests and hatch in 3 to 4 days. Because Green Sunfish spawn simultaneously with other species of *Lepomis*, hybridization is not uncommon. Bluegill and Green Sunfish crosses occur most frequently, and in these cases the offspring are males that are unable to reproduce.

Like other sunfish, the species may become stunted, or attain only small sizes in confined environments. Average lengths of fish aged 1 to 4 years are 3.8, 5.3, 6.5, and 6.8 inches. The diet consists of a variety of small animals that are eaten throughout the water column. Preferred foods are dragonfly and mayfly nymphs, caddisfly larvae, midges, freshwater shrimps, beetles, Mosquitofish, and small sunfish.

Fishing. This small species is of no commercial importance, and is not highly regarded as a game fish. Green Sunfish are usually caught by anglers fishing for other centrarchids using small artificial lures such as dry flies and spinners, and with live worms. Many muddy piedmont creeks that offer little in the way of angling opportunity are good locations for catching Green Sunfish.

Preparation. The flesh resembles that of Bluegill and Shellcracker in texture and taste. Although seldom eaten, the meat is best deep fried

after rolling it in seasoned cornmeal. Other methods of preparation that require fish with white, lean flesh may also be followed when cooking this species.

Suggested Readings. 24, 108.

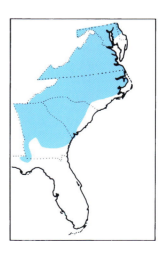

PUMPKINSEED
Lepomis gibbosus
Speckled Perch, Bream

Habits. The Pumpkinseed is a brilliantly colored, medium-sized sunfish that inhabits brackish waters in the southeastern United States. In addition to low-salinity estuaries, the species is found in quiet, slow-flowing streams, weedy lakes, and coastal ponds. Pumpkinseed occur east of the Rocky Mountains in North America from North Dakota east to Quebec and south to northeastern Georgia, Ohio, and Iowa. They are olive-green above, bluish-orange with gold on the lower sides, and orange underneath. Distinctive blue and orange streaks radiate from the mouth onto the cheeks. The dark opercular flap has a bright red spot on the posterior border. The long pointed pectoral fin, short stiff gill rakers, and coloration easily separate this species from other centrarchids.

Spawning takes place in the spring and early summer when waters warm to about 68°F. Both males and females reach sexual maturity during the second year of life. During the prespawning period, males construct nests in shallow water (less than 5 feet deep), often near aquatic vegetation. The circular nests are 4 to 16 inches in diameter and are built singly or in small groups. Mating involves considerable display behavior as both fish swim in a circular path around and above the nest before the eggs are released. The number of eggs produced by a female varies only slightly with age (size). A 2-year-old female may lay 1 thousand eggs, whereas a fish 5 years old is capable of laying approximately 3 thousand in a season. The eggs are adhesive and stick to the bottom before hatching, which takes place in about 3 days at 82°F. After the young fish leave the nest, the male often clears it in preparation for a second spawning. Because several species of sunfish often spawn in the same area simultaneously, there is frequent hybridization in the genus *Lepomis*. In nature, Pumpkinseed hybridize with Warmouth, Bluegill, Redbreast, and other sunfishes.

Pumpkinseed feed on a variety of small animals, including dragonfly nymphs, ants, small salamanders, amphipods, mayfly nymphs, midge larvae, worms, snails, and water beetles. Although most Pumpkinseed are small (about 4 to 6 inches), some reach a length of 12 inches and are believed to be about 10 years old. Average lengths for fish aged 1 to 8 years are 2.6, 4.2, 4.9, 5.6, 6.1, 6.8, 7.3, and 7.8 inches.

Fishing. Many writers describe the Pumpkinseed as a small fish, one that is too easily caught, and therefore of little interest to fishermen. This is

not always the case. Fish in the 8- to 10-inch size class may be very plentiful in a given area, yet these fish may be anything but easy to catch. Pumpkinseed of all sizes bite very timidly. It takes an experienced eye and hand to notice a bite. Most Pumpkinseed are caught on worms or crickets. Cane or fiber glass poles are rigged with tiny hooks and split shot. Good fishing spots are coastal creeks with a heavy detrital layer on the bottom and a periphery of cattails and needlerush. Anglers fishing from small boats in April and May usually catch Pumpkinseed by casting close to the vegetation. Later in the season, fish may be taken on dry flies and small popping bugs.

Preparation. The flesh is white, flaky, and sweet. It is delicious rolled in seasoned cornmeal and fried.

Suggested Readings. 24, 78, 108, 133.

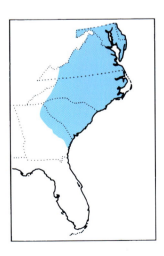

WARMOUTH

Lepomis gulosus

Openmouth, Perch, Goggle Eye

Habits. At first glance it is difficult to tell whether the Warmouth more closely resembles a bass or a bream. It is related to both and has a stout, deep body similar to that of a Bluegill or Shellcracker, yet has a large bass-like mouth. The species may be easily separated from other sunfishes by a combination of three characteristics: short anal fins, three anal spines, and teeth on the tongue. Warmouths vary from brassy to dark olive-green overall with a nondescript pattern of dark spots on the sides. Three dark bars radiate from the eyes and may be used to identify individuals of all sizes. Warmouths inhabit slow-flowing mud-bottom creeks, ponds, and swamps from the Great Lakes to the Gulf of Mexico on both sides of the Appalachian Mountains. They have been widely introduced elsewhere. The species is fond of hiding around aquatic vegetation, stumps, and snags, and under the banks of streams and ponds.

Like other centrarchids, Warmouths spawn in the late spring and summer. Spawning usually begins when waters warm to about 70°F and continues through the warmer months (April through August). Multiple spawning is common. Individuals spawn for the first time when they are 3 to 4 inches long, being from 1 to 3 years old depending on local conditions influencing growth. The male builds a shallow, bowl-shaped nest that occurs singly or with others to form a small group of nests in water less than 5 feet deep. Favorite nesting sites are in sand or rubble bottom with a thin covering of silt or detritus near patches of lily pads, cattails, and grasses, or at the base of trees standing in shallow water. Polygamy is common, with the number of females laying eggs in one nest determined by the number of ripe females available to a male. Fecundity ranges from 3 to 23 thousand eggs, which hatch in about 35 hours at temperatures of 77° to 80°F. Eggs are guarded constantly by the parent.

Warmouths are capable of living for at least 8 years and may reach a length of 12 inches and a weight of approximately 1 pound. Average lengths of fish aged 1 to 8 years collected from several geographical areas are 2.5, 4, 5, 6, 7, 8, 9, and 9.5 inches. Because of their large mouths, Goggle Eyes have a more diverse diet than most species of *Lepomis*, eating fish as well as invertebrates. Small sunfishes, darters, Mosquitofish, crayfish, snails, freshwater shrimps, dragonflies, and other insects are important food items.

Fishing. Warmouths are easily caught by anglers using cane poles and natural baits, spinning tackle with small topwater lures and shallow-running spinners, and on wet and dry flies. Although Warmouths strike hard, frequently breaking the surface of the water, they possess the fighting qualities of a stick. After the initial hit, Warmouths generally lay back and are retrieved with mouths agape. Most are caught by people who are fishing for bass or bream, yet they add meat to a successful day's creel. The best way to catch Goggle Eyes is to fish in shallow water around trees, stumps, or vegetation, from a small boat or the bank. Preferred natural baits are worms and minnows, while Beetle Spins, Rebels, Rapalas, and popping bugs are the best artificials. Commercial fishermen catch the species while fishing for catfish and anadromous species using traps and nets. In most states the commercial harvest of sunfish is illegal, and the fish must be returned to the water alive.

Preparation. Like other centrarchids, Warmouths are good to eat even though they are small and bony. The meat is usually prepared by deep frying after rolling it in seasoned cornmeal.

Suggested Readings. 24, 53, 108.

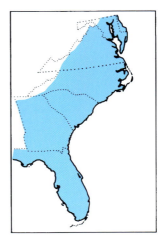

BLUEGILL
Lepomis macrochirus

Bream, Blue Bream

Habits. More Bluegills are caught by anglers fishing the fresh waters of the southeastern United States than any other fish. In terms of providing sport for the largest number of people, the Bluegill is the most important form of wildlife in the South. The original distribution, which extended from southern Ontario through the Great Lakes and Mississippi River drainages south to Florida, Texas, and northeastern Mexico, has been greatly expanded by the construction of thousands of farm ponds throughout the country. Besides ponds, Bluegills prefer the quiet waters of lakes and slow-flowing rivers and streams with sand, mud, or gravel bottoms, bordered by aquatic vegetation.

Like most lepomids, Bluegills have small mouths and oval-shaped, almost rounded, bodies. The color is highly variable, but generally olive-green above, with dark vertical bands along the sides that fade into a light green-yellow underside. The lower cheeks are dark blue, thus the common name. Two distinctive characteristics are the prominent blue-black opercular flap and the dark spot at the base of the posterior portion of the dorsal fin.

Spawning is from April to September, commencing when water temperatures warm to about 70°F. Multiple spawning is common, and individuals may reproduce several times. The age of sexual maturity, and size and age in general, vary from one region to another. Bluegills attain first maturity when they are 2 or 3 years old, some as young as 4 months. The male acts as mate, nest builder, and guardian of eggs and newly hatched young. Shallow, bowl-shaped nests (6 to 24 inches in diameter, and 2 to 6 inches deep) are constructed in water 1 to 6 feet deep over a sand, gravel, or mud bottom. Bluegill beds occur in colonies of up to 500 nests in a small stretch of shoreline. In dense concentrations, beds touch and resemble honeycombs, emitting a distinctive earthy odor. A female may lay 2 to 63 thousand eggs, which hatch 30 to 35 hours after fertilization. One fish may lay eggs in several nests, and one nest may receive eggs from more than one female. Males stand vigil throughout the incubation period and fan the eggs to keep them clean and aerated.

Growth is so variable that it is difficult to relate fish size with age. Average lengths of Bluegills aged 1 to 9 years from different areas of the country are 1.9, 3.7, 5.1, 6, 6.4, 7.1, 7.8, 8, and 8.4 inches. Bluegills feed on a variety of small foods, foraging at different levels in the water

column according to temperature. Important foods are spiders, insects, crayfish, fish eggs, and small fishes.

Fishing. This species is a popular sport fish because it is easily caught by novice and experienced anglers in relaxing surroundings. Bluegills may be caught year around, but most are caught when they are bedding or when surface waters cool in the fall. The most effective way to catch Bluegills is to locate their nests by smell or sight and fish with poles rigged with small hooks, corks, and split shot, using worms or crickets as bait. The angler must be quiet because the nests are in shallow water and the fish are alert while protecting them. Fly fishing is productive in spring and fall. During hot weather, Bluegills move to deep water and feed less often, so in summer one should fish deep. Slowly retrieved spinners such as Beetle Spins and Panther Martins as well as live baits will allow one to catch summer Bluegills.

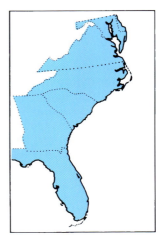

Preparation. Bluegills are excellent to eat. The meat has a mild flavor and is generally rolled in cornmeal or dipped in pancake batter before frying. Bream can be filleted, but those who do so discard the sweetest meat.

Suggested Readings. 24, 108.

LONGEAR SUNFISH
Lepomis megalotis

Habits. The Longear Sunfish occurs sparsely in the southeastern United States. The present distribution includes the western portions of Virginia, North Carolina, Georgia, Florida, and possibly South Carolina. Longears are found in the east-central section of North America, west of the Appalachian Mountains from southern Quebec to the Gulf of Mexico. Longears are replaced by the closely related Dollar Sunfish, *Lepomis marginatus*, in peninsular Florida. The Longear Sunfish is a beautifully colored, small centrarchid that seldom attains a length greater than 9 inches. Consequently, it is of minor importance to sport fishermen and of no commercial value. The species inhabits small streams and upland sections of rivers, and more recently, reservoirs. Longear Sunfish are usually absent from downstream lowland portions of rivers and streams.

Like most lepomids, Longears are deep-bodied, laterally compressed, short fish with a single dorsal fin. To fishermen, they are probably more similar in appearance to the Redbreast, *L. auritus*, than to any other sunfish. Identification of adults is possible, however, by the opercular lobe. Longears have long, upward turned lobes that are at least as wide as the eye. Redbreasts have long, narrow opercular lobes. Longears have short, stiff gill rakers and 36 to 45 scales along the lateral line. The body is olivaceous above with a dull orange-red breast and belly. Breeding males are brilliant iridescent green or turquoise and orange on the sides. The opercular flap is usually black, edged with white to red or yellow.

Spawning occurs over a gravel bottom from late May to mid-August, when the water temperature ranges from 75° to 86°F. Although some fish are capable of reproducing when they are only 1 year old, most spawn for the first time when they are aged 2. Males defend territories and build typical sunfish nests that are shallow and saucer shaped in waters 8 inches to 2 feet in depth. The nesting cycle lasts for 2 weeks, and the eggs hatch in about a week. Many beds are usually found close together. The number of eggs laid during the season by one fish ranges from approximately 600 for fish 3.5 inches long, to more than 4 thousand for larger females. Longears are capable of living for 8 years and attaining a length of 9 inches. Males grow faster and live longer than females. Average lengths for both sexes aged 1 to 7 years are 2.9, 3.7, 4.4, 4.7, 5.2, 5.5, and 6 inches. The species feeds throughout the water column. Sometimes Longears pick immature aquatic insects,

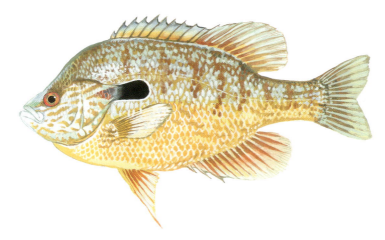

worms, crayfish, and fish eggs off the bottom, and occasionally they rise to the surface to gulp a struggling insect that has fallen into the water.

Fishing. Although small, the Longear is an excellent game fish on light tackle. The fighting qualities are enhanced by the fact that fish generally are caught in areas of moderate to swift currents. The species readily takes natural baits such as crickets, worms, minnows, and crayfish as well as small artificial flies and spinners. In general, the same fishing techniques described for the Redbreast apply to the Longear Sunfish.

Preparation. The white and sweet flesh is excellent when rolled in seasoned cornmeal and fried.

Suggested Readings. 27, 133.

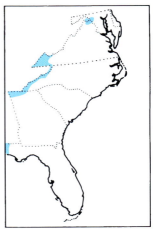

REDEAR SUNFISH
Lepomis microlophus

Shellcracker, Bream

Habits. Because Redear Sunfish fight hard on light tackle, attain a large size for a panfish (many 2 to 3 pounds), and can be caught in large numbers, they are a popular sport fish. Native to the southeastern United States and the Mississippi and Rio Grande drainages, the species has been introduced in other States including Ohio, Indiana, and California. The preferred habitat is nonflowing waters such as farm ponds, lakes, and reservoirs.

Redears are olivaceous with yellow-orange breasts. Five to 10 vertical bars are more or less evident on the sides, depending on the size of the fish. The species is distinguished from other centrarchids by having short gill rakers, long pointed pectoral fins, and red-bordered opercular flaps; thus the name Redear Sunfish. The frequently used name, Shellcracker, is derived from its ability to crush snails and other hard-bodied animals with the molarlike teeth located on the lower pharyngeal arches.

Some Redear Sunfish are capable of spawning in hatchery ponds when they are only 5 inches long and 1 year old. Older fish in natural environments seem to inhibit spawning by young fish so that most reproduce when they are 2 years old or older. Spawning begins when the waters warm to about 70°F, as early as March in Florida, and extending throughout the spring, summer, and early fall. Like most sunfish, Shellcrackers build nests in which the 6 to 45 thousand eggs are deposited. Males build and guard the shallow, circular nests, which are approximately 1 foot in diameter and several inches deep. Nesting sites are often near aquatic vegetation such as water lilies, cattails, lizardtails, and maidencane, in water ranging in depth from 2 to 8 feet. The substrate may be sand, limestone, shell, or roots of water lilies. Some nests occur solitarily, but they are most often in large concentrations. As many as 300 beds have been observed in an area of 1,500 square feet. Size of fish for a given age varies geographically, being larger in the more southern part of the range. A study in Oklahoma revealed fish aged 1 to 5 years were 6, 7, 8, 9, and 10 inches. Redear Sunfish are opportunistic bottom feeders, foraging mainly during daylight hours on a variety of invertebrates. Primary food items in the diet are midge larvae, snails, amphipods, and mayfly and dragonfly naiads. Foods of secondary importance are copepods, clams, fish eggs, crayfish, and damselfly naiads.

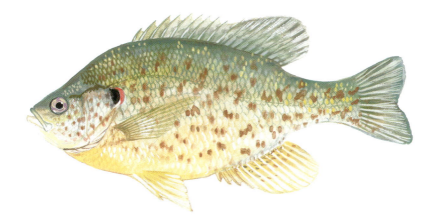

Fishing. Redear Sunfish are caught exclusively by sport fishermen using hook and line. Most fish are taken on cane or fiber glass poles with small hooks, corks, and split shot for weight. Favorite baits are crickets and worms fished in the spring and summer during the bedding season. Many anglers strap on bait buckets, don waders or tennis shoes and quietly wade the edges of vegetation, presenting their baits in the open areas. Fly fishing with wet and dry flies and the use of light spinning tackle with small spinners (Beetle Spins, Rooster Tails, and Shysters) also produce good results. The trained nose can sniff out the earthy smell of bream beds; thus the angler avoids fishing nonproductive locations.

Preparation. The suggested method of cooking bream is by frying. The fish should be cleaned and then rolled in cornmeal that has been generously salted and peppered. Some prefer dipping the fish in pancake batter rather than cornmeal before frying. Larger fish may be filleted, but with a loss of flavor.

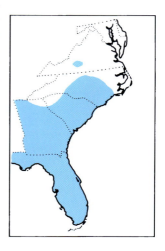

Suggested Readings. 164.

SPOTTED SUNFISH
Lepomis punctatus

Stumpknocker

Habits. There are several species of sunfish in the region that are widespread geographically, yet seldom are caught by fishermen. Some, such as the Bluespotted Sunfish, *Enneacanthus gloriosus*, Banded Sunfish, *E. obesus*, Blackbanded Sunfish, *E. chaetodon*, and Dollar Sunfish, *Lepomis marginatus*, are too small. Others, like the Orange-spotted Sunfish, *L. humilis*, and Spotted Sunfish are somewhat larger but are not very common, and therefore unfamiliar to most fishermen. The last probably is the most frequently caught of this group.

Spotted Sunfish, or Stumpknockers, are distributed along the eastern coast of the United States from North Carolina to Florida. They also occur throughout the Gulf Coast and up the Mississippi Valley as far north as southern Indiana. In the Southeast the species is most abundant in central Florida, although even there it is not an important game fish. The preferred habitat is slow-flowing, heavily vegetated streams and rivers with limestone, sand, or gravel substrates. Its northern ecological counterpart is probably the Redbreast. Spotted Sunfish are plain olivaceous overall with numerous brown or black spots scattered over the sides. The opercular lobe is short and black, with a bony margin.

Sexually mature fish, or those 2 years old and older, spawn throughout most of the year when water temperatures range from 64° to 91°F. Peak spawning takes place from May through August (81° to 84°F). Nesting and courtship behavior are similar to that of other centrarchids. Very little information is available on age and growth. Approximate average lengths for fish from Oklahoma aged 1 to 4 years are 2, 3.5, 4.5, and 6 inches. Spotted Sunfish feed on a variety of plants and animals that are usually associated with aquatic vegetation, brush, or rubble. Favorite foods are filamentous algae, diatoms, amphipods, caddisflies, and midges. The species generally feeds on the bottom, but occasionally it will rise to the surface to take food.

Fishing. The same methods of fishing discussed for the Redbreast apply for the Spotted Sunfish. It has no commercial fishery value.

Preparation. Pan Fried Sunfish are excellent. The ingredients are 6 dressed sunfish, 2 cups of cornmeal, salt and pepper, and cooking oil. Roll the fish in cornmeal that has been seasoned with salt and pepper. It is particularly important when cooking freshwater fish that the cornmeal be adequately seasoned. Put enough oil in a large frying pan to equal

about one-half of the thickness of the fish. Heat the oil until it is very hot. Put the fish in the pan and fry them on both sides until they are brown and the meat is flaky. Remove them from the pan and place on paper towels to drain excess oil. Serve immediately with baked beans, coleslaw, and cornbread. Serves 4.

Suggested Readings. 23, 27, 78.

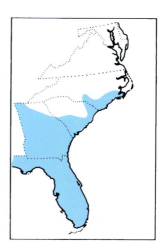

SPOTTED BASS
Micropterus punctulatus

Kentucky Bass

Habits. The Spotted Bass is very similar in appearance to the Large-mouth Bass and Smallmouth Bass, especially the former. There has been, and still is, confusion regarding its identification. The species was first described by Rafinesque in 1819 as *Calliurus punctulatus*, but it was not until 1927 that the Spotted Bass was placed in the familiar genus, *Micropterus*. By close examination, the adults can be distinguished because the upper jaw does not extend past the posterior margin of the eye as it does in the Largemouth Bass. Unlike the Smallmouth Bass, the Spotted Bass has a longitudinal stripe of connected black blotches on the sides of the body. The back is olive-green, the belly white, the scales are spotted, and the fins are dusky.

The native range extends throughout the central and lower Mississippi basin and along the Gulf Coast from western Texas through northwestern Florida. There are several subspecies that extend the distribution eastward into western Virginia, North Carolina, Georgia and Alabama. Additionally, there are two basses—the Redeye Bass, *M. coosae*, and the Suwannee Bass, *M. notius*—found in the southeastern United States, but both have very restricted ranges and are of little importance to fisheries. The former occurs in parts of Alabama, Georgia, and South Carolina, and the latter in the Suwannee River, Florida. An undescribed species, the Shoal Bass, is found in the Apalachicola River drainage in Florida. Spotted Bass prefer large, cool streams, and rivers with gradients less than 3 feet per mile, although they have adapted well to deep, oligotrophic reservoirs. When inhabiting the same stream, Smallmouth Bass often prefer riffles, Largemouth Bass weedy oxbows, and Spotted Bass sluggish pools.

Spawning takes place in the spring when the water warms to about 60° to 65°F. Sexually mature fish, or those 2 to 3 years old or older, construct saucer-shaped nests on a soft, clay bottom or on gravel bars. The eggs hatch in 4 or 5 days, yielding 2 to 3 thousand fry per nest. Although the Spotted Bass grows faster than Smallmouth Bass and slower than Largemouth Bass, it does not attain as large a size as the other species. Average lengths for fish aged 1 to 8 years are 4, 8, 12, 14, 15, 16, 17, and 18 inches. The major foods are crayfish, shad, and aquatic insects. The species is less piscivorous than the other black basses and seems to be more selective in its feeding habits.

Fishing. Spotted Bass are caught almost exclusively by sport fishermen. The species is noted for its speed, endurance, and power as a game fish. However, unlike the Largemouth Bass and Smallmouth Bass, it seldom leaps when it is hooked. Most of the fish are caught in the spring in shallow water on spinning tackle or cane poles. Good natural baits are salamanders, crayfish, and minnows. Jigs, artificial worms, and deep-running lures are effective artificials.

Preparation. Spotted Bass are excellent to eat and may be prepared like the other freshwater bass. A suggested dish is Baked Fish with Cheese Sauce. The ingredients are a 2- to 3-pound dressed fish, 1 chopped onion, 8 ounces of grated cheese, 1½ tea-spoons of Worcestershire sauce, 1 teaspoon of dry mustard, 1 teaspoon of salt, ½ tea-spoon of pepper, and 1 cup of milk. Place the onion and half of the cheese in the cavity of the fish. Put the remaining cheese on top of the fish. Add the other ingredients to the milk and pour it over the fish. Bake at 400°F for 25 to 30 minutes. Serves 4.

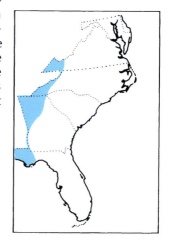

Suggested Readings. 2, 78, 133.

LARGEMOUTH BASS
Micropterus salmoides

Chub, Bigmouth, Black Bass

Habits. More anglers using artificial lures fish for Largemouth Bass than any other inland game fish in the southeastern United States. The species, and its close relative the Smallmouth Bass, *Micropterus dolomieui*, is a member of the sunfish family, Centrarchidae. Largemouth Bass are distributed from southern Canada through the Great Lakes drainage south into Mexico and throughout the Southeast. It has been widely introduced elsewhere. In Florida, a subspecies, the Florida Largemouth Bass, has gained fame because of its large size and has been stocked in other states.

Coloration is highly variable, ranging from a silvery background to dark olive-green, influenced by genetics and also by habitat, notably water clarity. Generally, Largemouth Bass are dark green above with silvery sides and belly. A dark stripe runs longitudinally, but usually breaks up in larger individuals. Three dark bars are found on the sides of the head back of and below the eyes. The Smallmouth Bass has a similar body shape, but has continuous dorsal fins, a smaller mouth in proportion to the body, very small scales, and more rows of scales (17) on the cheeks than does the Largemouth Bass (9 to 10). Largemouth Bass occupy brackish to freshwater habitats, including upper estuaries, rivers, lakes, reservoirs, and ponds. The species is replaced in colder, more rapidly flowing waters by trouts, Smallmouth Bass, and pikes.

Although some individuals spawn by the end of their first year, most spawn for the first time when they are 2 years old. Size at maturity ranges from 9 to 12 inches. Spawning begins as early as March or as late as June when the water warms to 67°F. Bass are territorial and build nests 7 to 10 feet apart. Males build saucer-shaped nests, 20 to 30 inches in diameter, in hard-bottom areas where the water is 1 to 8 feet deep. Depending on her size, the paired female lays 2 thousand to 1 million eggs, which are fertilized as they settle into the bed. The male guards the nest and eggs until they hatch.

Largemouth Bass may live for 13 years and weigh 20 pounds. Approximate lengths for ages 1, 2, 5, 10, and 13 years are 8, 13, 17, 20, and 23 inches. Growth is more rapid in the southerly part of the range. Largemouth Bass are voracious carnivores and eat minnows, sunfish, Gizzard and Threadfin Shads, insects, frogs, and occasionally snakes.

Fishing. The species is not a commercial fish in any state, and its capture by commercial gear and sale are usually prohibited. Largemouth Bass rank very high as sport fish. The variety of items in the diet makes it possible to fish by trolling, casting, and jigging artificials as well as with live minnows, worms, frogs, and salamanders. Light spinning and bait-casting outfits are becoming more popular as anglers use topwater plugs, spinners, rubber worms, spoons, and other deep-running lures. Fly fishing with popping bugs, streamers, and even wet flies, is effective in spring and summer. Fishing is best early in the morning or late afternoon. In recent years, Largemouth Bass tournaments offering large cash prizes have created a multitude of professional fishermen who, like tennis and golf pros, travel the "pro circuit."

Preparation. The eating qualities of Bass are directly dependent upon the way the fish are cleaned and prepared. The strong weedy taste of Bass caught in some waters may be eliminated by skinning the fish and generously salting and peppering the fillets before battering. Most Largemouth Bass are fried, although the larger ones may be baked.

Suggested Readings. 2, 23, 30, 133.

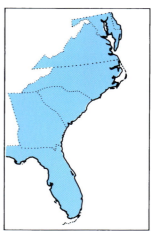

WHITE CRAPPIE
Pomoxis annularis

Speckled Perch

Habits. There are two species of crappies: *Pomoxis annularis*, the White Crappie, and *P. nigromaculatus*, the Black Crappie. Both have characteristically compressed bodies, small heads, and arched backs. Crappies are the only sunfishes that have only five to eight dorsal spines and anal fins as long as their dorsal fins. The two species may be identified by the number of dorsal fin spines; White Crappies have five or six, whereas Black Crappies have seven or eight. The coloration of the White Crappie is dark above with silvery sides flecked with small dark spots that occur in seven to ten vertical bars.

The original distribution extended from the Great Lakes south to Texas and Alabama. The range now covers much of North America. Both species inhabit ponds, lakes, reservoirs, and low-gradient streams and rivers. Although White Crappies seem to grow better in small lakes and ponds, Black Crappies can become stunted in these confined environments. White Crappies are more tolerant of turbid conditions than Black Crappies, but are somewhat less comfortable in cold waters. Both species concentrate around cover such as brush, fallen trees, and stumps.

Spawning occurs from March to July, depending on latitude, when waters warm to 58° to 64°F. Like most other centrarchids, male White Crappies select and clear nest sites and guard the eggs. Nests are located near brush piles, stumps, or rock outcroppings in water 3 to 8 feet deep. Sexual maturity is attained when fish are 2 to 3 years old, or about 7 to 10 inches long. Age is more important than size, for stunted fish as small as 4 inches may spawn. The number of eggs ranges from 1 to 213 thousand. Although White Crappies are known to live at least 9 years, most of the fish caught are 5 years old or younger. Average lengths for fish aged 1 to 8 years compiled from throughout the United States are 2.9, 7.2, 9.7, 11.4, 12.4, 13.3, 13.6, and 15 inches.

White Crappies feed on a variety of animals, depending on their size. Recently hatched crappies feed on zooplankton, fish less than 6 inches long eat aquatic insects, and larger crappies eat fishes. Major foods are insects, freshwater shrimps, amphipods, and small fishes.

Fishing. Crappies are excellent sport fish because large numbers are easily caught, they are game fighters on light tackle, and are good to eat. The best time to catch White Crappies is early morning or late afternoon in the spring or fall. In some areas night fishing is popular

where anglers use lanterns to concentrate bait fish, which in turn attract crappies. Both natural and artificial baits are effective. Small, lively minnows hooked through the lip or back with long-shanked small hooks are the preferred live bait. Fiber glass and cane poles and spinning outfits are used. Artificial lures such as Mini-jigs and small spinners are also good baits. The key to good crappie fishing is to fish confined, brushy areas. Although many crappie are caught from the bank, most are caught from boats, which enable fishermen to cover large areas to locate schools. Underwater brush, tree tops, stumps, and shell and limestone ledges are good fishing spots. Depth recorders are valuable for locating fish. Some ambitious anglers place brush or tires on the bottom to attract crappies. Commercial fishermen catch the species with nets and traps while fishing for other species. In most states the commercial harvest of crappies, as well as other sunfish, is illegal.

Preparation. The meat is usually prepared by rolling in cornmeal or dipping in pancake batter and deep frying. The roe is also cooked in this manner.

Suggested Readings. 5, 24, 108.

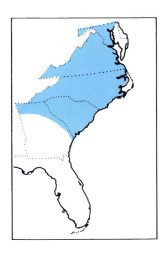

BLACK CRAPPIE
Pomoxis nigromaculatus

White Perch, Speck, Speckled Perch

Habits. In appearance, the Black Crappie differs from the White Crappie in only two major characteristics: the dorsal fin spines (Black Crappies have seven or eight, White Crappies have five or six), and coloration. The dark blotches on the sides of the Black Crappie are much less ordered than the vertical bars on the White. Overall, Black Crappies appear much darker, although the coloration of both species may vary with the waters inhabited; thus color alone may not be a reliable means of identifying the species. For sure identification, count the dorsal spines.

The native range extends from the upper St. Lawrence River and Manitoba south to northern Texas and Florida. The species is now distributed throughout much of North America. Black Crappies are more tolerant of cold water than White Crappies, but do not grow as well in turbid waters. In the Southeast, Black Crappies are most abundant in the clear, organically stained waters of the coastal plain and in the lakes and rivers of central Florida.

Spawning takes place in the spring, but at slightly warmer temperatures than those initiating the reproduction of White Crappies. Optimum temperatures are 64° to 68°F. Males select nest sites and clear beds in water 3 to 8 feet deep over gravel or mud bottom. Fecundity ranges from approximately 11 to 188 thousand eggs. Black Crappies become sexually mature when they are 2 or 3 years old. Size for a specific age reveals much variation, compounded by the fact that stunting may occur in small, restricted environments, such as ponds, where the fish are overcrowded. Average lengths of Black Crappies from throughout the United States for ages 1 to 8 years are 3.4, 7.3, 9.8, 10.6, 11.8, 12.7, 14.1, and 14.5 inches.

The diet of the two species is very similar. Black Crappies of all sizes tend to eat more benthic insects in the spring than do White Crappies; larger fish adopt a piscivorous feeding behavior during other seasons.

Fishing. Under optimum conditions of season, time of day, and habitat, Black Crappies are excellent game fish and are highly regarded by bait fishermen and artificial-lure anglers alike. Fishing methods discussed for the White Crappie apply for both species.

Preparation. Usually deep fried, Black Crappies may also be used to make a quick New England Fish Chowder. Cut a 1-pound fillet in about 1-inch cubes. Fry 4 teaspoons of bacon or diced salt pork until crisp and

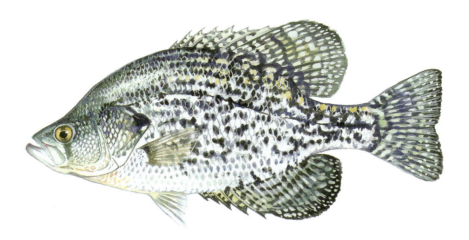

golden brown. Add ½ cup of chopped or sliced onions and brown slightly. Add 3 cups of hot water and 3 cups of diced potatoes, and cook for 10 minutes or until the potatoes are partially tender. Add the fish, turn the heat to simmer, and cook until the fish can be flaked easily with a fork. Add 3 cups of milk; salt and pepper to taste, and heat but do not boil. Serve immediately with chopped parsley sprinkled over the top. For additional flavor, add bay leaves and thyme. Serves 5 or 6.

Suggested Readings. 5, 24, 108.

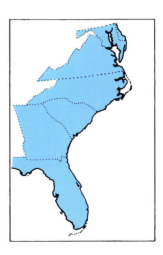

ANADROMOUS-
UPPER ESTUARINE FISHES

ATLANTIC STURGEON
Acipenser oxyrhynchus

Sea Sturgeon, Common Sturgeon

Habits. Sturgeons are members of the family Acipenseridae, and the decline of these once plentiful fish is a sad chapter in the American fisheries heritage. The Atlantic Sturgeon and Shortnose Sturgeon, *Acipenser brevirostrum*, were once common spring visitors to Atlantic estuaries and rivers. However, overfishing, deterioration of water quality, and the damming of rivers have taken their toll on the populations. Today, Atlantic Sturgeon are sparsely distributed along the East Coast from Labrador to the St. Johns River, Florida.

Sturgeons are large, primitive-looking fish. The mouth is protractile and is located underneath a pointed snout. Four barbels line the front of the mouth, giving the fish a whiskered appearance. Five rows of scutes extend the length of the body—one on the back, two on the sides, and two on the belly. Atlantic Sturgeon are either dark brown or olive-green, and may be distinguished from the Shortnose Sturgeon by their much longer snouts.

The species is anadromous and the spawning season begins as early as February in Florida, April in Chesapeake Bay, and June in the Gulf of Maine. Males in Florida attain first maturity when they are 7 to 10 years old, whereas those farther north are unable to reproduce before they are 22 to 28 years old. This extreme late age of maturity poses problems for management of the species. Heavy fishing pressure and destruction of habitat severely reduce the chances of an adequate number of fish reaching an age, or size, for reproduction.

Average fecundity ranges from about 1 to 2.5 million eggs. However, a 352-pound female had one ovary that contained 3.8 million ova. Sturgeon eggs are two to three times larger than most fish ova and are laid in flowing fresh water up to 60 feet deep. The adhesive eggs sink to the bottom in stringy clumps. The incubation time varies from 94 to 168 hours, depending on the water temperature. After hatching in fresh water, the young remain there for as long as 5 years before they journey to the sea. Adults inhabit tidal bays and sounds and may range as far as 900 miles from their natal rivers and offshore to depths of 150 feet.

Atlantic Sturgeon may live as long as 60 years, reaching a length of 14 feet and a weight exceeding 800 pounds. Approximate average lengths for fish age 1, 5, 10, 16, and 20 years are 1, 3, 5, 6, and 7 feet. Sturgeon feed on the bottom, using their protractile mouths and barbels to root in the mud and sand for worms, insect larvae, crabs, and small fishes.

Fishing. Important commercial fisheries for Sturgeon once flourished along the East Coast. These developed as Indians and white settlers realized the value of the meat and roe. Fishermen worked the Hudson, Delaware, Susquehanna, Potomac, York, James, St. Marys, and St. Johns Rivers. Large drifting gill nets have been used for more than 200 years to catch the species. Nets once were up to 1,500 feet long and 21 feet deep with a stretch mesh of 13 inches. As the size of the Sturgeon decreased over the years, smaller meshes were set. Besides gill nets, the species is caught today using haul seines, pound nets, fish slides, and weirs. The fishing season coincides with upstream spawning migrations in the spring, but a minor commercial fishery occurs in the fall when the adults return to the sea. Sport fisheries are much smaller and localized by comparison. Sturgeon are caught by fishing on the bottom with natural baits.

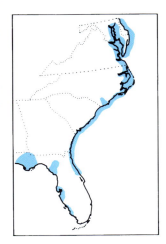

Preparation. The roe, or caviar, is a well-known delicacy. The meat is also excellent and may be cooked in fish stews or prepared as fish cakes.

Suggested Readings. 111.

BLUEBACK HERRING
Alosa aestivalis

Glut Herring, River Herring

Habits. Each spring coastal rivers and streams along the eastern United States are inundated by two species of river herrings, the Blueback Herring and the Alewife, *Alosa pseudoharengus*, which return to their natal waters to spawn. The Blueback Herring is distributed from Nova Scotia to the St. Johns River, Florida, and is the more important of the two south of the Chesapeake Bay. Alewives are more common farther north. Blueback Herring are small clupeids, reaching a maximum size of about 15 inches and a weight of 1 pound.

They are bluish above and silvery on the lower sides and belly. A faint shoulder spot is followed by rows of scales, which have more or less distinct dark lines. The fins are plain and slightly green or yellow in life. Blueback Herring are very similar to Alewives in size and body shape but can be distinguished by: (1) the blue back (Alewives are relatively gray), (2) silvery head (Alewives have brassy heads), (3) black peritoneum (Alewives have a white or dusky peritoneum), and (4) 41 to 51 gill rakers on the lower limb of the first arch (Alewives have 59 to 73).

Some herring reach sexual maturity as 3-year-olds, and all are capable of reproducing by age 4. The species begins to ascend rivers and streams in late winter and early spring when water temperatures are about 55°F. Spawning may occur in tidal zones or as far as 150 miles upstream in fresh water. Peak spawning along much of the southeastern United States takes place from the end of March to the first of May when water temperatures range from about 57° to 68°F. Spawning fish are often observed splashing along shorelines, releasing ova and milt into the spring currents. The average-sized female lays about 250 thousand demersal and somewhat adhesive eggs, which hatch in 2 to 3 days. Scientists believe that drastic alterations of waterways, such as channelization and clearing debris and aquatic vegetation, are detrimental to egg survival. After spawning, the adults return to the sea, where they probably overwinter in deep water offshore. Young Blueback Herring remain in lower rivers and estuaries for 5 to 6 months before migrating to sea.

Although Blueback Herring have been aged as old as 7 years, most of the fish caught are 4 to 6 years old. Approximate lengths for fish 1 to 7 years are 5, 7, 9, 9.5, 10, 10.5, and 11 inches. Adult herring feed on small animals—copepods, insects, pelagic shrimps, worms, and some fishes. Undoubtedly, one of the most important roles of the River

Herring is as food for important piscivorous sport and food fishes such as Striped Bass, Bluefish, catfish, White Perch, trouts, and flounders.

Fishing. Although some Blueback Herring are caught by sportsmen fishing for American Shad and Hickory Shad with small artificial lures, most are caught by commercial fishermen. During their annual spring pilgrimage, herring are confronted with a maze of fishing gear—drift gill nets, set gill nets, seines, skim and dip nets, fyke nets, pound nets, fishing machines, weirs, and trawls—which stand between them and the spawning grounds. Prospective buyers and the curious flock to landing sites, which since colonial times have provided food and entertainment.

Preparation. The flesh and roe are marketed. Fresh fish are almost always notched (scored) and fried crisp in deep fat. They are also salted (corned), pickled, and vinegar-cured. In colonial times, the naturally oily backbones were used as lamp wicks.

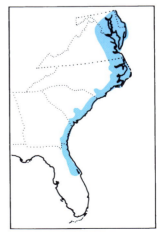

Suggested Readings. 15, 51, 152.

HICKORY SHAD
Alosa mediocris

Shad, Hick, Roe Herring, Tailor Shad

Habits. The Hickory Shad is a medium-sized anadromous clupeid (herring family). It is smaller than the American Shad and larger than the Alewife or Blueback Herring. Although the species may occasionally attain a length of 2 feet, most of the fish caught by fishermen are less than 18 inches. Major identifying characteristics are the prominently projecting lower jaw, 19 to 21 gill rakers on the lower limb of the first arch, and the pale-colored peritoneum. Hickory Shad are gray-green along the back, shading gradually to iridescent silver on the lower sides and belly. There is a dark shoulder spot which is usually followed by several obscure spots. These spots become more prominent when the scales are removed. The sides of the head are brassy and the tip of the lower jaw is dusky.

Shad are distributed along the East Coast from the Bay of Fundy, Canada, to Florida. They enter coastal rivers in the spring to spawn. Both sexes reach sexual maturity when they are 2 years old and about 12 inches long. Spawning occurs from March through May when water temperatures range from 55° to 69°F, with the peak occurring between 62° and 66°F. Spawning takes place in freshwater zones as far as 125 miles from estuaries, often in creeks, ponds, lakes, and other backwaters tributary to main river courses. A 2-year old female is capable of laying 61 thousand eggs and a 6-year old more than 300 thousand, which are fertilized by accompanying males. Juvenile Hickory Shad linger in the lower rivers, sounds, and bays before migrating to sea. In late spring and early summer these small fish are found primarily in fresh waters, but by fall and early winter they have moved into more saline waters.

Hickory Shad are considered to be more piscivorous than other anadromous clupeids. They feed on a variety of small freshwater, estuarine, and marine fishes as well as on fish eggs, small crabs, aquatic insects, and squids. A study of the age and growth of Shad inhabiting the Neuse River, North Carolina, indicates that fish aged 1 to 8 years are 7, 12, 14, 14, 14.5, 15, 15.5, 16, and 16.5 inches in length.

Fishing. Hickory Shad are of minor importance as food fish because the meat is bony and is considered to be of inferior flavor. Commercial crews fishing for American Shad and river herrings catch Hickory Shad by set gill nets, drift gill nets, haul seines, pound nets, fyke nets, trawls, and fishing machines. The flesh is frequently discarded, but the eggs from roe shad are marketed.

Although the species is of minor commercial value, it has contributed to sport fisheries along many southeastern coastal rivers during the spring spawning migrations. In North Carolina, the small town of Grifton has an annual Shad Festival featuring a parade, arts and crafts displays, a Shad Queen, and sport-fishing contests.

Anglers use light spinning outfits with 4- to 8-pound monofilament line to cast shad darts and other small artificial lures. One of the most effective lures is a shad dart with a red head, white body, and yellow-dyed hair tail. Experienced fishermen know exactly when and where to fish. Tying up to the right tree or stump in March or April and casting into just the right current means the difference between catching many Shad or no Shad at all.

Preparation. As far as palatability is concerned, the roe is held in high esteem. It may be baked and served on toast or rolled in cornmeal and fried. The flesh is most often baked for 3 or 4 hours at 300° to 350°F. Leftovers can always be fed to the cat.

Suggested Readings. 51, 117, 152.

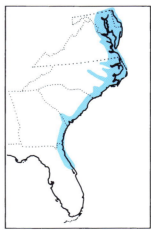

ALEWIFE
Alosa pseudoharengus

River Herring, Branch Herring, Goggle Eye, Grayback, Forerunner Herring

Habits. The Alewife is closely related to the Blueback Herring, and in some areas along the East Coast they occur simultaneously. Usually, however, Alewives are more common north of Chesapeake Bay. In streams where they occur with Blueback Herring, Alewives precede them by 2 to 3 weeks, thus earning the common name, Forerunner Herring.

Alewives are distributed along the East Coast from the Gulf of St. Lawrence to southeastern North Carolina. The species has been introduced into landlocked reservoirs and lakes, particularly in the Southeast, as forage for large predatory fishes. Alewives are gray-blue along the upper sides and back, and silvery on the belly and lower sides. The peritoneum is generally pale silver, with dark punctuations giving it a dusky appearance. The pale peritoneum, brassy head, and number of gill rakers separate the species from Blueback Herring.

Mature fish, 4 years old or older, ascend coastal rivers and streams when water temperatures range from 52° to 60°F from March through May. Alewives have been observed spawning in salt water behind barrier islands and in fresh water as far inland as 150 miles. The spawning act has been described as a pair of fish whirling in a close spiral, terminating as they reach the surface with a splash. Spawning waterways vary from large rivers such as the Merrimac, Potomac, and Roanoke to streams only inches deep, so small one could jump across them. Females may lay 48 to 360 thousand demersal, adhesive eggs, which adhere to ropes, fishing gear, brush, pilings, and other objects. Eggs hatch in 2 to 6 days, depending on the water temperature. After spawning, adults return to the sea and overwinter there. Juveniles congregate in the estuaries before migrating to sea in the fall.

Alewives may live as long as 8 years. Lengths at a given age are similar to those of Blueback Herring. Alewives feed on small animals such as diatoms, copepods, ostracods, shrimps, amphipods, insects, fishes, squids, and fish eggs.

Fishing. Most Alewives are landed by commercial fishermen using the same methods discussed for Blueback Herring. Unfortunately, landing statistics for the two are usually combined, making it virtually impossible to tell which species is being caught when, where, or by what type of fishing gear.

Preparation. In addition to frying and corning, herring may be pickled. Scale and rinse the fish in cold water. Either fillet the fish, or remove the head and viscera and cut the body into chunks about 1-inch wide. Place a layer of fish in a nonmetallic container, and sprinkle heavily with non-iodized salt. Add another layer, sprinkle with salt, and continue until the supply is used up. After a day or two, when a heavy brine has formed, add enough distilled vinegar to make a 50 percent solution. Store in a cool place for 5 to 10 days. To pickle, prepare the following mixture: Boil ½ gallon of water with 1 to 2 ounces of mixed pickling spices and 8 ounces of sugar. After cooking, add ½ gallon of distilled vinegar. Remove the fish from the solution and rinse. In pint or quart jars, alternate layers of fish with layers of sliced onions and a few slices of lemon. Fill to the top with the pickling mixture, cover tightly, and store in a cool place. Remove the skin, cut into bite size pieces, and mix with onions and sour cream to serve.

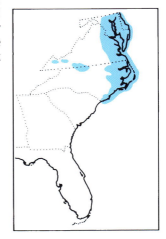

Suggested Readings. 15, 51, 133.

AMERICAN SHAD
Alosa sapidissima
Shad, White Shad

Habits. American Shad, like Atlantic Menhaden and Striped Bass, were important sources of food and fertilizer to Indians and later to settlers during the colonization of the North American east coast. The species is the largest member of the herring family in the United States, averaging 3 to 4 pounds and occasionally attaining a weight of 12 pounds. Shad are anadromous, spending most of their lives in the ocean but ascending rivers to spawn. The species has a compressed body, single soft-rayed dorsal and anal fins, and, like other members of the family Clupeidae, large, easily-shed scales that come together to form a ragged cutting edge along the belly. Shad are silvery white overall, with green to dark blue along the back. The back fades to brown as adults migrate into fresh water to spawn.

The range of the American Shad on the Atlantic Coast is from the Gulf of St. Lawrence, Canada, to St. Johns River, Florida. Fish have been introduced into the Mississippi River drainage, streams in Colorado, the Great Lakes, and the Sacramento and Columbia Rivers on the West Coast.

Most American Shad spawn for the first time when they are 4 to 5 years old. A few males reach sexual maturity at 2 to 3 years, and some females when they are 3 to 4 years old. Shad may ascend rivers as far as 300 miles to spawn when water temperatures range from 41° to 73°F. The peak migrations usually occur when waters are 55° to 61°F. Migrations may start as early as mid-November in Florida and as late as May or June in the northern extremes of their Atlantic range. The majority of the spawning along the southeastern United States occurs from February through April. A ripe female may lay 100 thousand to 600 thousand eggs in open water, after which the eggs are carried by the currents and, being slightly heavier than water, sink. Hatching takes place 3 to 8 days after fertilization, depending on the water temperature (6 days at 68°F). Young Shad remain in the lower rivers and estuaries until fall and then migrate to sea. Tagging studies indicate that American Shad travel long distances and return to spawn in rivers where they were hatched. Shad from the Neuse River, North Carolina, aged 1 to 6 years were 7, 11, 14, 17, 19, and 20 inches long. Adult Shad are plankton feeders, swimming with their mouths open and gill covers extended while straining the water for minute food. Major foods are small crustaceans, insects, fish eggs, and algae.

Fishing. Indians captured American Shad for spring festivals with bush nets, spears, weirs, and bow and arrows for centuries before the white man arrived. The early settlers undoubtedly learned how to catch Shad by watching the Indians fish. As early as 1850 American Shad populations began to decline as a result of overfishing and river alterations. Landings on the Atlantic Coast decreased from over 50 million pounds in the 1890s to less than 10 million pounds in the 1960s. Fortunately, populations have started to respond favorably to management programs, which use hatcheries, pollution abatement, and fish passages around man-made obstructions to restore the stocks. Today, commercial fishermen use nets, weirs, trawls, and fishing machines to harvest these prized food fish. Sport fishermen catch Shad in the spring, using light spinning tackle to cast small artificial lures from boats and from riverbanks.

Preparation. The bony American Shad is best prepared by baking. Fish may be wrapped tightly in foil with butter, potatoes, and onions, and cooked for 3 or 4 hours at a moderate temperature. Addition of lemon juice, tomatoes, or other acids tends to assist the baking process in dissolving the small intramuscular bones.

Suggested Readings. 161.

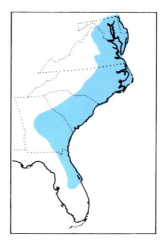

WHITE PERCH
Morone americana

Gray Perch, Blue-nosed Perch

Habits. The White Perch is a temperate species related to the Striped Bass and the White Bass. However, it is much smaller by comparison. Most of the fish caught are only 6 to 8 inches long and weigh less than a pound. White Perch are most easily identified by their three stout anal spines. Unlike those of the White Bass and Striped Bass, the anal spines of the White Perch are not graduated in length. The second and third spines are approximately equal.

The native distribution includes both brackish and fresh waters along the Atlantic Coast from Nova Scotia to South Carolina. The preferred habitat is large, low-salinity sounds such as Chesapeake Bay and Albemarle Sound. The species also thrives in the fresh waters of coastal rivers, lakes, and ponds and in some inland reservoirs. The body is mostly silvery, often dark green, gray or blue along the back and upper sides. The lower sides are occasionally brassy, and usually have several irregular dark horizontal lines.

In their natural habitat, White Perch are semianadromous, migrating from brackish water to fresh to spawn. Populations tend to make predictable migrations before and after spawning. During other times of the year, movements are more local and random. Spawning takes place in the spring from April through June, when water temperatures range from 51° to 60°F. In Virginia and North Carolina, the peak activity is in April and early May. Males initially outnumber females on the spawning grounds. They attain sexual maturity much earlier and at smaller sizes than females. All males are capable of reproducing as 2-year-olds, compared with age 4 for females. The eggs are released in shallow water (1 to 12 feet). After fertilization they settle to the bottom where they adhere to sticks, rocks, and other submerged objects. Fecundity varies from about 20 to over 300 thousand eggs. A 6-inch female may lay 21 thousand eggs, an 8-inch fish 96 thousand, and a 10-inch fish 230 thousand. The incubation time may be as long as 6 days at 51° to 53°F, or as brief as 30 hours at 68°F.

Although White Perch may live as long as 17 years, reaching a length of 19 inches and a weight of 4 to 5 pounds, most are much smaller and live for only 5 to 7 years. Average lengths for Perch aged 1 to 10 years are 3, 5, 6, 7, 8, 9, 9.5, 10, 11, and 11.5 inches. Females live longer than males, and by age 7 may outnumber their counterparts by as much as 12 to 1. White Perch are predaceous carnivores whose diet changes with the size of the fish. Smaller individuals eat zooplankton and

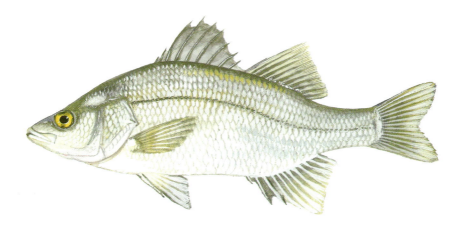

aquatic insects, whereas larger Perch feed on crabs, shrimps, and small fishes such as anchovies, and juvenile Atlantic Menhaden, Alewives, and Blueback Herring.

Fishing. The White Perch is one of the most important fish to commercial fisheries operating in the sounds and coastal rivers of the Mid-Atlantic States. Landings are largest in the spring during the spawning season and in the fall from September through November when the fish school and feed on emigrating clupeids. The most effective fishing gear are haul seines, purse seines, traps, pound nets, fyke nets, and gill nets. Recreational fishermen also catch large numbers of White Perch. The seasons parallel those of the commercial fisheries. Favorite techniques are to drift fish using live minnows and to cast or troll small artificials in the vicinity of surface-feeding schools. Jigs, spoons, and spinners are good lures.

Preparation. The white, flaky flesh of the White Perch is among the best. It is excellent fried, and may also be broiled or baked.

Suggested Readings. 64, 78, 94, 118, 133.

STRIPED BASS
Morone saxatilis

Rock, Rockfish, Striper

Habits. In their natural habitat, Striped Bass are anadromous, moving from the ocean up rivers to spawn in fresh water. In recent years the species has been introduced into rivers, lakes, and reservoirs throughout the southeastern United States as well as in California, the Soviet Union, and South Africa. The scientific name means "rock dweller." Centuries ago when New World animals were being named, Striped Bass were first observed spawning among rocks of piedmont waterways.

Along the Atlantic Coast, Rockfish are distributed from the St. Lawrence River, Canada, to St. Johns River, Florida. There are nine major Atlantic populations: St. Lawrence River, Nova Scotia, Hudson River, Delaware River, Chesapeake Bay, Roanoke River-Albemarle Sound (North Carolina), Cape Fear (North Carolina), Santee-Cooper River system (South Carolina), and St. Johns River. Striped Bass are silver overall and dark olive-green or gray on the back with seven or eight black horizontal stripes along the sides. The species has been hybridized, notably with the White Bass, *Morone chrysops*. Hybrids may be identified by the broken or irregular stripes.

Males reach sexual maturity during the second or third year, females between their fourth and fifth years. Males as small as 7 inches and females as small as 14 inches have been observed spawning. Spawning occurs in the spring when water temperatures range from 60° to 70°F, as early as February in Florida to as late as July in New England. Eggs are released and fertilized when one female and many males form a violently thrashing aggregation that fishermen refer to as "fights." A large female may lay 3 or 4 million semi-buoyant eggs. Unless held suspended by water currents, they settle to the bottom and perish.

Females grow larger than males, and most fish older than 11 years and longer than about 39 inches are females. The largest Striped Bass on record weighed 125 pounds and was believed to be between 29 and 31 years old. Average lengths for fish aged 1, 5, 10, and 13 years are 7, 22, 35, and 45 inches. In salt water, Striped Bass feed on menhaden, anchovies, silversides, herrings, crabs, and shrimps. In fresh water, Gizzard and Threadfin Shads, herring, Golden Shiners, minnows, amphipods, and mayflies are preferred foods.

Fishing. Rock are caught by fishermen in fresh and salt water. Fishing techniques vary depending on water conditions and according to local tradition and laws. Commercially, the species is taken by nets, trotlines,

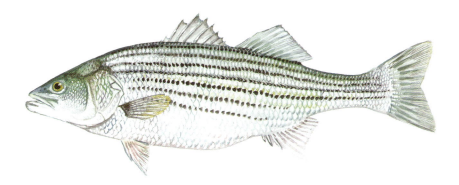

and fishing machines. Landings have declined drastically during recent years.

Sport fishermen troll, cast, or jig artificials and float or bottom fish with natural baits. Ocean fishermen surf cast with spoons or heavy lures, or fish with live crabs, bloodworms, or eels. Fishermen bottom fish in rivers with cut herring or cut sucker, float fish with live herring or shiners, or cast Rapalas, Rebels, Cordell Hot Spots, or Bucktails. Reservoir fishing may be by deep trolling or plugging on the surface. Best fishing along the coast is during the spring spawning run and in the fall. Inland fishing is productive all year.

Preparation. Rock are excellent eating fish and may be prepared in many ways. Smaller fish are usually fried and larger ones are baked. A favorite method is to cook a Rock "muddle," a thick stew made of fish, bacon and drippings, potatoes, and onions.

Suggested Readings. 135.

YELLOW PERCH

Perca flavescens

Raccoon Perch, Redfin Perch

Habits. Anglers who enjoy fishing cool-water lakes and reservoirs are familiar with the Yellow Perch, a species frequently caught along with Walleye, Sauger, Smallmouth Bass, Northern Pike, and Muskellunge. Perch also inhabit coastal rivers, streams, and low salinity estuaries, along with Striped Bass, White Perch, Pumpkinseed, Spot, and Atlantic Croaker. Yellow Perch are native to the northeastern part of the United States and Canada. The present range along the East Coast extends from Canada through South Carolina.

Yellow Perch have six or seven vertical brown bands that extend across the back. The lower fins are yellow or sometimes bright red. Like other members of the family Percidae, the species has the characteristic separated dorsal fins and only one or two anal spines (Yellow Perch have two).

Spawning takes place in shallow water in the spring, March through May, when water temperatures range between 45° and 55°F. Males attain sexual maturity when 2 years old, as small as 5 inches, and females at age 3, as small as 6 inches. During the spawning season, each gravid female is accompanied by 15 to 25 males that fertilize the eggs as they are released. Fecundity has been estimated from about 3 thousand eggs for small females to more than 150 thousand for large individuals. The eggs are laid in a gelatinous strand, often several feet long. The egg strands weave in and around aquatic vegetation and submerged branches of fallen trees. There is no parental care, and many eggs are lost each year through predation, washing up on shore, and being stranded by low water. The eggs hatch in 2 to 3 weeks at normal water temperatures.

The size of Yellow Perch at specific ages varies greatly from one geographic area to another. Average lengths for fish aged 1 to 10 years are 3.2, 5.5, 7.3, 8.2, 9.2, 10, 10.6, 11, 11.2, and 11.4 inches. Perch are known to live as long as 13 years and to reach a weight of 4 pounds. However, a fish weighing 2 pounds is considered large; most are only a few ounces and 5 to 8 inches long. The diet is diverse and includes benthic insect larvae (mainly chironomids and mayflies), leeches, amphipods, crayfish, and small fishes such as shiners, Threadfin Shad, and Alewives.

Fishing. Although Yellow Perch contribute to daily creels, they are seldom sought after by fishermen. Certainly, most anglers fishing for

crappie and bass in the early spring have encountered Yellow Perch. These feisty fish are often too small to keep, yet are voracious enough to keep one busy groping around in the minnow bucket or dislodging artificial lures from their tiny mouths. An occasional keeper, bright colors splashing on the surface of the cold water, makes all the trouble worthwhile.

Besides being caught in the spring on light spinning tackle, Perch are also taken by fishing through ice in colder climates. Holes are cut in the ice and short, light rods with tip-ups of various kinds are used to signal the angler when a fish has been caught. Hooks baited with minnows, worms, and insect larvae are attached to a spring or hinged device on the surface, which will release a marker when a fish is hooked. Commercial fishermen using gill nets, hoop nets, fyke nets, traps, pound nets, and trawls also land the species, which is marketed fresh or frozen.

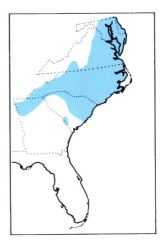

Preparation. Yellow Perch have deeply embedded ctenoid scales, which makes scaling very difficult. Fish should be cleaned as soon as possible after they are caught. Because most Perch are small, they are usually fried.

Suggested Readings. 24, 75, 77.

HOGCHOKER
Trinectes maculatus

Habits. The Hogchoker, a small flatfish of the family Soleidae, is of little consequence to fisheries. To handle one, however, is an unforgettable experience. The fish have a seemingly hairy texture because of the tiny, rough scales, and they vigorously adhere to objects—bottoms and sides of buckets and boats, fishermen's boots, and the palms of hands. The species is very hardy and is capable of living out of the water for an extended period of time. The name is reported to have originated from the fact that hogs, which are fed trash fish in some sections of the country, have choked on them. Some fishermen cautiously cull Hogchokers from fish that are to be fed to livestock.

The body is round; the head, eyes, and mouth are very small; and pectoral fins are absent. The eyed side is brownish-gray, usually crossed with seven or eight thin black bars. The blind side varies from plain white to light brown with pale spots. The Hogchoker is a marine and estuarine species that ascends coastal rivers into fresh water from Massachusetts to southern Mexico. It is most abundant in the southern part of its range.

Spawning takes place in late spring and summer over wide salinity and temperature gradients. Eggs have been collected from waters with salinities of 0 to 24 ppt, and temperatures ranging from 59° to 86°F. Most of the spawning activity occurs in July in moderately saline (10 to 16 ppt) waters that are about 77°F. Fish reach sexual maturity when they are 2 years old and are capable of laying thousands of eggs during a season. A 6.5-inch female contained 54 thousand ripening ova. The eggs have a short incubation period of 26 to 34 hours. Recently hatched young migrate upstream in coastal rivers and congregate in a low-salinity nursery area near the freshwater-saltwater interface.

Hogchokers may live for at least 7 years and attain a length of 8 inches. Females grow larger and live longer than males. Average lengths for both sexes aged 1 to 7 years are 2.1, 3.1, 3.9, 4.6, 5.2, 5.6, and 6 inches. Feeding occurs on the bottom where fish search through detritus, mud, and aquatic vegetation for worms, crustaceans, and immature insects.

Fishing. Hogchokers are not caught by sport fishermen and are infrequently landed by commercial fishing gear. Some are caught incidentally to commercially important species in bottom trawls, haul seines, traps, and hoop nets.

Preparation. The flesh is reported to be flavorful. However, it would be a very hungry or adventurous soul indeed, who would sit down to eat a plate of Hogchokers.

Suggested Readings. 42, 76, 78, 95.

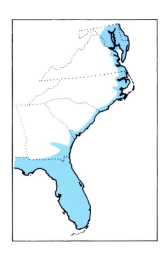

COASTAL
GROUND FISHES

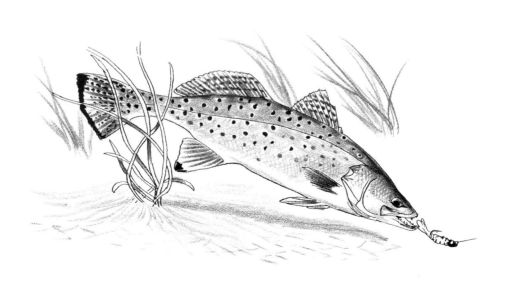

TIGER SHARK
Galeocerdo cuvieri

Habits. Because if its name, large size (up to 18 feet long) and agressiveness, the Tiger Shark is one of the most feared of all sharks, particularly in the West Indies. It is one of the more abundant of the larger sharks inhabiting the warmer waters of the western Atlantic Ocean. Tiger Sharks are found from Massachusetts to Uruguay, although most occur south of Cape Hatteras.

The species is easily identified by its short, rounded snout, sharp-pointed tail, coloration, and teeth that are characteristically serrated on both edges. Tiger Sharks are gray or brownish gray with darker brown or black spots that often form irregular oblique or transverse bars on the sides. These markings fade as the fish attain larger sizes. The Sand Tiger, *Odontaspis taurus*, is also grayish-brown and has brown spots on the sides of the body. This species belongs to a different family however, has a longer snout, larger second dorsal fin, and strongly projecting teeth.

Young Tiger Sharks develop ovoviviparously and are approximately 18 or 19 inches long at birth. The broods are large and many gravid females contain 30 to 50 embryos. An 18-foot specimen captured off Cuba contained 82 young. Smaller females may produce as few as 10 to 14. Although little information is available on the size of the species at a given age, some length and weight data have been recorded. Sharks 5½ feet long weigh about 37 pounds, whereas those 10 feet, 11 to 12 feet, 12 to 13 feet, and 13 to 14 feet weigh approximately 366, 710 to 825, 850 to 1,325, and 1,028 to 1,395 pounds. Tiger Sharks are classical scavengers of the sea, feeding on fishes, birds, turtles, mammals, invertebrates, and garbage. Capable of swallowing small prey whole, they render large animals into consumable portions by savagely tearing them apart with vicious twisting motions of the head. Some of the food items found in the stomachs include spiny lobsters, horseshoe crabs, squids, stingrays, mackerel, skates, turtles, sea lions, and birds.

Fishing. Tiger Sharks are caught by recreational fishermen throughout the region. The fishing techniques described for Dusky and Scalloped Hammerhead Sharks apply equally well for this species. Most commercial fishermen in the United States today regard the Tiger Shark as a threat to their nets and to the fish that they seek. This was not always true. Longliners once provided thriving industries with sharks that were used to produce leather goods and liver oil extracts.

Preparation. The flesh is edible, and it is marketed both fresh and salted. A suggested dish is Shark Marseillaise. The ingredients are 2 pounds of shark fillets, 2 large onions, 2 tablespoons of olive oil, 4 tomatoes, 1 clove of garlic, 1 pinch of saffron, salt and pepper to taste, and 1 glass of water or fish stock. Chop the onions very fine and fry in the olive oil. Add the tomatoes cut into small pieces, the garlic, saffron, salt and pepper, and the water or fish stock. Place the shark fillets in the mixture, and allow to boil fast for 15 to 20 minutes. Keep the kettle covered tightly. Remove the fish and place on slices of French bread that have been browned in the oven. Boil the liquid down a few minutes so that it will not be watery, correct the seasoning, and pour it over the shark. Serves 4 to 6.

Suggested Readings. 12, 46, 132.

SMOOTH DOGFISH
Mustelus canis

Sand Shark

Habits. The Smooth Dogfish is one of the most common sharks along the Atlantic coast of the United States. The small gray-brown shark discarded on a pier or beach in the spring of the year is probably a Smooth Dogfish. It is a medium-sized shark reaching a maximum length of about 5 feet, although fish in the 1- to 3-foot class are more common.

The species has a slender body with two dorsal fins nearly equal in size. The second dorsal fin is positioned slightly ahead of the anal fin. Other distinguishing characteristics are the narrow, catlike eyes, the large spiracle behind each eye, and the caudal fin, which has a small lower lobe. Another species, the Spiny Dogfish, *Squalus acanthias*, also is found in the region, although it is more common north of North Carolina. It is easily recognized by the spine that is located in front of each of the two dorsal fins. Smooth Dogfish are tannish-gray, slate-gray, or brown above. The lower sides and belly are white, grayish-white, or yellow. A sooty spot is often found near the tip of the upper lobe of the caudal fin. The species is distributed from New Brunswick, Canada, to Uruguay, and inhabits the bottoms of estuaries and coastal waters out to a depth of about 650 feet. During the spring and summer, most of the sharks are found in waters less than 60 feet deep.

Spawning occurs in coastal waters from May through July over most of the range. Males are sexually mature when they are 1 to 2 years old, females when they are 2 or 3. Fertilization is internal, and after a 10-month period, the female births 4 to 20 (average 14 or 15) 14-inch pups. The sexes grow at different rates. Females are larger at a given age than males, and attain a larger maximum size (59 inches compared to 43). Average lengths for the sexes combined for ages 1, 5, 10, and 15 years are 16.9, 43.9, 50, and 52 inches. Smooth Dogfish use their senses of sight and smell to scavenge for prey, usually during the hours of darkness. Favorite foods are crabs, fishes, squids, clams, worms, and lobsters.

Fishing. In the spring and early summer, small Dogfish are caught by surf fishermen and by anglers fishing from small boats. Most of the sharks are caught by those who are bottom fishing for flounder, Spot, Atlantic Croaker, or trout with shrimp or squid baits. The young sharks may be so plentiful that they are a nuisance to fishermen. Large numbers of Smooth Dogfish are also caught by commercial fishermen using trawls, bottom longlines, pound nets, and gill nets. Dogfish are usually discarded for

they are not deemed suitable as food fish in the United States; however, they are highly esteemed in Europe.

Preparation. If cleaned quickly after capture, Dogfish fillets may be broiled, or basted over charcoal.

Suggested Readings. 12, 28, 46, 50.

SCALLOPED HAMMERHEAD
Sphyrna lewini

Hammerhead

Habits. Sharks such as the Hammerhead, that have their eyes positioned on lateral extensions of their heads belong to the family Sphyrnidae. Four species occur in the region: Scalloped Hammerhead, Smooth Hammerhead, *Sphyrna zygaena*, Great Hammerhead, *S. mokarran*, and Bonnethead, *S. tiburo*. The last species is easily distinguished from the others because it has a shovel-shaped, as opposed to a hammer-shaped head. The first three species are more difficult to separate. The Scalloped Hammerhead, the most frequently caught of the group, is recognized by smooth teeth and by an indentation in the front margin of the head at its midpoint. The Great Hammerhead has teeth with serrated margins, and a relatively smooth midline on the head. The Smooth Hammerhead is rarely encountered.

Scalloped Hammerhead are powerful swimmers that make extensive north-south and inshore-offshore migrations. The species is distributed in the western Atlantic from New Jersey to southern Brazil, including the Caribbean, Gulf of Mexico, and Central American coast. It is gray, grayish-brown, or olivaceous above, shading to white below. In life, the pectoral fins may be black tipped. Scalloped Hammerheads are viviparous, and studies suggest that the young are approximately 16 to 18 inches long at birth. Sexual maturity is not attained until the sharks are large (6 feet for males).

Age and growth information is not conclusive at this time. The species spends much of the day along coastal dropoffs and leaves these areas at night, probably to search for food in the surrounding pelagic waters. It feeds on fishes and squids near the surface, and also on crabs, stingrays, and other bottom-dwelling animals. Grouping, or schooling, by Scalloped Hammerheads has been observed in the northern Gulf of Mexico and off California. The average size of these groups is about 20 sharks, but groups of more than 100 are not uncommon. Scientists wonder whether the sharks group for reproduction, feeding, defense, or swimming efficiency.

Fishing. Hammerheads are caught far from land by commercial longliners and by sport fishermen, and also in shallow coastal waters including sounds and bays. Many are landed by recreational fishermen who bottom fish at night from piers and from the surf. Placement of the bait is the trick. This is easily done from a pier by merely casting the heavy weight and baited hook. It gets exciting from the beach, however. There,

the angler is unable to cast the terminal tackle; he must carry it out, either by surf board (or similar conveyance) or by hand while swimming. Imagine setting a shark bait at night while swimming. The terminal tackle may consist of an 8/0 to 16/0 hook baited with a whole fish, chicken, or cat and weighted by a heavy sinker. Strong line is required, not only because of the size of the quarry, but also because the line is subject to constant abrasion against the sand. Sturdy fiber glass rods with roller line guides are suggested.

Preparation. Hammerheads are marketed fresh and salted, usually in the Caribbean and along the Central American coast. The flesh is reported to be of good quality and may be served after broiling or cooking over charcoal.

Suggested Readings. 12, 46, 132.

CLEARNOSE SKATE
Raja eglanteria

Skate, Briar Skate

Habits. Skates are strange looking fishes with triangular shaped bodies and long tails. From the underside, skates are said to resemble hooded Klansmen because of their pointed snouts, white bellies, smiling mouths, and air spiracles that look like eyes. Skates are elasmobranchs and are related to other cartilaginous fishes—the sharks and rays. The Clearnose Skate is by far the most common skate along the southeastern United States. It inhabits shallow coastal waters out to a depth of about 390 feet from Massachusetts to central Florida. This species is brown on the back, with numerous darker brown elongated spots and bars. The underside is white. The Clearnose Skate derives its name from the translucent spaces on either side of the snout. It is also known as the Briar Skate because of the spines or thorns that occur in a single row along the midridge of the back and in patches on the large pectoral fins and near the eyes.

There are probably two populations of Clearnose Skate off the eastern coast of the United States. One occurs from North Carolina to Massachusetts and migrates northward and inshore in the spring, and southward and offshore in the fall. The other population is found from South Carolina to Florida and is believed to be nonmigratory, remaining in local coastal waters all year.

Members of the family Rajidae, including the Clearnose Skate, reproduce oviparously—they lay eggs. Following internal fertilization, each developing egg is encapsulated in a dark, leathery case, which is then deposited. Hatching takes place outside the body. These cases are found on the beach and referred to as devil's or sailor's purses. Sperm from one mating is sufficient to fertilize 2 to 5 eggs, which are laid inshore in the spring and summer. Repeated matings occur throughout the warmer months. A female may lay as many as 66 eggs in a year. Young skates are approximately 5 to 6 inches in length (measured from the tip of the snout to the second dorsal fin) at hatching. Skates mature when as small as 21 inches long, although most are not sexually active until they reach about 26 inches.

No information is available on the age and growth of the species, although the Clearnose Skate is known to reach a length of at least 38 inches. Skates are bottom dwellers, partly burying themselves in the sand. They feed primarily at night on fishes, crabs, worms, shrimps, and clams. Because their mouths are located on the underside, they must swim over and settle on their prey before consuming it.

Fishing. Because they occur close to shore, Clearnose Skate are caught from beaches, piers, jetties, bridges, and small boats. These spring visitors are considered nuisances by both commercial and sport fishermen. However, they are harmless, put up a good fight, and can be fun to catch on light tackle. The standard two-hook bottom rig baited with shrimp, squid, or cut fish is most effective. Commercial fishermen land the species with pound nets, gill nets, seines, and trawls.

Preparation. The flesh is seldom marketed in this country, but it has been sold by European fish vendors for centuries. The meat is white, somewhat cartilaginous and scallop-like. It is best prepared deep fried or sautéed with sherry.

Suggested Readings. 14, 64.

SOUTHERN STINGRAY
Dasyatis americana

Stingray

Habits. Like other rays, stingrays have long, slender tails and very broad pectoral fins. Unlike some of their relatives, all stingrays (family Dasyatidae) possess one or two barbed, venomous spines on their tails. Four species are fairly common along the southeastern United States: the Southern Stingray, *Dasyatis americana*; Bluntnose Stingray, *D. sayi*; Roughtail Stingray, *D. centroura*; and the Atlantic Stingray, *D. sabina*. The last species often enters fresh water, particular in Florida. The Southern Stingray is encountered most frequently by fishermen. It is easily distinguished from the Atlantic and Bluntnose Stingrays, which have rounded pectoral fins, because its pectoral fins are more pointed. Although the Southern and Roughtail Stingrays have similarly shaped pectoral fins, the latter species has numerous prickles and thorns along the length of its tail. Tails of Southern Stingrays are smooth by comparison.

Southern Stingrays inhabit coastal waters from New Jersey to Brazil, including the Caribbean and the Gulf of Mexico. They may be found partially buried on the bottom with only their eyes and breathing spiracles visible above the sand. The coloration of the body is highly variable and changes with the shading of the surrounding substrate. The upper sides vary from slate gray to brown, but the undersides are always white. The whip-like portion of the tail is dark brown or black. Occasionally, a pale spot is located on the midline of the snout, just in front of the eyes.

The species reproduces oviviparously in late spring and summer. Three to five eggs develop and hatch within the female, and the young are born alive. Young rays are approximately 8 inches wide at birth. Southern Stingrays feed on a variety of bottom-dwelling animals such as worms, clams, shrimps, crabs, and small fishes. They possess powerful, grinding teeth that enable them to crush the toughest shells. Rays often locate their prey by using the digging motion of their pectoral fins to excavate the substrate, exposing the animals buried in the mud. No information is available on age and growth, but Southern Stingrays as large as 5 feet in width have been caught.

Fishing. Although they are seldom sought by fishermen in the United States, stingrays create a great deal of excitement when they are landed. The curious flock to beaches, piers, and bridges to gawk at rays that

have been caught on rod and reel, and comment on their ugly mouths, wing-like fins, and most of all, their poisonous spines.

Commercial fishermen, upon finding rays in their nets, believe that the animals have gorged themselves on every clam, oyster, and scallop in sight. Stingrays are caught by bottom fishing with shrimp or cut bait, and also with pound nets, seines, trawls, gill nets, and bottom longlines.

Preparation. The flesh is highly esteemed in other countries and is sold fresh, frozen, and salted. In the United States, the meat of the pectoral fins is often prepared by frying, sautéeing in butter, and broiling. The flesh is also used to make gelatin and cooking oil.

Suggested Readings. 14, 46.

COWNOSE RAY
Rhinoptera bonasus

Habits. The Cownose Ray is one of the most abundant elasmobranch fishes found in the coastal waters of the South Atlantic Bight. It is distributed along the East Coast from Cape Cod to the Florida Keys and in the Gulf of Mexico to Louisiana. The species has wide, winglike pectoral fins and a long, whiplike, spined tail. It also has a peculiar indention in the anterior contour of the head, which gives it a bilobed appearance, like a cow's nose. Cownose Rays are large animals, with males averaging about 24 pounds and females 30. The species is much smaller than the gigantic Manta Ray, *Manta birostris*, which has a large, conspicuous fleshy lobe on each side of the mouth.

Cownose Rays are chocolate brown above, sometimes with a yellowish tint. The underside is yellow-white, and the outer edges of the pectoral fins are dark brown.

The species inhabits estuaries and coastal waters out to a depth of about 100 feet. Cownose Rays have been collected in waters ranging from 59° to 84°F with salinities of 8 to 30 ppt. Large schools migrate north in the spring and south in the fall. A typical spring migration may find Rays off northeastern Florida in mid-March, off Cape Lookout in mid-April, and in the upper Chesapeake by early June. They move out of the estuaries in fall, and generally offshore, as they travel south. Rays probably overwinter in deeper waters throughout the South Atlantic Bight.

Cownose Rays reproduce ovoviviparously. Embryos are birthed alive, but there is no placental connection between parent and young. The size of rays is measured as disk width from the tip of one pectoral fin to the tip of the other. Males, which are easily identified by claspers, mature at a disk width of about 31.5 inches. Adult females probably have an 11- to 12-month gestation period. Birthing occurs in June and July in Chesapeake Bay, followed by a second mating with internal fertilization. A gravid female usually carries three or four eggs, but only one develops into a young ray, which averages 16.5 inches at birth.

The sexes grow at different rates; females grow faster than males and attain larger sizes. The maximum size for females is about 45 inches and a weight of 60 pounds. Disk widths for fish aged 1 to 10 years are 21.1, 24.5, 27.3, 29.6, 31.6, 33.3, 34.6, 35.8, 37.9, and 38.7 inches. Cownose Rays feed on shellfish, worms, crustaceans, and other benthic animals by stirring the bottom with their pectoral fins, and then protruding both jaws into the sediment. Feeding excavations are often

visible as bowl-shaped pockmarks measuring 3 feet in diameter and 8 to 12 inches deep.

Fishing. Both commercial and sport fishermen catch rays. Nets, rod and reel, and longlines are used to land the species, usually incidental to other, more desirable fish. In some areas, bow and arrow fishing is a popular sport. Because schools are easily seen from the water and from the air, they are vulnerable to commercial fishing. Haul seine sets take in thousands of pounds to remove the nuisance fish, not to market them. In recent years oyster and clam growers have reported substantial losses to Cownose Ray predation. Fencing shellfish beds with large mesh netting is effective but expensive. A better solution to the problem may be to establish domestic or foreign markets for the flesh.

Preparation. The pectoral fins of Cownose Rays can be chunked and fried like scallops. The fish should be handled carefully, for the serrated tail spines can cause painful puncture wounds. Application of meat tenderizer to the wound may provide temporary relief.

Suggested Readings. 144.

BONEFISH
Albula vulpes

Habits. Regarded as one of the premier saltwater game fishes, the Bonefish inhabits warm coastal waters of the Atlantic from Massachusetts to Rio de Janeiro, including the Bahamas and Bermuda. It is most common around southern Florida, and is rarely seen north of Florida. The silver color, elusive habits, and swimming speed undoubtedly contributed to the scientific name, *Albula vulpes*, which means "white fox." The species is the only representative of the family Albulidae and is most closely related to the Tarpon and Ladyfish. It is unlike the former, however, because it does not have a protruding lower jaw, and differs from the latter by having its mouth under its snout rather than at the end of it. The body is bright silver overall. The back and upper sides are blue-green, punctuated by numerous faint horizontal lines that extend from the head to the tail.

The life history is poorly understood. Spawning presumably occurs at sea during the late winter and early spring, and the larvae undergo a leptocephalus stage similar to that of young Ladyfish and Tarpon. The species may attain a length of 30 inches and a weight of nearly 20 pounds. Bonefish move onto the shallow sand and mud flats to feed on animals that live on the bottom. They use their conical snouts to root around the bottom to dislodge worms, mollusks, shrimps, and crabs. At times the fish may be seen literally standing on their heads with their tails sticking out of the water.

Fishing. Bonefish are caught almost exclusively by sport fishermen who are guided by professionals. Most guides take their clients on one-day fishing trips in small, low-sided outboard boats that have flat or slightly V-shaped bottoms. Once the party arrives on the fishing grounds, the guide poles the boat over the flats. Best fishing is on sunny days with very little wind. Because the water is shallow and clear, care must be taken not to startle the fish. This is one type of fishing where it is imperative to keep quiet and still.

A favorite method of fishing is to anchor or stake the boat and chum the area with crushed shrimp. To chum Bonefish successfully, fishermen must know the stage of the tide, how currents will be running on a particular flat, and from what direction the fish will approach. Usually, anglers chum so that the shrimp are carried away from the boat over open sand, where the fish are more easily detected. Once sighted, Bonefish may be caught with live shrimp on a bottom rig or with a small

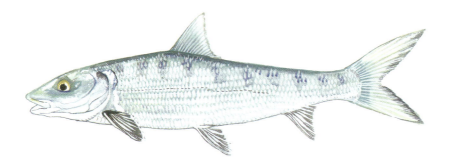

jig (¼ to ⅜ ounce) or streamer fly. The Bonefish is famous for its hard strike and determined run once it is hooked.

Preparation. The flesh is very bony and is seldom eaten in the United States.

Suggested Readings. 15, 46.

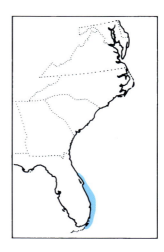

CONGER EEL
Conger oceanicus

Sea Eel, Silver Eel

Habits. The Conger Eel closely resembles the American Eel, *Anguilla rostrata*, but is distinguishable by its longer snout and the very large dorsal fin that originates much closer to the pectoral fins. The Conger is also larger, frequently attaining a weight of 10 to 20 pounds and a length of 5 to 7 feet. Its European cousin, *Conger conger*, is even more spectacular, occasionally tipping the scales at 130 pounds and measuring over 12 feet in length. The American Conger is gray above and white underneath. The dorsal and anal fins have broad black margins. Overall, the Conger appears much lighter than the freshwater eel, thus the common name Silver Eel. The species is distributed from Massachusetts to south Florida and in the Gulf of Mexico westward to Mississippi.

Spawning probably occurs offshore during the summer. The only information available on fecundity is old and pertains to two European specimens that contained 3 million and 7 million ripe ova. Like the American Eel, young Conger metamorphose through an intermediate, ribbonlike leptocephalus stage. When searching for food, the Conger Eel is a night stalker. It feeds during the hours of darkness on fishes, crabs, worms, and other bottom-dwelling animals that it stealthily approaches and grabs.

Fishing. The Conger Eel is caught in baited fish and crab traps as well as on hook and line, but seldom in nets because the fish can squirm through them. Conger caught by anglers may cause a great deal of excitement. The fish are large, they fight hard, and are very difficult to remove from the hook. The species readily takes shrimps, squids, and other cut baits that are fished on the bottom.

Preparation. In years past, the species was marketed fresh and salted in the Chesapeake Bay region, but today it supports no commercial fishery in the United States and is rarely eaten. The Conger Eel is an important food fish in parts of Europe, Africa, and Asia. Other than deep frying, perhaps the best way to cook the species is by smoking. The following procedure may be used to smoke most fish. The ingredients are 6 dressed, 1-pound fish, 1 cup of salt, 1 gallon of water, and ¼ cup of salad oil. The Eel should be prepared by removing the head, viscera and skin. Add the salt to the water and stir until it is dissolved. Pour the brine over the fish and let them soak for about 30 minutes. Remove the fish from the brine and rinse them in cold water.

To smoke, use a charcoal fire in a covered grill. Let the fire burn down to a low, even heat. Cover the coals with hickory chips that have been presoaked overnight in water. Place the fish on a well-greased grill, skin side down if they are split open, and about 4 inches above the smoking coals. Add more chips as needed to keep the fire smoking. Brush the fish with the oil, and cook for about 15 minutes. Baste again, cover and cook for 10 minutes longer or until the meat is lightly browned. This recipe serves 6.

Suggested Readings. 46, 64.

INSHORE LIZARDFISH
Synodus foetens

Sand Pike

Habits. There always seems to be a dead lizardfish drying in the sun on an ocean fishing pier, or thrown up on the beach behind a surf fisherman. In the United States, anglers dislike these fish because they are small (usually 6 to 8 inches), they steal bait, and they are not considered a food fish. Ranging from Massachusetts to Brazil, the Inshore Lizardfish is the most abundant species of lizardfish along the southeast and Gulf coasts. It is found in shallow saltwater creeks, rivers, and sounds, as well as along outer beaches offshore to a depth of about 300 feet. Lizardfish prefer sand and mud bottoms.

Like other members of the family Synodontidae, Inshore Lizardfish have cylindrical bodies, pointed reptile-like heads, tiny sharp teeth, and a single dorsal fin followed by an adipose fin. The large, oblique mouth gives it a grinning or laughing countenance, even in death. Lizardfish are similar in overall appearance to another family member, the Snakefish, *Trachinocephalus myops*. However, Snakefish have shorter, stouter bodies, are more vividly colored, and occur in slightly deeper water than Inshore Lizardfish. Inshore Lizardfish are dull brown with a series of white spots dorsally, and have darker brown diamond-shaped markings on the lower sides. The belly and throat are usually white.

Little is known about the life histories of the lizardfishes, except their feeding habits. The species are voracious piscivores that dart up from the bottom to grab their prey. Lizardfish often lie on the bottom with the head and upper parts of the body elevated, or they may bury themselves in the sand with only their eyes exposed. They have been known to strike with enough force to trip fishermen's planers. Planers are hydrodynamically designed pieces of metal that are attached in front of unattended, trolled lures. The appearance of the planer at the surface indicates that a fish, usually a mackerel or Bluefish, has struck the lure. Imagine the surprise of a fisherman who retrieves his tripped line only to find a 4-ounce lizardfish.

Fishing. Although lizardfish are caught by anglers who are trolling with lures or fishing with cut bait on the bottom, they are usually discarded because of their small size. They are seldom, if ever, sought by sport fishermen. The species is not targeted by any large commercial fishery in the United States, although it is caught by bottom trawls, fish traps, and handline. In southeast Asia, the family is of much greater commercial

importance. Recently, small local markets have been developed in Florida, catering to the demands of Oriental restaurants.

Preparation. Lizardfish may be broiled or deep fried.

Suggested Readings. 16, 46, 64.

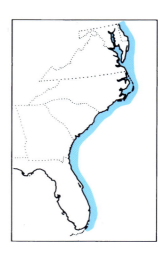

HARDHEAD CATFISH
Arius felis

Sea Catfish, Silver Catfish

Habits. There are two species of saltwater catfishes found along the southeastern and Gulf coasts of the United States, the Hardhead and the Gafftopsail, *Bagre marinus*. Both are caught by fishermen in the southerly part of the region; however, they are not usually regarded as food fish or sport fish. Marine catfishes are considered nuisances by fishermen because they tangle gill nets and steal anglers' baits. The Hardhead Catfish is the more common of the two species on the East Coast, ranging from the Florida Keys northward occasionally to North Carolina. Most are caught in coastal waters off Florida and Georgia.

The body is plain brown or dark blue on the back, shading to white on the undersides. The Hardhead differs from the Gafftopsail in having three pairs of barbels (one on the upper jaw, two on the lower) and in lacking extremely long filaments on the dorsal and pectoral spines. Hardhead Catfish inhabit turbid waters over sand and mud bottom. Although it prefers marine environments, the species occasionally enters brackish and fresh waters.

The life history of the Hardhead Catfish is relatively unknown. The little information that is available pertains to reproduction. Spawning occurs in or near bays and inlets in the summer from June through August. The male uses his mouth to incubate the fertilized eggs, which are very large and number fewer than 100.

Fishing. Hardhead Catfish are often plentiful and are easily caught on many types of natural baits and table scraps. The fish are aggressive feeders and seldom allow more desirable species to take the bait. Although there is no commercial market for the species in this country, it is caught with gill nets, traps, and trawls. Marine catfishes should be handled with caution. Their sharp spines may produce painful puncture wounds.

Preparation. The flesh is edible but seldom eaten. For an out of the ordinary recipe, one might try Fish Creole. The ingredients are 2 pounds of fish fillets, 2 cups of stewed tomatoes, 1 cup of water, 3 cloves, 1 sliced lemon, 1 sliced small onion, 2 tablespoons of butter, 1 tablespoon of flour, and a dash of salt and pepper. Place the tomatoes, water, cloves, and onion in a pan and heat. Mix the butter and flour together, stir them into the sauce when it boils, and add salt and pepper. Cook for about 10 minutes and pour into a bowl. Poach the fish in

boiling water for about a minute. Remove the fish, season it with salt and pepper, and lay it in a casserole dish. Put the lemon on top, then pour half of the tomato sauce around the fish and bake at 400°F for 30 to 40 minutes. Baste the fish several times as it bakes. Serve the fish covered with the remaining sauce on a hot platter. Rice is an excellent side dish. Serves 6.

Suggested Readings. 46, 78, 79.

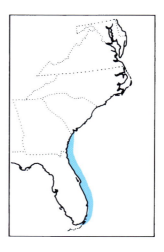

OYSTER TOADFISH
Opsanus tau
Mud Toad, Oyster Cracker

Habits. The Oyster Toadfish is a grotesque, demersal marine species that occurs from Maine to the West Indies. It is replaced in the Gulf of Mexico by the closely related Gulf Toadfish, *Opsanus beta*, and by the Leopard Toadfish, *O. pardus*. The ugly appearance of the Oyster Toadfish is accentuated by the broad flattened head, the bulging toad-like eyes and the fleshy protrusions that abound on the head and around the mouth. The slimy, scaleless skin is brownish-yellow, mottled with dark brown oblique bars that extend onto the fins. The outer portions of the pectoral fins have a series of brown concentric bands.

Oyster Toadfish conceal themselves around pilings, oyster reefs, and garbage dumps in shallow water as well as in crevices of rocky outcrops in offshore waters as deep as 150 feet. The species is capable of contracting the muscles attached to the air bladder, thus emitting sounds. Two sounds have been described. One is gruntlike and is produced when the fish are alerted to food or danger. The other, which sounds like a boat whistle, is used by males during the spawning season to call females.

Spawning takes place from early May through October, depending on the latitude, when water temperatures range from about 64° to 80°F. Unlike most marine species, the male Oyster Toadfish selects the nest site, usually under a board or in a can, jar, or old shoe. After the male prepares the nest, he enters it and uses the boat-whistle call to entice a mate. Anywhere from one to several females, each laying 20 to 800 eggs, may contribute ova to one nest. Each egg has an adhesive disk that cements the ovum to the hard substrate. When the spawning is completed, the female retires to deep water, and the male maintains his vigil throughout the incubation period, 5 to 12 days, until the tadpole-shaped young mature from a dependent, clinging stage to a free-swimming life style. No information is available on the age and growth of Oyster Toadfish; however, the species is probably slow-growing and may attain a maximum length of 15 inches. Toadfish are stealthy nocturnal predators that both stalk prey and lie in wait for it. The mouth is large enough to allow Oyster Toadfish to swallow most prey whole. The diet includes crabs, fishes, shrimps, amphipods, and worms.

Fishing. Ask any small child who has caught an Oyster Toadfish and a flounder on the same day which fish he remembers, and he will

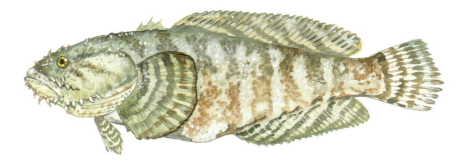

certainly describe the Toadfish. Even with this vote of confidence, the species ranks low among fishermen in the United States. It has no commercial value. Although lively on light tackle, it has a slimy body and powerful snapping jaws that make it very difficult to remove from a hook. Toadfish are caught throughout their range in traps, seines, and trawls, and by anglers fishing on the bottom with cut bait.

Preparation. The flesh is reported to be sweet and palatable, but it is seldom eaten, probably because of the fish's ugly appearance.

Suggested Readings. 55, 58, 64.

GOOSEFISH
Lophius americanus

Monkfish, Anglerfish, Allmouth

Habits. The family Lophiidae includes large, flat-headed fishes with enormous mouths and tapering bodies. They are unlike any other fish in the region, and it would be difficult to confuse them with other species. Also referred to as Monkfish, Allmouth, and Anglerfish, Goosefish have their first dorsal spine modified for a special purpose. The spine possesses a flap of skin at its tip which acts to lure prey when it is wiggled back and forth like a worm on the end of a slender reed. Behind its head, the Goosefish has a group of short dorsal spines that are connected by a black membrane. Another, more southerly species, the Blackfin Goosefish, *Lophius gastrophysus*, lacks the interspinous membrane and has longer dorsal spines. The Goosefish is dark chocolate brown above, sometimes mottled, and light tan below. It is a benthic species occurring in coastal waters and out to depths of at least 1,500 feet from New Brunswick, Canada, to northern Florida. Goosefish inhabit sand, mud, and broken shell bottoms in waters ranging from about 32° to 75°F.

Spawning occurs offshore from spring to early fall, depending on the latitude. Reproductive activity commences as early as March off North Carolina and as late as September off New England. The pelagic eggs are deposited in huge gelatinous masses. These ribbonlike egg veils are seasonally observed by sea-going fishermen, for they may be 20 to 36 feet long and 2 to 3 feet wide. The purplish-brown eggs, numbering 1 to 2 million, are clustered in small groups of several ova, each in compartments within the floating mass. Hatching takes place in continental shelf waters that are 41° to 65°F.

Goosefish are among the most gluttonous of all fishes. Not only do they ambush small prey, aided by their fishing appendage, but they also engulf large food items. Foods identified from Goosefish stomachs include Spiny Dogfish, skates, eels, herrings, Weakfish, Tautog, Butter-fish, puffers, Cod, Haddock, flounders, sea birds (loons, seagulls, scoters, and mergansers), lobsters, crabs, worms, shellfish, sand dollars, and starfish. One Goosefish contained 21 commercial-size flounders and a Spiny Dogfish; another had eaten 75 herrings; and a third consumed 7 wild ducks. No information is available on the age and growth of this species.

Fishing. Goosefish are seldom caught on hook and line. Undoubtedly, they put up a fierce fight when they are hooked. Most are caught with

commercial fishing gear such as trawls and pound nets. The species is of considerable commercial importance in Europe, where it is marketed fresh and frozen as Monkfish.

Preparation. The species is an excellent food fish, being relatively free of bones and having sweet-flavored white flesh. Baked or broiled and dipped in melted butter, the flesh resembles that of crab or lobster.

Suggested Readings. 13, 46, 64.

COASTAL GROUND FISHES

ATLANTIC COD
Gadus morhua
Cod, Codfish

Habits. The Atlantic Cod is a widely marketed food fish in the United States and Europe. It is a bottom-dwelling species that occurs on both sides of the Atlantic Ocean from Cape Hatteras, North Carolina, to Greenland, and from Iceland southward along the European coast to the Bay of Biscay off France and Spain. Four geographically distinct stocks are hypothesized for Atlantic Cod in American waters: Georges Banks, Gulf of Maine, Nantucket Shoals, and the Mid-Atlantic Bight. All but the last are believed to be nonmigratory. The species inhabits waters that are 32° to 50°F, and range from 200 to 1,300 feet in depth.

Cod have heavy, tapering bodies, three dorsal fins and two anal fins, and a prominent chin barbel. The species may be distinguished from its relative the Pollock, *Pollachius virens*, by the projecting upper jaw. Although many color phases have been noted for Cod, most fish are either olive-green or deep red. Green, brown, or reddish spots occur along the back and sides, sometimes extending onto the fins.

Sexually mature fish, those older than 3 years, spawn in December and January off the Mid-Atlantic Bight, and from February through April farther north. Fecundity ranges from about 1 to 9 million eggs depending on the size of the fish. The eggs are transparent and buoyant and hatch in approximately 40 days at 32°F, and in 17 days when the surgace water temperature is 41°F. The slow-growing Atlantic Cod is capable of living for about 22 years. Average lengths for fish aged 1 to 15 years are 4.7, 8.3, 11.8, 15.7, 19.3, 23.2, 27.6, 31.1, 33.5, 35.4, 37.4, 39, 39.8, 40.5, and 40.9 inches. Cod feed on, or near the bottom, on many kinds of animals. Favorite foods are crabs, worms, clams, and fishes.

Fishing. Atlantic Cod are caught by anglers fishing from small private boats and party boats, and by commercial fishermen using hook and line, traps, and trawls. Commercial fishing vessels may be as small as one-man dories, or as large as 2,000-ton trawlers. Fishermen have braved the fog-shrouded, cold waters of the North Atlantic for hundreds of years fishing for Cod. Disembarking from larger vessels to their dories, men made their lonely and often dangerous treks to and from the fishing grounds.

Today, most Cod are caught from ships operating off Iceland, in the Barents Sea, off Newfoundland and Greenland, and in the Norwegian Sea. The most productive fishing areas are between the 35th and 80th

north parallels. The Atlantic Cod is but one of many species of bottomfish that support important commercial fisheries along the northeastern United States. Besides the Cod and Pollock, others are Silver Hake, *Merluccius bilinearis*, Atlantic Tomcod, *Microgadus tomcod*, Haddock, *Melanogrammus aeglefinus*, and Atlantic Halibut, *Hippoglossus hippoglossus*.

Preparation. Cod are marketed fresh, frozen, and salted. A suggested dish is Cod Soufflé. The ingredients are 1 cup of cooked, flaked fish, 2 cups of chopped potatoes, 2 tablespoons of cream, 2 eggs, 1 tablespoon of butter, and ¼ teaspoon of white·pepper. Place the fish and potatoes in enough boiling water to cover them, and boil until the potatoes are done. Drain thoroughly, mash the fish and potatoes, and beat them well with a fork, adding white pepper, butter, and cream. Beat in well-stirred yolks of 2 eggs, and fold in the well-whipped egg whites. Pour the soufflé mixture into a greased baking dish and bake at 375°F for 20 minutes, or until it is brown. Serve with pickles, horseradish, or fresh cucumbers.

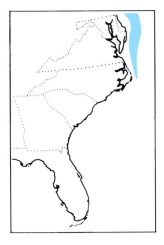

Suggested Readings. 167.

ATLANTIC NEEDLEFISH
Strongylura marina

Garfish

Habits. The habit of surface swimming, particularly at night around lighted piers and bridges, makes the Atlantic Needlefish one of the most visible of saltwater fishes to coastal residents and tourists. Also referred to as Garfish, the species has a very slender body and long jaws armed with sharp teeth. The species is blue-green above and silvery below. A conspicuous dark-blue stripe extends horizontally from behind the pectoral fins to the tail.

There are other fish in the region that have elongated jaws and resemble Needlefish in gross appearance. The Houndfish, *Tylosurus crocodilus*, is almost identical, but possesses a lateral keel on the caudal peduncle and is much larger (up to 40 to 45 inches long). The Ballyhoo, *Hemiramphus brasiliensis*, and Halfbeak, *Hyporhamphus unifasciatus*, are small, surface-swimming species of another family. Although their lower jaws are extended, their upper ones are very short. Both species are excellent baits for oceanic pelagic fishes such as tuna, Wahoo, and billfish. They may be identified from each other by the positions of the dorsal and anal fins. Those of the Ballyhoo are opposite, whereas the dorsal fin of the Halfbeak originates in front of the anal fin.

The Atlantic Needlefish is found in coastal waters—salt, brackish, and fresh—of the western Atlantic from Massachusetts to Brazil. It is distributed throughout the Gulf of Mexico and along the Central American coast, but is absent from much of the West Indies.

Very little is known about its life history. The spawning season is reported to occur during the summer when large numbers of eggs, all produced by a single ovary, are deposited in estuaries. The maximum size is approximately 25 to 30 inches.

Fishing. Atlantic Needlefish are of no direct importance to fisheries. They are occasionally landed in seines and gill nets, or by casting and trolling artificial lures. Needlefish, alive or dead, are excellent baits for many of the important recreational species such as Dolphin, King Mackerel, and tunas. It should be noted that the Houndfish, although infrequently hooked, makes spectacular twisting leaps when it takes a bait.

Preparation. Atlantic Needlefish are not marketed in the United States. The truly adventuresome may try deep frying small fish whole. This is a

method of cooking usually used with smelts, anchovies, silversides, and juvenile herrings and referred to as Fried Whitebait. The fish should be scaled and washed thoroughly in cold water. They are then fried after they have been dipped in milk and rolled in seasoned flour.

Suggested Readings. 46, 64.

SNOOK
Centropomus undecimalis
Linesider

Habits. Many fishermen consider the Snook to be the finest of all game fishes. When hooked, it takes unpredictable, explosive runs, making the fish very difficult to turn and reel in. Snook are found in warm waters from southern Florida to Rio de Janeiro, including the eastern Gulf of Mexico, Caribbean coast of Central America, and most of the West Indies. The species is occasionally found as far north as North Carolina.

Snook have long, pointed heads with strongly projecting lower jaws. The back is gray, with a yellow-green tint, and is separated from the silvery lower sides and belly by a black lateral line. An appropriate name given the species by fishermen is Linesider. It is the largest (up to 4 ½ feet in length and a weight of 51 pounds) and by far the most common of the four species found in the region. The other species are Swordspine Snook, *Centropomus ensiferus*, Fat Snook, *C. parallelus*, and Tarpon Snook, *C. pectinatus*. These are seldom caught and have pelvic fins that, when extended backward, overlap the anus. Snook are year-round residents of mangrove-lined bays, estuaries, canals, and lower reaches of streams and rivers where the water temperature is 60°F or warmer. The species is seldom caught in water deeper than 65 feet. During the spawning season, fish may be seen congregating around passes between islands and mouths of rivers.

The spawning season extends from May through November with a peak in May and June. Approximately one-half of the fish are mature when they are aged 3. Not much is known about spawning in the wild; however, Snook have been raised in the laboratory. There, the average female produces about 49 thousand eggs per pound of body weight. Or, on a length basis, a female 31 inches long lays about 1.6 million eggs during a spawning season. The eggs hatch in 24 to 30 hours at 82° to 87°F. Information on age and growth is limited to the first 7 years. Average lengths for ages 1 to 7 are 7, 14, 18, 23, 26, 29, and 32 inches. Snook are agressive predators that seek their prey throughout the water column. Foods include both freshwater and saltwater species of crustaceans and fishes. Some of the items identified in the stomachs are crayfish, shrimps, crabs, Pinfish, Pigfish, mullet, anchovies, and Mosquitofish.

Fishing. Most Snook landed in the United States are caught by sportsmen fishing in Florida with live bait or artificial lures. Anglers fish primarily in May and June when they wade or use small boats to drift

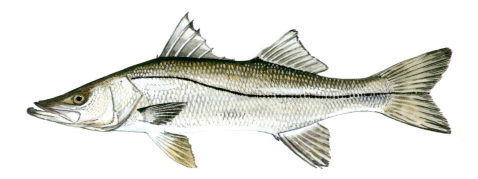

among the mangroves. A popular method is to free spool a live minnow on the surface. Bait such as menhaden, small mullet, or silversides are chummed with catfood and caught with a cast net. Some minnows are crippled and released, others are retained for bait. As the Snook move in to feed on the crippled minnows, a minnow is placed on a 2/0 or 3/0 hook and allowed to drift over the feeding fish. A stiff rod and medium-size bait-casting reel with 12- to 18-pound test line is standard. Artificial lures, both the plastic commercial variety and the homemade wooden clothespins, are popular. Favorite colors are silver or red. Spoons and Mirro-lures are also good baits. The lures are retrieved with a twitching, fluttering motion. The best times to fish are at night, during cloudy weather or other times when boat traffic is reduced, and during the 2 ½ hours before or after high tide. Commercial fishermen catch Snook with gill nets, beach seines, and handlines. Recent declines in catches have resulted in drastic management regulations in Florida.

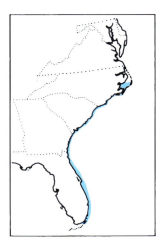

Preparation. The flesh is usually marketed fresh and is delicate and flaky. It is probably best broiled or baked.

Suggested Readings. 1, 46, 78, 96, 136, 160.

FLORIDA POMPANO
Trachinotus carolinus

Common Pompano

Habits. The Florida Pompano is a beautifully colored, delicately textured member of the family Carangidae and is highly esteemed as a food fish. Unlike most jacks, it lacks scutes on the caudal peduncle and may also be identified by its short, blunt snout. It is one of the few fish that is more vividly colored after death than when alive. The belly and fins are a beautiful golden hue and the sides are whitish-platinum. When removed from the water the body is dark green-blue above and silvery-white below.

The range extends from Massachusetts to Brazil, although the species is more common south of Virginia. It occurs irregularly in the West Indies. Adults are found along sandy beaches, in high-salinity (usually greater than 32 ppt) estuaries, and in shallow coastal waters out to a depth of approximately 130 feet. Large schools tend to migrate northward along the Atlantic coast in the summer and south in the fall, thus remaining in relatively warm (62° to 89°F) waters. The preferred water temperatures seem to range from 82° to 89°F.

Spawning takes place at sea, primarily from April through June, followed by lesser spawnings in the summer and fall. The species probably attains sexual maturity at the end of the first year, and is capable of laying thousands of pelagic eggs. A female 16 inches long contained more than 600 thousand ripe ova. The species grows rapidly, attaining a length of about 8 inches by the end of the first year of life. Longevity is estimated to be 3 or 4 years. Juvenile Florida Pompano feed on pelagic invertebrates—amphipods, crab larvae, copepods, isopods, and young fishes. Adults eat small surf clams (coquinas), amphipods, crabs, shrimps, and mussels.

Fishing. The Pompano is considered to be a gourmet food item by many and consistently demands the highest price per pound of any saltwater fish in the continental United States. It is an excellent game fish for its size and is caught by anglers fishing from bridges, jetties, piers, the surf, and small boats.

Most are caught by fishing on the bottom with natural baits, although some are caught by casting and trolling small artificial lures. Late summer and early fall are the best times to catch Pompano along the Carolinas, and spring and fall are the most productive fishing seasons along the east coast of Florida. Runs are sporadic, rarely sustained, and last only for several days. During these times the word quickly spreads,

and anglers flock to the coast with their spinning and bait-casting outfits.

Terminal tackle favored by most fishermen consists of two or three No. 1 or 1/0 claw hooks tied on short dropper loops one above the other. Sand fleas, shrimp, clams, and small crabs are good baits. The best fishing conditions are early in the morning or late afternoon, on an incoming or high tide with light to moderate surf and clear water. The baits should be allowed to rest on the bottom for a few minutes and then retrieved slowly. Pompano hit the bait hard and fast, usually hooking themselves. Occasionally, sport fishermen use small (1/8 to 3/8 ounce) yellow and white jigs sweetened with a piece of shrimp. Commercial landings in the United States are made primarily with gill nets, trammel nets, pound nets, trawls, and hook and line.

Preparation. The flesh is marketed fresh and is considered to be of excellent quality prepared in a variety of ways. Perhaps the best way is to broil, or lightly fry, and cover with gently browned melted butter (Pompano *buerre noir*).

Suggested Readings. 11, 46, 47.

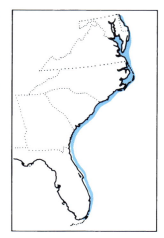

TRIPLETAIL
Lobotes surinamensis

Habits. The Tripletail has a compressed, deep body somewhat similar to that of a freshwater crappie. The dorsal and anal fins are rounded, extend far back on the body, and with the tail fin appear as a single three-lobed caudal fin, or as three tails. The profile of the head is concave, and the preopercle is strongly serrated. Compared with other saltwater fishes, Tripletails probably most resemble groupers, but lack teeth on the roof of the mouth. The color is drab, various shades of yellow-brown to dark brown, with obscure spots and mottling on the sides.

The species occurs in tropical waters of the Atlantic, Indian, and western Pacific Oceans. Although distributed from New England to South Florida along the eastern coast of the United States, the species becomes more abundant south of Virginia where it is observed offshore, lying on its side near buoys or other floating objects. Infrequent and seasonal landings suggest a northerly and inshore transport or migration as waters warm in the spring and summer.

Because of their limited abundance, only a few fish have been examined by scientists to gather life history information. It seems that Tripletails attain sexual maturity at the end of the first year of life, and that spawning occurs in the spring and summer. Ripe females have been collected off North Carolina from June through August. Some data indicate that fish in the Gulf of Mexico may move inshore to spawn. However, along the southeastern United States, juveniles have been collected in estuaries and from patches of *Sargassum* far offshore in the Gulf Stream.

Although Tripletails may live for as long as 7 to 10 years, and reach a maximum weight of 45 pounds, most caught by fishermen are only 1 to 3 years old. Approximate average lengths for fish aged 1 to 3 years are 19, 23, and 25 inches. These sizes for the given ages look questionable. Tripletails are almost exclusively piscivorous. Foods listed in order of importance are Thread herring, menhaden, Butterfish, Spot, anchovies, Atlantic Croaker, shrimps, crabs, and squids.

Fishing. Even though Tripletails are occasionally caught throughout their range, they are unimportant to commercial fisheries outside Florida. There, a few thousand pounds are landed annually by haul seines, gill nets, and hook and line. The flesh is marketed fresh and is reported to be of excellent quality, especially when baked. Sport fishermen usually

catch Tripletail around wrecks, buoys, and offshore pilings from May to October.

A unique method used by some Mississippi anglers is to place pine trees in the bottom to attract fish. The trees are several inches in diameter and 15 to 20 feet long. They are placed vertically in water 8 to 10 feet deep by driving them into the soft mud bottom. To fish the trees, anglers wait a month or so and then return with medium-size spinning or bait-casting tackle rigged with a float, 6/0 to 9/0 hook, and a live fish or shrimp for bait. Tripletails are often reluctant to bite, but when hooked provide a good fight and promise for the table.

Preparation. Tripletails may be prepared like any other species that has flaky, white meat (fried, baked, or broiled).

Suggested Readings. 46, 64, 103.

PIGFISH
Orthopristis chrysoptera

Hogfish

Habits. The Pigfish is one of the most popular pan fishes caught along the east coast of the United States. It belongs to the grunt family, but unlike most of its relatives, the Pigfish inhabits warm-temperate, rather than tropical waters, and it is found as far north as Cape Cod. The species is most abundant south of Chesapeake Bay in coastal waters over sand and mud bottom.

Pigfish are separated from other grunts by the long sloping snout, color, and 12 to 13 anal fin rays. They make a grunting sound when removed from the water. The color is pale blue-gray above, shading to silver below. The cheeks and upper sides have brassy or golden variable markings that often form oblique lines. The fins are yellow-bronze with dusky margins. The color in death is a dull brown-gray.

Considering its abundance and importance to fisheries, one would expect the Pigfish to have been studied extensively. This is not the case. Only brief descriptions of spawning, food habits, and longevity are available. Spawning occurs inshore in the spring and early summer in open ocean waters just prior to the fish's migration to estuaries. Pigfish are believed to mature during the second year of life, when the fish are as small as 7 inches. Pigfish are bottom feeders that root through the sediments searching for a variety of benthic invertebrates including worms, mollusks, amphipods, shrimps, and crabs. The maximum size attained by the species is approximately 19 inches and a weight of 2 to 3 pounds. Few fish reach the age of 3 years, very few 4.

Fishing. Pigfish are important to commercial and recreational fisheries. They are easily caught in late summer and fall, August through November, by bottom fishing with a standard two-hook rig baited with shrimp, squid, or bloodworms. Commercial fishermen land the species in gill nets, pound nets, trawls, and seines.

Preparation. Pigfish are marketed fresh and are preferred by many coastal residents over all other finfish. Because of their small size, Pigfish usually are not filleted, but are prepared by removing the scales, head, tail, and viscera. The meat is then fried. Pigfish are also corned or salted as is done with herrings, mullets, and mackerels.

After cleaning the fish, wash them thoroughly in ice water. Layer the fish and non-iodized salt in a container such as an ice chest. The fish must be completely surrounded by salt. Cover the container and store in

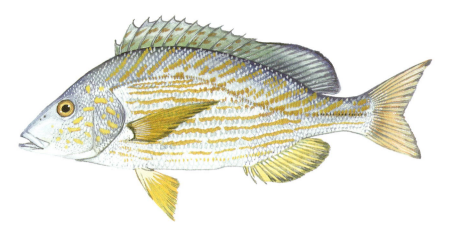

a cool place for 7 to 10 days. This is called striking the fish. Pour off the thick, dark liquid that has accumulated. Again, wash the fish thoroughly. Make a brine solution that is strong enough to float an unbroken raw egg. The volume will depend on the amount of fish being corned. Place the fish in storage containers, usually plastic or glass gallon jars. Do not pack them too tightly. Fill each container with the brine (½ teaspoon of ascorbic acid per gallon will increase the shelf life). Seal the top (to prevent rusting, put plastic or aluminum foil between the jar and lid). Store in a cool place. To cook the fish, remove from the brine and soak them in water overnight. Salt fish are excellent pan fried after they have been rolled in cornmeal.

Suggested Readings. 38, 46, 64.

SHEEPSHEAD
Archosargus probatocephalus

Convict Fish

Habits. The Sheepshead is a large sparid that is found in coastal waters browsing around jetties, wharfs, pilings, shipwrecks, and other structures covered with barnacles, mussels, and oysters. The species ranges from Nova Scotia to Cedar Key, Florida, along the Atlantic coast of North America. There are two other populations of the species that are regarded as subspecies, but they occur in the western Gulf of Mexico and in the South Atlantic to Rio de Janeiro.

Sheepshead are greenish-gray, with a laterally compressed body marked vertically with five or six dark bars. Another common name, Convict Fish, stems from these markings. The mouth is medium sized, with strong incisors and molars that enable the fish to pick up and crush shellfish and sea urchins. Although a saltwater species, Sheepshead are often found in brackish waters of coastal rivers.

During the spawning season, Sheepshead swim in schools and appear to prefer sandy shores. The dark, pelagic eggs are deposited near shore, where they hatch in about 40 hours at 76° to 77°F. The young often inhabit grassy flats and feed on small, soft animals and plants before they disperse to more high-relief, hard-bottom areas. In Florida, and as far north as South Carolina, the Sheepshead may be a winter resident. Farther north, however, the species is scarce in winter and most abundant from April through November. The preferred water temperature is probably not below 60° to 65°F.

Sheepshead commonly attain a length of 30 inches and a weight ranging from 5 to 15 pounds. Fish as large as 20 to 25 pounds are caught occasionally.

Fishing. A number of methods are used to catch Sheepshead. Anglers may choose handlines, cane poles, and spinning tackle. Fiddler crabs, barnacles, oysters, clams, crabs, and shrimp are used for bait. The experienced fisherman chums the area with crushed oysters or crabs before fishing. Because Sheepshead are bottom feeders, bottom and float rigs are the principal fishing methods.

Fishing around jetties and pilings on a half-flooded tide produces good results. Many fishermen use conventional or spinning gear rigged with a float, 4-foot wire leader, and a treble hook baited with a live shrimp. A popular method is to cast from a boat anchored adjacent to a jetty, allowing the tide to carry the bait across the rocks. Perhaps the best

way to catch Sheepshead is to fish next to a piling with a cane pole, strong line, small split shot, and a 2/0 hook baited with a fiddler crab.

Preparation. Sheepshead are a favorite food fish. They are excellent fried, baked, or broiled. The flesh is white and dry, and the large bones are easily avoided.

Suggested Readings. 46, 64, 78.

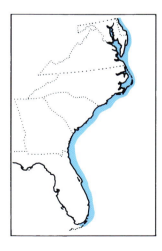

PINFISH
Lagodon rhomboides

Sailor's Choice, Canadian Bream

Habits. The Pinfish is the most abundant member of the porgy family (Sparidae) along the southeastern United States. Although small in size, the species is popular with many anglers, particularly children. It is easily recognized by the oval body, small mouth, incisor-like teeth with deeply notched edges, and color. The body is silvery with yellow and blue longitudinal stripes and a black spot behind the gill cover. Four to six diffuse vertical bars also occur along the sides. The pectoral and caudal fins are yellow and the dorsal fin is blue and yellow striped.

Pinfish are usually found around pilings, rocks, and vegetated areas in shallow waters from Cape Cod to Yucatan, Mexico, including the Gulf of Mexico, Bermuda, and the northern coast of Cuba. The species is tolerant of a wide range of environmental conditions: salinities of 1 to 37 ppt, water temperatures of 42° to 95°F, and depths of from several inches to at least 240 feet.

Sexual maturity may be reached when fish are as small as 5 inches and as young as 1 year, although most reproduce initially when they are larger (older). Spawning occurs from about mid-October to March as larger individuals move offshore. Peak spawning along most of the southeastern United States takes place in December and January. The eggs are pelagic and number from 7 to 90 thousand, depending on the size of the female. Age and growth information is available for only the first 7 years. Approximate average lengths for ages 1, 2, 3, and 7 are 4, 6, 8, and 12 inches. Like other porgies, Pinfish probably live longer than 7 years. The maximum size is about 16 inches, a length that far exceeds that for a 7-year old. The species has been described as a catholic grazer, one that feeds on plants, detritus, and various small bottom-dwelling animals. Small food items are swallowed whole; larger ones are nibbled into pieces by the incisor teeth. Pinfish most often eat worms, crustaceans, and mollusks found on or near rocks, pilings, and seagrasses. Feeding occurs primarily during daylight hours.

Fishing. Pinfish are categorized as trash fish or scrap fish by commercial fishermen because their market value is very low in the United States. This was not the case in the 1800s, when thousands of pounds were sold annually at fish markets in Charleston, Savannah, and Florida (Indian River). Today, the species appears as an incidental catch with important fishes in trawls, seines, pound nets, gill nets, and traps. Pinfish are caught by anglers bottom fishing from piers, docks, bridges,

146

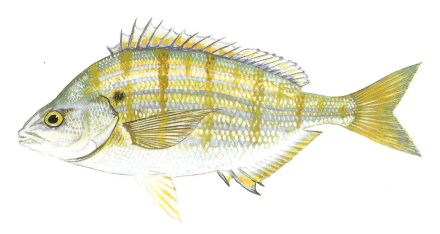

and small boats using standard two-hook rigs baited with shrimp, squid, or bloodworms. Children generally are prouder of their Pinfish catches than are adults. The species is used commercially to produce pet food, and is excellent bait for mackerels, Bluefish, Tarpon, Cobia, Red Drum, and groupers.

Preparation. The flesh is edible and is usually prepared by frying. It is not popular, however, because it is oily and has a strong fishy flavor.

Suggested Readings. 22, 46, 62, 64.

SCUP
Stenotomus chrysops

Porgy

Habits. There are two species of *Stenotomus*: the Scup, *S. chrysops*, and the Longspine Porgy, *S. caprinus*. Although both are caught by saltwater fishermen along the east coast of the United States, the Scup is more important, particularly to commercial fisheries. Scup inhabit the nearshore region of the continental shelf from Nova Scotia to South Carolina. Longspine Porgy replace Scup in southern areas, particularly the Gulf of Mexico. Scup prefer hard bottom such as rock outcroppings and wrecks, in waters 45°F or warmer. The species is found inshore in late spring and summer, entering tidal bays and sounds, and offshore in fall and winter, shoreward of the 120-foot contour.

Scup are deep bodied and have very spiny fins. The front teeth are incisor-form and are very narrow, almost conical. There are two rows of molars in the upper jaw. Longspine Porgy are similar but may be readily identified by their elongated dorsal spines. Scup are dusky colored. They are brownish, somewhat silvery below with bright reflections. The fins are mottled with dark brown in the adults, and the young may be faintly barred.

Sexual maturity is attained when fish are 2 years old and about 8 inches long. In the more northerly part of the range, spawning occurs from May through August. The eggs and larvae are pelagic and are carried by currents and winds before finally settling to the bottom. Scup may live to be 15 years old, reaching a length of 18 inches and a weight of 3 pounds. Approximate lengths for fish aged 1, 5, 10, and 15 years are 5, 10, 14, and 15 inches. Like other members of the family Sparidae, Scup are browsers; they nibble on invertebrates that live on the ocean bottom. Foods in the diet are crabs, shrimps, worms, clams, snails, starfish, sea urchins, and occasionally small fishes. Scup are able to grasp foods with their incisors, and then crush even hard-shelled animals with the strong molars.

Fishing. Scup have been caught commercially since colonial times. Historical records vividly describe fishing for Scup as well as more prestigious fishes such as Striped Bass, Bluefish, Black Sea Bass, and mackerels. Commercial fishermen use otter trawls, traps, pound nets, seines, and hand lines to capture Scup. The largest fisheries by far are in the Northeast.

Sport fishermen have found Scup to be game fighters on light tackle, and more importantly, abundant and easy to catch during certain times

of the year. Porgy are caught bottom fishing with natural baits and by jigging small artificial lures. For bottom fishing, anglers anchor their boats and use weighted chum pots baited with cut clams to attract fish. A light, 6-foot boat rod or 7-foot spinning rod matched with a medium-sized saltwater reel spooled with 10- to 15-pound test line is all the fisherman needs to catch Scup. Terminal tackle may be two No. 1 sproat hooks with short, 12-inch leaders attached to a heavy leader with a dropper loop. The first hook is placed about 6 inches above the 4- to 16-ounce sinker, and the second is fastened about a foot above the weight. Baits often used are clams, shrimp, bloodworms, or squid.

Preparation. Porgy are tasty and very easy to prepare. They keep well and may be frozen for months without loss of meat texture or taste. They may be served after frying, broiling, or baking. Scup also make excellent milk or tomato chowders.

Suggested Readings. 106.

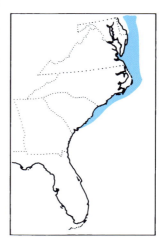

SILVER PERCH
Bairdiella chrysoura

Sand Perch

Habits. The Silver Perch is a small sciaenid that is seasonally abundant in the sounds, bays, and beaches along the Atlantic seaboard from Connecticut to south Florida and throughout the Gulf of Mexico. The species has an olivaceous to bluish back with bright silvery or brassy sides and belly. It may be distinguished from other drums and croakers by its terminal mouth, lack of chin barbels, and strong spines on the margin of the preopercle.

Spawning occurs in late spring or early summer, beginning later and having shorter duration at higher latitudes. Spawning lasts from June to August off New Jersey, from May to July in the Delaware Bay, from April to August off Beaufort, North Carolina, and in April and May off Georgia. The pelagic eggs, which number about 53 thousand for a 6-inch female, are broadcast in coastal waters, particularly around inlets.

Very little information is available on age and growth. Approximate lengths for fish aged 1 to 3 years are 3.8, 5.4, and 7.1 inches. The diet of the Silver Perch is diversified, changing as the fish grow larger. Small Silver Perch feed on crustaceans (amphipods, copepods, mysids, and crab larvae), whereas larger fish eat silversides, anchovies, and herring. In the fall, schools of Silver Perch are often mistakenly identified as Bluefish as they scatter prey fishes across the water's surface.

Fishing. Because of their small size, Silver Perch are usually discarded by fishermen, although the meat has an excellent flavor. The species is caught in pound nets, seines, and trawls, as well as by hook and line incidentally to species that are more important to commercial and recreational fisheries. While Silver Perch are seldom served as food for man, they are excellent live bait for Bluefish, mackerel, and Striped Bass.

Preparation. Silver Perch are best deep fried or broiled. To broil, place the fish on a greased broiler rack, skin side down. Put in a broiler with the pan about six inches from the source of heat. Brush the fish with melted butter and lemon juice and broil for 8 to 10 minutes or until the fish flakes easily with a fork. Turn thicker pieces, such as pan-dressed fish, halfway through the cooking time and baste. Sprinkle paprika over the fish and serve on a hot platter.

Fish that have been cleaned by removing scales, head, and viscera may be deep pan fried after rolling them in seasoned cornmeal. Many cooks prefer a well-seasoned cast-iron skillet for pan frying fish. The British method of pan frying is to dredge the portions in steel-cut oatmeal (seasoned to taste with salt and pepper) and to use just enough cooking oil to cover the bottom of the pan. Sauté the fish over medium-high heat until brown on both sides. The meat should be flaky but not dried out. Serve immediately with oatcakes instead of hushpuppies.

Suggested Readings. 64, 120, 150.

SPOTTED SEATROUT
Cynoscion nebulosus

Speckled Trout, Southern Spotted Weakfish

Habits. The Spotted Seatrout is a member of the family Sciaenidae (drums, croakers, and Weakfish) and is prized as a game and food fish. Its geographical range is from New York to the northern part of Mexico. The species is euryhaline; it tolerates a wide range in salinity, but prefers the low to medium salinity of coastal waters and brackish estuaries. It is a year-round resident of coastal waters in the southern portion of its range, whereas populations north of North Carolina tend to leave the estuaries in early winter and return the next spring.

The Spotted Seatrout has a relatively long, slender body. The upper jaw possesses two large, curved canine teeth. The back is usually a dark silvery gray with a bluish tint; the sides are silvery. Round black spots are distributed on the back, upper sides, and the second dorsal fin. One way to distinguish the Spotted Seatrout from its close relative, the Weakfish or Gray Trout, *Cynoscion regalis*, is by the spots. The Spotted Seatrout has spots extending onto the second dorsal fin; the Gray Trout does not.

The Spotted Seatrout has an extended spawning season, from spring through early fall. The number of eggs produced by a female ranges from 100 thousand to 1.1 million (for fish 10 and 26 inches long, respectively). The average is probably between 500 and 600 thousand. Age at the size of sexual maturity varies among estuarine populations. As a general rule, fish mature between their first and third years of life. Spotted Seatrout may live as long as 10 years and weigh as much as 10 pounds. However, the average catch consists of fish ranging from 1 to 5 pounds, representatives of the first few age classes. Average lengths for fish aged 1 to 8 years are 8, 12, 15, 18, 22, 25, 27, and 30 inches. Spotted Seatrout are voracious predators that feed on a variety of animals found near the bottom and at midwater. Fishes most often encountered in the diet include mullet, menhaden, Atlantic Croaker, Spot, anchovies, and silversides. The species also feeds on shrimps and crabs. Schools of Trout seem to be constantly searching for food. Adults form small schools and with the incoming tide move onto shoals to feed.

Fishing. The species is taken on light to heavy spinning tackle. Ultra-light spinning gear is thought by some to provide the most sport. Popular natural baits include live and dead shrimp and live minnows. Bucktails and plastic grubs are preferred artificials. These brightly colored lures are retrieved very slowly along the bottom. Because

Spotted Seatrout feed throughout the water column, both bottom and float rigs are effective terminal tackle. Anglers fishing from small boats take Trout by anchoring, drifting, or trolling slowly in deep holes or near pilings and shell banks. Peak catches are made during the fall, although May and June are productive months.

Preparation. The white flesh and excellent flavor make the Spotted Seatrout a highly esteemed fish for the table. The meat does spoil rapidly, and care should be taken to chill it at all times and to prepare it as soon as possible. Trout may be fried, baked, or broiled after stuffing them with crabmeat.

Suggested Readings. 46, 153.

WEAKFISH
Cynoscion regalis

Gray Trout, Gray Seatrout, Squeteague

Habits. The Weakfish, or Gray Trout, is one of more than 30 members of the family Sciaenidae found along the Atlantic, Gulf, and Pacific coasts of the United States. Collectively these fishes are known as drums or croakers because most make drumming or croaking sounds by vibrating their air bladders with specialized muscles.

Gray Trout occur in coastal waters from Cape Cod to Mobile, Alabama, but tend to be more abundant in the northern part of their range (South Carolina and northward).

The species is silvery overall, with the top part of the body dark olive-green and flecked with many dark blotches, some forming wavy lines that run down and forward. The dorsal and tail fins are dusky, while the ventrals, anal fin, and margin of the caudal fin are yellow. Two large canine teeth are in the upper jaw. Weakfish are migratory, and the smaller, younger fish move offshore and south along the Atlantic Coast in fall and winter, some as far south as Florida. Older fish move farther offshore than do the young ones, and most migrate south, but only as far as North Carolina.

Spawning occurs in nearshore and estuarine waters from May to October, with peak activity in May and June. Some fish are mature by the end of their first year, and all are capable of spawning by the end of the second. A female 16 inches long may lay more than 1 million eggs, and a fish 20 inches long may spawn 2 million eggs at one time. Gray Trout grow rapidly and live as long as 9 years. A 1-year-old fish is about 7 or 8 inches in length, a 2-year-old about 10, and a Trout at age 7 is about 19.5 inches long. Feeding takes place throughout the water column. Smaller fish generally eat shrimps, crabs, and small clams on the bottom, and large fish consume Butterfish, herrings, silversides, anchovies, and other fishes.

Fishing. Sport fishermen have found that catching Gray Trout may be perplexing. One does not usually have a fair day; it is an all or none proposition. There are many good anglers, some living on the coast, who have never caught a Gray Trout. Live bait such as shrimp, shedder crabs, and fish, as well as artificials, are effective baits. The best type of lure is a hammered steel-headed jig with a brightly colored rubber tail. These are bumped on the bottom of deep holes or ship channels and retrieved slowly with casting or spinning rigs with 4- to 20-pound monofilament line. The fishing season on the Atlantic Coast is from

April through November. Commercial fishermen land Gray Trout by gill nets, seines, pound nets, and trawls. Thousands of pounds of young Gray Trout are caught each year by the winter trawl fishery off North Carolina and Virginia.

Preparation. The flesh is very tender and easily torn, thus the name Weakfish. Fish should be iced immediately and cleaned as soon as possible. Gray Trout are easily filleted and are usually fried. Large Trout may be stuffed with crabmeat or scallop dressing and baked.

Suggested Readings. 102, 166.

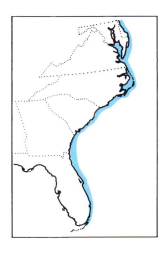

SPOT

Leiostomus xanthurus

Norfolk Spot

Habits. The Spot may have brought more enjoyment to marine anglers along the mid-Atlantic and southeastern United States than any other saltwater fish. The species is also very important to commercial fishing interests in the region. Spot inhabit estuarine and coastal waters from Massachusetts to Mexico. They are most abundant from Delaware Bay to Georgia in the summer and fall. Seasonally, Spot tend to occur in shallow waters during the summer from Delaware to Georgia, and then move offshore in the winter to occupy much of the shelf edge from Cape Hatteras to central Florida. Like its close relative the Atlantic Croaker, the Spot can tolerate a wide range in water temperature (35° to 95°F) and salinity (fresh to 37 ppt). Severe winters, however, have been known to cause extensive mortalities to estuarine populations of juveniles. Adult fish are easily separated from other sciaenids by the lack of chin barbels and by their color. The body is grayish-silver overall, with golden reflections along the upper sides, and 12 to 15 oblique dark lines extending from the dorsal fins to below the lateral line. A characteristic prominent black spot, about the same size as the eye, is located behind the gill cover. The dorsal and caudal fins are dusky, whereas the other fins are generally pale yellow.

Spawning takes place at sea in the fall and winter where water temperatures range from 59° to 79°F. The spawning season is extended and lasts from September through November off Chesapeake Bay, from October through February off North Carolina, and from December through March along Florida. Sexual maturity is first attained when fish have completed their second year of life or have started their third. Although good information on fecundity is not available, the numbers of eggs produced by Spot approximate those for Atlantic Croaker, 100 thousand to 1.7 million. The eggs and larvae are pelagic and are carried shoreward by currents and winds. Extended periods of offshore-directed winds or unfavorable currents during these critical life stages may cause drastic reductions in a year class of Spot as well as other species of ocean-spawning, estuarine-dependent fishes. Once on the estuarine nursery grounds, the juveniles move into less saline areas, sometimes into fresh water where they spend the winter. They return to more saline waters as they grow older.

Growth is rapid for the first year because the estuaries are very productive and offer a variety of foods—crustaceans, clam siphons, detritus, worms, and small fishes. Although Spot are capable of living as

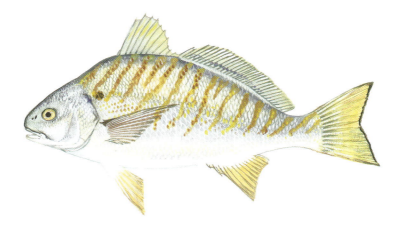

long as 5 years, most of those caught by fishermen are only 1 to 3 years old. Approximate lengths for fish aged 1 to 5 years are 5.5, 8.5, 9.5, 11.5, and 13.5 inches.

Fishing. Millions of pounds of Spot are landed by both recreational and commercial fishermen each year. Commercial fishermen use trawls, pound nets, haul seines, and gill nets to catch the species during the summer and fall. The migratory habits of the species, which tend to concentrate fish in large schools close to shore, make commercial harvest by nets very efficient. Anglers fishing with light sporting tackle from piers, bridges, jetties, the surf, and small boats also catch many Spot. Tackle described for Atlantic Croaker works equally well for Spot.

Preparation. The flesh is excellent and is usually fried fresh, or after it has been stored in salt.

Suggested Readings. 46, 64, 150.

SOUTHERN KINGFISH
Menticirrhus americanus
Whiting, Sea Mullet, Virginia Mullet

Habits. Surf and pier fishermen along the southeastern United States are certainly familiar with the kingfishes, also known as Whiting, Sea Mullet, and Virginia Mullet. Three species occur in the region: the Southern Kingfish, the Northern Kingfish, *Menticirrhus saxatilis*, and the Gulf Kingfish, *M. littoralis*. The Southern is by far the most common of the three, and is distributed from Cape Cod to Argentina.

It is most abundant from Chesapeake Bay to Fort Pierce, Florida, where in the warmer months it inhabits sand- and mud-bottoms of sounds, inlets, and coastal waters out to depths of about 30 feet. During the winter, the species presumably moves southward and offshore to deeper water. The Southern Kingfish seems to tolerate a wider range of environmental conditions than either the Northern or Gulf Kingfishes, and is found in waters from 46° to 86°F where salinities vary from 6 to 35 ppt.

The species is a medium-sized member of the croaker family with a slender body, a small inferior mouth, and a single, rigid chin barbel. The back and sides are silvery-gray with seven or eight oblique dusky bars, which extend downward and forward to just above the white belly.

Spawning takes place from April through August when mature females (2 years old and older) lay their pelagic eggs miles offshore. The newly hatched larvae are carried into estuarine nursery areas by currents and winds, and remain there for months seeking food and shelter from predators. Little information is available on age and growth; however, the maximum age is probably 5 or 6 years and the maximum size is about 16.5 inches and 2 ½ pounds. Approximate lengths for the first 3 years are 5.3, 9.8, and 12 inches. Whiting are bottom feeders that consume a variety of small marine animals. Major foods are worms, shrimps, shrimp larvae, crabs, amphipods, and fishes. The relative importance of these food groups changes as the fish attain larger sizes.

Fishing. Whiting are very popular food and game fishes. They are caught commercially in otter trawls, haul seines, gill nets, and pound nets and are marketed fresh. Recreational anglers bottom fishing from piers, the surf, bridges, and small boats catch Whiting from April through November in coastal waters. Light spinning and bait-casting tackle outfits with two-hook rigs weighted by 1- to 3-ounce sinkers are the standard gear. Shrimp, mole crabs, bloodworms, and squid are excellent

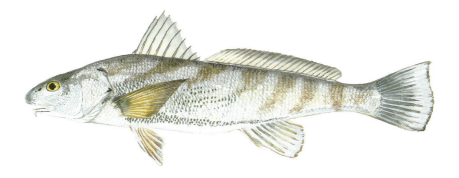

baits. Most anglers prefer to fish between the shore and a sandbar, or in other natural depressions, just before or after a high tide.

Preparation. The flesh is excellent fried, and many coastal residents prefer it over all other saltwater fish.

Suggested Readings. 7, 46.

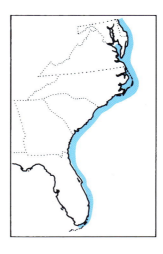

GULF KINGFISH
Menticirrhus littoralis

Whiting, Sea Mullet, Virginia Mullet

Habits. The Gulf Kingfish is similar to the Southern Kingfish in shape, but it has fewer scales along the lateral line (72 to 74 compared with 86 to 96). It is silvery below and darker on the back and upper sides, and lacks the dusky bars of the Southern Kingfish. Even with these distinguishing features, the species is often confused with the other kingfishes and all are referred to as Whitings or Sea Mullets.

The species is distributed along the Atlantic coast of the United States from Chesapeake Bay to south Florida and throughout the Gulf of Mexico to Brazil. It is most abundant south of Cape Hatteras, where it inhabits sand- and mud-bottom coastal waters, particularly the surf zone. The species occasionally enters high-salinity estuaries, where the salt content is greater than 25 ppt.

Spawning takes place offshore in May and June. The Gulf Kingfish is the largest of the three kingfishes, attaining a maximum length of approximately 18 inches and a weight of 3 ½ pounds. It uses its small underside mouth and its chin barbel to root around on the bottom for crabs, worms, and shrimps.

Fishing. Gulf Kingfish are caught commercially by trawls, pound nets, haul seines, and gill nets, and by recreational fishermen. Most are caught by anglers fishing shallow coastal waters from piers, bridges, and the surf. Light spinning tackle and bottom rigs consisting of 2- to 4-ounce pyramid lead sinkers and two hooks baited with shrimp, bloodworms, or squid are the standard equipment.

Preparation. The flesh is excellent, is usually deep fried, and is a favorite of coastal residents and tourists. A suggested method of cooking kingfish and other species with white, lean meat is Fish Fillets with Mushrooms. The ingredients are 1 pound of mushrooms, 1 ½ pounds of fish fillets, flour, 2 tablespoons of butter, 1 tablespoon of oil, ½ teaspoon of salt, dash of pepper, ½ cup of dry white wine, a pinch of nutmeg, and 1 tablespoon of lemon juice.

Separate the stems and caps of the mushrooms. Roll the fish fillets in flour and shake off the excess. Heat 1 tablespoon of butter and the oil in a large frying pan until it begins to splatter. Put the fillets in the pan and brown them on both sides. Add the mushrooms, salt, pepper, and white wine. Cover and let it simmer for about 5 minutes. Sprinkle in the nutmeg, and add the lemon juice and remaining butter. Stir by tipping

the pan back and forth. Spoon the sauce over the fish and serve on a hot platter. Serves 4 to 6.

Suggested Readings. 7, 46.

NORTHERN KINGFISH
Menticirrhus saxatilis

Whiting, Sea Mullet, Virginia Mullet

Habits. The Northern Kingfish is easily identified by its dark coloration and by the long spine on its first dorsal fin, which makes the fin higher than that of the Gulf and Southern Kingfishes. The back and sides are gray, sometimes blackish above, and always with five or six oblique, narrow bars. The fins are dusky or blackish; the spiny dorsal fin, anal fin, pectorals, and ventral fins are often tipped with dusky white. It is the only kingfish in the region that possesses a dark longitudinal stripe behind the pectoral fins.

The species is distributed from Maine to south Florida, but is most abundant north of Cape Hatteras. The Northern Kingfish prefers hard sandy bottom and forms large schools that occur in coastal waters, occasionally entering estuaries.

Spawning occurs in the spring and summer: April and May off North Carolina, and from June through August off the coast of Maine. Although some individuals are sexually mature at the end of their first year, most males reproduce initially as 2-year-olds, and females when they are three. The pelagic eggs hatch in about 46 to 50 hours in waters 68° to 70°F. Young fish are transported inshore to estuarine nursery areas by currents and winds. The species is known to live for at least 4 years and to attain a maximum length of 17 inches and a weight of 3 pounds. Approximate lengths for fish aged 1 to 4 years are 10.2, 13, 14.6, and 15.5 inches. Northern Kingfish feed on small animals that live on the bottom, such as worms, crabs, shrimps. and fishes.

Fishing. Northern Kingfish are caught commercially by trawls, haul seines, gill nets, and pound nets, and by recreational fishermen. Anglers fishing from the surf, ocean piers, and small boats use light spinning or bait-casting outfits and two-hook bottom rigs baited with shrimp, squid, clams, or bloodworms to catch Northern Kingfish. Sport-fishing techniques and equipment described for Spot, Atlantic Croaker, and Southern Kingfish apply equally well for this species.

Preparation. The flesh is excellent and is usually deep fried. Since the meat is white and lean, it may also be used to make a fish chowder or fish casserole. The ingredients for Fish Casserole are 1 pound of fish fillets, 1 sliced onion, 2 celery stalks sliced diagonally, 1 carrot sliced round, 1 yellow squash sliced round, 1 sliced fresh tomato, 1 bell

pepper cut in thin strips, salt and pepper, juice of 2 lemons, and ¼ cup of Worcestershire sauce.

Layer the fish, onion, celery, carrot, squash, tomato, and bell pepper in a square casserole dish, seasoning each layer. Pour the lemon juice and Worcestershire sauce over the top. Cover the casserole and bake at 350°F for about 1 hour or until the vegetables are tender. Serves 4.

Suggested Readings. 7, 46, 131.

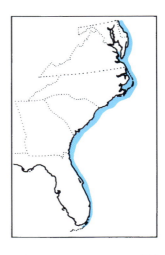

ATLANTIC CROAKER
Micropogonias undulatus

Croaker

Habits. The Atlantic Croaker is one of the most frequently caught estuarine and nearshore marine fishes along the eastern coast of the United States. The common name is derived from the deep croaking sounds created by muscular action on the air bladder. The species is a medium-sized member of the family Sciaenidae, attaining a maximum length of about 20 inches and a weight of 4 pounds. It is distributed from Massachusetts to Texas in North America, and along the South American coast from Surinam to Argentina. Atlantic Croakers are tolerant of a wide range of salinities (0 to 35 ppt) and temperatures (35° to 86°F), and they inhabit both mud- and sand-bottom areas.

Several characters separate this species from its close relatives: 3 to 5 pairs of small chin barbels, a strongly serrated preopercular margin with 3 to 5 spines at its angle, and 64 to 72 scales along the lateral line. Unlike the spot, *Leiostomus xanthurus*, which has a concave caudal fin, the Croaker has a convex tail. Atlantic Croakers are silvery overall, with a faint pinkish-bronze cast. The back and upper sides are grayish, with brassy or brown spots that form oblique wavy lines on the fish's sides. No other croaker has these markings.

Like most other sciaenids, Atlantic Croakers spawn at sea during the fall or winter. The spawning season is influenced by latitude and extends from late August off Chesapeake Bay to March off Cape Canaveral. Peak spawning months for much of the region are September, October, and November. The number of eggs spawned by an adult female, 2 years old or older, ranges from 108 thousand for an 8-inch fish to more than 1.7 million for one 15 inches long. The pelagic eggs and recently hatched larvae drift passively toward land. Later, the advanced larval stages and juveniles continue their landward migration by actively swimming into estuarine nursery areas, where they remain until the next fall.

Limited information is available on age and growth, but it is believed that 2- and 4-year old fish are 6 and 10 inches in length. Atlantic Croakers feed chiefly on animals and detritus that occur on the bottom, as evidenced by their inferior mouths and chin barbels. Schools of Atlantic Croaker search the flats and bars for food on an incoming tide and feed on crustaceans, worms, mollusks, detritus, and small fishes.

Fishing. Atlantic Croakers are seasonally important to both recreational and commercial fisheries along the Atlantic Coast and are caught in large numbers from March through October. Fish north of South

Carolina arrive in the estuaries in March and April and emigrate in the early fall, moving offshore to waters as deep as 60 to 300 feet. South of North Carolina the species is comparatively nonmigratory. Commercial fishermen land Croakers in bottom trawls, gill, trammel and fyke nets, haul seines, and pound nets. Over abundance often causes local market prices to plunge to only a few cents per pound. Recreational fishermen catch the species in the spring and fall by fishing on the bottom with cut baits. Typical tackle may consist of a light spinning outfit with a 2- to 6-pound test line, a 1- to 3-ounce sinker, and two 1/0 sproat hooks spaced about 12 inches apart on a heavy leader. Preferred baits include shrimp, clams, bloodworms, and squid. Fishing is best just before or just after a high tide in channels or deep holes.

Preparation. Because of their small size, Croakers are usually fried, either whole or filleted. The species is marketed fresh in the United States.

Suggested Readings. 62, 64, 107, 150.

165

BLACK DRUM
Pogonias cromis

Drum

Habits. The scientific name of the Black Drum is derived from the Greek words *pogonias*, meaning "bearded," and *cromis*, "to grunt" — and for good reason. The species has conspicuous chin barbels and utters a loud grunting sound when excited. Adults have dusky to black fins and are silver with a brassy luster in life, changing to dark gray after death. Young Drum possess four to six black vertical bars, and may be misidentified as juveniles of closely related species.

In the United States, Black Drum occur from southern New England to Mexico, and are commonly caught from New Jersey southward. Major fishing areas are Chesapeake Bay and the tidal waters of Georgia, Florida, Louisiana, and Texas. Black Drum are the largest members of the family Sciaenidae on the Atlantic Coast, reaching a length of 5 feet and a weight of 146 pounds. Preferred habitat is coastal waters including bays, sounds, and inlets where salinities range from near fresh to sea strength.

Sexual maturity is attained by the end of the second year when fish are about 12 inches long. Adults form schools and in the spring migrate to spawning grounds, which are at sea near mouths of rivers and bays. A large fish may lay 6 million eggs. The newly hatched Drum reside in estuaries for the first year of life, later moving offshore. Although the species is known to live for 35 years, most of the fish caught are 10 years old or younger. A 1-year-old Black Drum is about 9 inches long and weighs half a pound; a 5-year-old may grow to 34 inches and 19 pounds; and a 10-year-old is approximately 49 inches long and weighs 59 pounds. Black Drum feed on the bottom, aided in their search for food by the chin barbels, which serve as feelers. Food items include clams, mussels, oysters, crabs, worms, and some fishes. Strong throat teeth, pharyngeals, are capable of crushing shells of clams, oysters, and crabs to make them easier to digest.

Fishing. Black Drum are caught by both commercial and sport fishermen. On the East Coast, commercial landings are small compared to the Gulf, where 50 to 80 percent of the catch is made in Texas alone. Commercial fishermen use pound nets, seines, trawls, and gill nets to capture Drum.

Sport fishing on the East Coast is localized and seasonal. The Delaware Bay, Chesapeake Bay, and tidal waters of Georgia and Florida are all good fishing areas from May through Labor Day. Fish enter

estuaries to feed on a rising tide, and then leave as the tide drops. Best fishing occurs when the tide is about a half to three-quarters out. Anglers either cast slow-sinking mirror-sided lures or bump the bottom with fast-sinking spoons, Bucktails, or nylon jigs. Preferred natural baits are crabs, cut fish, clams, and shrimp. Ocean spinners and bait-casting outfits with 15- to 20-pound monofilament line are ideal rigged with 2/0 to 4/0 hooks and a medium-weight sinker.

Preparation. The flesh is white, flaky, and easily separated from the large bones. Drum are most often cooked in soups and chowders.

Suggested Readings. 141, 142.

RED DRUM
Sciaenops ocellatus

Channel Bass, Puppy Drum, Spottail Bass, Redfish

Habits. The Red Drum, or Channel Bass, is the second largest member of the drum family in the western Atlantic, reaching a maximum length of 5 feet and a weight of approximately 100 pounds. Only the Black Drum is larger. The Red Drum is distributed in coastal and estuarine waters from Massachusetts to Key West, Florida, along the southeastern United States and in the Gulf from southwest Florida to Tuxpan, Mexico. The species is readily identified by the inferior, or subterminal, mouth, by the lack of barbels on the chin, and by the one or more black ocellated spots on the upper sides near the base of the tail. It is the only sciaenid with large spots. Red Drum are iridescent silvery-gray overall, with a coppery cast that is usually darker on the back and upper sides.

Spawning occurs at dusk in coastal waters near passes, inlets, and bays from early fall to late winter (September to February) when water temperatures range from 64° to 82°F. Sexually mature fish, those 3 years old or older, engage in prespawning behavior, which includes chasing and butting, several hours prior to mating. During this time, males may change color and become dark red or bright bluish-gray above the lateral line. Released and fertilized at mid-depths, the eggs float to the surface where they hatch in 19 to 20 hours at 75°F. A female 35 inches long is capable of laying 3.5 million ova. The newly hatched larvae are carried by currents and winds into estuarine nursery areas where they remain for 6 to 8 months.

Although Red Drum probably live for at least 20 to 30 years, only those 1 to 10 years have been aged. Average lengths for fish of these ages are 13.1, 21, 26, 29.7, 32.6, 34.1, 35.6, 36, 36.5, and 37 inches. The species uses its senses of sight and touch to feed on animals that live on the bottom. Crabs, shrimps, sand dollars, and fishes such as menhaden, mullet, Pinfish, Pigfish, searobin, lizardfish, Spot, Atlantic Croaker, and flounder compose the bulk of the diet of large Drum. Smaller individuals feed on copepods, amphipods, and tiny shrimps. Channel Bass are often seen in a head-down position browsing and rooting the bottom in search of food.

Fishing. Red Drum are caught in the spring and fall. Commercial fishermen use haul seines, pound nets, and gill nets. Most of the commercial landings are made in the Gulf of Mexico, whereas recreational catches occur along the coasts of Virginia and North Carolina as well as in the Gulf. Surf fishing and sight casting are the two

methods preferred by anglers. Sight casting combines the thrills of hunting and fishing in one outing as fishermen search for schools of Drum in shallow water and then quietly maneuver their boats into an effective casting position. Both saltwater fly rods and stiff surf rods with large spinning reels are used to cast for Red Drum. Suggested baits are streamer flies, Hopkins lures, lead jigs, and medium-size floating plugs. These should be presented right in front of the fish. Surf fishermen use 10- to 11-foot surf rods with bait-casting or spinning reels and 20- to 30-pound test monofilament line. The bottom rig consists of one or two 9/0 hooks baited with large pieces of cut fish, and an 18-inch, 60-pound test shocker leader, all held on to the bottom by a 4- or 5-ounce lead sinker. Fishing is best on a rising tide as the Red Drum move into the shallows to feed.

Preparation. Red Drum are excellent food fish and are marketed fresh. Small fish may be fried, baked, or broiled; large fish make good stews.

Suggested Readings. 4, 46, 142.

TAUTOG
Tautoga onitis

Blackfish

Habits. The wrasse family (Labridae) is one of the largest groups of marine fishes in the world. Most are warm-water species that occur in the tropics. The Tautog, or Blackfish, is one of the few exceptions and is found in temperate nearshore waters of the western Atlantic from Massachusetts to the Carolinas. It is most abundant from Cape Cod to Delaware, although it is occasionally plentiful in Chesapeake Bay and off North Carolina. Tautog are large, ugly fish that inhabit irregular bottoms such as rock piles, jetties, bridge pilings, wrecks, and artificial reefs.

The species may be identified by the high dorsal profile, blunt snout, thick lips, and high-set eyes. Unlike the Cunner, *Tautogolabrus adspersus*, another temperate wrasse, it has no scales on the gill covers. Tautog vary from chocolate brown to greenish-black above with irregular black blotches or bars on the sides. The mottling pattern is more evident on some fish than it is on others.

Adult Tautog make daily and seasonal migrations but both are limited in extent compared with the movements of most coastal species. One consists of a move from the night resting area to a nearby feeding ground, usually less than ¼ mile. The other, influenced by water temperature, is from deep water to shallow water in the spring and back to deep water in the winter.

Sexually mature fish, or those 3 years old or older, spawn in the spring and summer, from about May through August. The species is slow growing and very long lived. The maximum age and size are about 34 years and 36 inches (23 pounds). Average lengths for fish aged 1, 5, 10, 15, 20, and 27 years are 2.4, 11.3, 17, 19.2, 20.2, and 23.1 inches. Blackfish feed on the bottom, using their incisors to pick up food and their molars to crush it. Favorite foods are mussels, barnacles, crabs, shrimps, and worms. Tautog often take food in their mouths, spit it out, and eat it again. This action tends to make shelled food more digestible.

Fishing. The Tautog is a popular sport and commercial fish, particularly from Virginia northward. Commercial fishermen catch the species with handlines and baited traps. Sport fishermen use handlines, as well as bait-casting and spinning outfits to catch Blackfish from rowboats, private inboard and outboard motorboats, and large party boats. The most productive fishermen are those who know exactly where rock piles are, or use depth recorders to locate good bottom. Boats are anchored

and anglers bottom fish directly over the rocks. A typical bottom rig consists of two 6/0 sproat hooks rigged high and low about 2 feet apart. Sturdy boat rods, heavy line and 4- to 16-ounce lead sinkers are required. Bloodworms, clams, squid, mussels, fiddler crabs, blue crabs, and green crabs are good baits.

Preparation. The lean, firm flesh is excellent when it is skinned and filleted. It may be baked, basted with butter and covered with cracker crumbs. Another method of cooking is to place fillets in the oven, and add tomato paste, white wine, onions, green peppers, and dashes of Tabasco and Worcestershire sauces. Tightly cover the dish and bake at moderate heat until the meat is easily flaked with a fork.

Suggested Readings. 19, 33, 64.

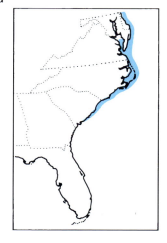

BUTTERFISH
Peprilus triacanthus

Habits. The Butterfish is a small oval-shaped fish with a blunt snout and very long anal and dorsal fins. A near-surface, dense-schooling species, the Butterfish occurs along the continental shelf of the North American east coast from Nova Scotia to Florida. It is absent from Bermuda and the Caribbean, and reportedly is replaced in the Gulf of Mexico by *Peprilus burti*, the Gulf Butterfish. These two species are almost identical in shape, coloration, and general appearance, although differing in the number of vertebrae. Both have 17 to 25 large pores below the dorsal fin. These pores are not found on the Harvestfish, *P. alepidotus*, a close relative that has a much rounder and deeper body.

Butterfish are plain—pale blue along the back and upper sides, and silvery below. The back and upper sides are often mottled with dark spots, markings not found on *P. burti*. Butterfish are found in coastal waters less than 180 feet deep, and where temperatures range from about 40° to 74°F. Two stocks are believed to occur in the region: one north of Cape Hatteras, which tends to migrate inshore and northward during warmer weather, and the other south of Cape Hatteras, which is nonmigratory.

Butterfish attain sexual maturity when they are 2 years old (about 8 inches long) and spawn only one time each year. Spawning takes place offshore from May through August depending on the latitude. The buoyant, transparent eggs hatch in less than 48 hours in waters 65° to 72°F. After hatching, juveniles move from offshore surface waters to estuarine nursery areas, often hiding from predators in masses of floating *Sargassum*, or among the tentacles of jellyfish. The species is short lived and fast growing. Approximate lengths for fish aged 1 to 4 years are 5.5, 8, 8.8, and 9 inches. Since the maximum size is about 14 inches, individuals probably live longer than 4 years. The Butterfish is one of only a few species of fishes that feed on such low-nutrition foods as jellyfish, ctenophores, and salps. In addition, amphipods, copepods, annelids, small shrimps, squids, and fishes are found in the diet.

Fishing. The species is of no direct value to recreational fisheries. It is caught commercially in trawls along with squid, hake, Scup, flounder, and skate, primarily in the spring and summer when large schools migrate inshore and northward. Butterfish are also landed in pound nets and seines.

Preparation. Marketed fresh and frozen, the Butterfish is highly regarded as a food fish. However, its greatest value to fishermen may be as food for other species important to recreational and commercial fisheries.

Suggested Readings. 43, 46, 110.

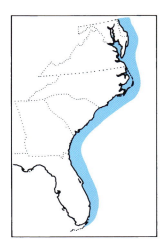

NORTHERN SEAROBIN
Prionotus carolinus

Searobin

Habits. Searobins are fish with broad, spiny heads and large fan-like pectoral fins that have modified rays for feeling or "walking" on the bottom. There are at least nine species found along the Atlantic coast of the United States. The two most common in the Southeast are the Northern Searobin and Striped Searobin, *Prionotus evolans*. A third species, the Barred Searobin, *P. martis,* occurs in the Gulf of Mexico.

The Northern Searobin is the species most frequently caught. It may be distinguished from its relatives because it has a dusky spot near the center of the first dorsal fin and, unlike the Striped Searobin, lacks horizontal stripes. The body is very tapered, almost triangular, and is colored gray or reddish above and dusky white or yellow below. Along the back are five dark, saddle-like blotches. The yellow or orange pectoral fins are marked with two broad dark bars. The species occurs from the Gulf of Maine to South Carolina (occasionally Florida) and inhabits sandy bottoms from shallow estuaries to the deep waters at the edge of the continental shelf. There are two populations, one north of Cape Hatteras, which migrates inshore from deep water in April, and the other south of Cape Hatteras, which is scattered over the shelf and does not migrate.

Spawning occurs in summer and early fall, from July through September. Some females mature at age 1, but most do so between their second and third years (8 inches). No information is available on the number of eggs spawned. Searobins grow slowly. A 1-year-old fish is about 6 inches long and a 5-year-old only 10 inches; one at age 11 is approximately 11 inches long and weighs slightly less than a pound. Searobins feed on the bottom by using their modified pectoral rays to feel food and also to stir up sand, weeds, and debris, thus dislodging small animals from their hiding places. Shrimps, scuds, squids, and worms are favorite food items.

Fishing. Although Northern Searobins are good fighters on light tackle and may be eaten, they are considered nuisances to most fishermen because they steal bait, are small, and are unpleasant to handle. Many an angler has been unpleasantly surprised to find a Northern Searobin, fins flared, tugging on the line. They are considered trash fish by commercial fishermen and are caught incidentally to food fishes in trawls.

Preparation. Searobins are eaten occasionally. There is little meat, but it is tasty. The best method of cooking is to batter and fry.

Suggested Readings. 126.

SUMMER FLOUNDER
Paralichthys dentatus

Flounder

Habits. Flatfishes that have both eyes on the left side of the body are called left-eyed flounders and belong to the family Bothidae. There are three species of bothids that commonly occur along the southeastern United States: Summer Flounder, Southern Flounder, *Paralichthys lethostigma*, and the Gulf Flounder, *P. albigutta*. The Summer Flounder is distributed from Massachusetts to Florida, but is most abundant from Delaware to Cape Lookout, North Carolina. The other species have more southerly ranges.

The three species may be distinguished by the numbers of gill rakers, anal fin rays, and lateral line scales in addition to their color patterns. Summer Flounders have five small, ocellated, dark brown spots on the back, Gulf Flounders have three, and Southern Flounders lack conspicuous spots. Summer Flounders inhabit shallow coastal and estuarine waters during the spring and summer, but they move offshore to waters that are 120 to 600 feet deep during colder weather. The species has been collected from brackish to sea-strength waters ranging from 35° to 81°F.

Spawning takes place at sea in the fall and winter, and the larvae are then transported to coastal and estuarine nursery areas by currents and winds. Sexual maturity is attained during the third year of life at sizes as small as 12 inches for males and 14 inches for females. Summer Flounders are capable of living at least 10 years and may reach a length of 35 to 40 inches and a weight of about 30 pounds. Females live longer and grow larger than males. Average lengths for fish aged 1 to 9 years are 8.5, 11.3, 14.9, 16.9, 19.3, 20.2, 21, 22.3, and 23.6 inches. Like other bothids, Summer Flounders feed by partially concealing themselves with sand and then darting forth to capture prey that ventures too close. Flounders occasionally pursue schools of small fish to the surface. Favorite foods are menhaden, silversides, sand lances, herrings, anchovies, Weakfish, squids, shrimps, and crabs.

Fishing. Summer Flounders are caught by both commercial and recreational fishermen. Although some are caught commercially from April through November in fyke nets, weirs, traps, and pound nets, most are landed in the winter by trawls from deep waters off Virginia and North Carolina. Using cut bait or live minnows, sport fishermen catch the species from the surf, from ocean piers, and also from anchored or drifting boats.

Because Summer Flounders tend to concentrate in narrow lanes associated with deep channels, ridges and sand bars, fishermen prefer to drift so that fish can be located more easily. Once fish are found, anglers either anchor or make repeated drifts over the productive bottom. The standard tackle is a moderate-weight spinning or bait-casting outfit with 10- to 20-pound test monofilament line and a bottom rig. The terminal tackle is usually a long shank No. 2 hook preceded by a spinner and fluorescent orange bead on an 18- to 24-inch leader. A three-way swivel separates the hook line and main line from a 3- to 6-inch line with a 1– to 3-ounce sinker. Live killifish, silversides, mullet, or menhaden are used as bait. When strong winds and the tide run in opposite directions, the effectiveness of drifting is reduced; then anglers may troll or anchor. When anchored, fishermen often use chum pots to attract fish.

Preparation. Flounders are highly regarded as food. The flesh is mild, white, and flaky. It may be fried, baked, or broiled. A suggested method of preparing is to stuff the fish with crabmeat or scallop dressing and bake.

Suggested Readings. 46, 119, 145.

SOUTHERN FLOUNDER
Paralichthys lethostigma

Flounder

Habits. The Southern Flounder, as its name implies, is found in the more southerly latitudes of the United States. The range is discontinuous, extending on the Atlantic Coast from the Albemarle Sound, North Carolina, to the Loxahatchee River, Florida, and in the Gulf of Mexico from the Caloosahatchee estuary to Corpus Christi, Texas.

The Southern Flounder is left-eyed, and is most readily separated from its close relatives by the lack of prominent ocellated spots on the body. It does possess numerous diffuse dark spots and blotches on the olive-brown eyed side and fins, but these are not conspicuous and tend to disappear in large fish. The species is very tolerant of a wide range in water temperature (50° to 90°F) and salinity (0 to 36 ppt). In fact, Southern Flounders are frequently found in brackish and even fresh waters, where salinities fluctuate from 0 to 20 ppt. No other flounder inhabiting the east coast of the United States is regularly encountered in this type of environment.

Spawning takes place offshore in the fall and winter as sexually mature fish, those 2 years old and older, move out of estuaries and bays from October through December. Postlarval and juvenile flounders immigrate to estuarine nursery areas from January into early summer. In the laboratory, three females were induced to spawn more than 120 thousand eggs, which hatched in 61 to 76 hours in water 63°F.

Information on age and growth is sketchy; however, females appear to grow faster and live longer than males. Approximate average lengths for females aged 1 to 5 years are 8, 14.4, 19.9, 21.8, and 24 inches. Southern Flounders feed by partly burying themselves in the sand and then waiting to ambush their prey. The diet changes as the fish grow. Small Flounders feed on mysid and penaeid shrimps and other small crustaceans, whereas larger flounders eat blue crabs, penaeid shrimps, and fishes—anchovies, mullets, menhaden, Atlantic Croaker, and Pinfish.

Fishing. The Southern Flounder is a prized catch to both commercial and recreational fishermen. Commercially, the species is captured in shrimp trawls, gill and trammel nets, and beach seines, as well as by spearing. Sportsmen take the species by bottom fishing, trolling natural baits, and gigging.

Gigging is accomplished at night on a high, clear tide using a three-pronged, long-handled spear and a strong light. Wading the

periphery of salt marshes, or poling the tidal creeks in a shallow-draft boat, the experienced fisherman can discern the outline of a buried flounder, cautiously approach it, and then plant his gig. This sport is interesting because the lantern illuminates multitudes of fishes, crabs, shrimps, and other marine life.

Another method used to catch Southern Flounder is to bump live minnows over the bottom of inlets and tidal creeks by slowly trolling against the current with a small outboard motor. A light bait-casting reel, 15-pound test monofilament line, and a medium-action 7-foot rod is the standard outfit. Two 2/0 hooks baited with a small killifish or finger-size mullet, positioned 6 and 18 inches off the bottom, and weighted with a drop sinker make up the terminal rig. Fishing is best from early spring through fall.

Preparation. Southern Flounder are marketed fresh and are considered excellent food fish. Prepare by broiling, baking, or frying. Baked flounder may be stuffed with crabmeat or scallop dressing.

Suggested Readings. 46, 119, 151.

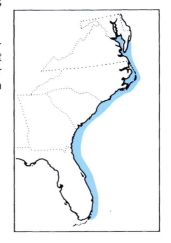

GULF FLOUNDER
Paralichthys albigutta

Flounder

Habits. The Gulf Flounder is by far the least caught paralichthid flounder occurring from Delaware to Florida. It has the familiar olive-brown background as do the Summer and Southern Flounders, but has three prominent ocellated dark spots arranged in a triangle on its eyed-side. One spot is above and another below the lateral line, while the third is on the middle of the line. These three spots may become obscure in larger fish. The species has 53 to 63 anal fin rays, which is fewer than the 63 to 73 found on the Southern Flounder. Gulf Flounders inhabit high-salinity (16 to 36 ppt) bays, inlets, and coastal waters from North Carolina to Laguna Madre, Texas.

Spawning occurs from October through February off the southeast and Gulf coasts as water temperatures drop from approximately 73° to 57°F. Both sexes reach sexual maturity when they are 2 years old. Juveniles begin to immigrate into estuarine nursery areas from January through April; their arrival coincides with a seasonal pulse in productivity, affording the young fish an abundance of food.

Small fish eat mysid shrimps and other small crustaceans, whereas larger Flounders feed on penaeid shrimps, blue crabs, and fishes. Like the Southern Flounder, female Gulf Flounder live longer and grow faster than males. Approximate average lengths for females aged 1 to 3 years are 9.8, 13.8, and 15.8 inches. The species is believed to live much longer than 3 years.

Fishing. This species accounts for less than 5 percent of the flounders landed along the southeastern United States coast. Most are caught by hook and line, by gigging, and in bottom trawls and trammel nets. The methods of fishing described for the Southern and Summer Flounders also apply for this species.

Preparation. Gulf Flounder are excellent food fish. Flounder Stuffed with Crabmeat is a favorite dish. The ingredients are six pan-dressed flounders, about ¾ pound each, ¾ cup of melted butter, ⅓ cup of lemon juice, 2 teaspoons of salt, paprika, and crab stuffing.

The crab stuffing is made with 1 pound of crabmeat, ½ cup of chopped onion, ⅓ cup of chopped celery, ⅓ cup of chopped green pepper, 2 cloves of garlic, ⅓ cup of fat or oil, 2 cups of soft bread crumbs, 3 well-beaten eggs, a tablespoon of chopped parsley, 2 teaspoons of salt, and ½ teaspoon of pepper.

The onion, celery, green pepper, and garlic are cooked until tender in the fat or oil. The other stuffing ingredients are mixed in thoroughly. To make a pocket in the fish for the stuffing, the fish is positioned on a cutting board, light side down. Cut down the center of the fish along the backbone from the tail to about 1 inch from the head end. Turn the knife flat and cut along both sides of the backbone to the tail, allowing the knife to run over the ribs. Stuff the fish loosely. Wrap the fish tightly in heavy-duty aluminum foil and cook over charcoal, or bake for 25 to 30 minutes at 350°F.

Suggested Readings. 46, 119, 151.

NORTHERN PUFFER
Sphoeroides maculatus

Swell Toad, Puffer, Blowfish, Blow Toad, Toadfish

Habits. Northern Puffers are small to medium-sized fishes with blunt bodies capable of rapid inflation by the intake of water and air. The generic name, *Sphoeroides*, is derived from the Greek meaning "resembling a sphere." This species is the most commonly occurring member of the puffer family along the southeastern United States, ranging from Cape Cod, Massachusetts, to northeastern Florida. Northern Puffers are demersal, and may be found over sand bottom, near or amid sea wrack in waters ranging from three to over 180 feet deep.

The species is gray-brown on the back and upper sides, and yellow-white on the lower sides and belly. Tiny jet-black spots are scattered over most of the body, being particularly evident on the cheeks. A row of 7 to 10 vertical bars occurs along the sides. These markings distinguish the Northern Puffer from its close relative, the Southern Puffer, *Sphoeroides nephelus*, which has dark spots rather than bars. It also has 14 pectoral rays, whereas the Northern Puffer has 16.

Puffers reach sexual maturity early in life, between their first and second years, and as small as 3½ inches in length. Spawning takes place inshore during the warmer months, extending from late spring in the more southern part of the range to early fall farther north. Fecundity studies suggest that a 5-inch female may lay 62 thousand eggs, a 10-inch fish 241 thousand, and a 12-inch one more than 340 thousand during a spawning season. The eggs are demersal with a smooth adhesive covering that causes them to attach to objects on the bottom. Occasionally, thousands of eggs clump together in a large gelatinous mass. After hatching, the larvae undergo a pelagic phase before settling to the bottom. The maximum age of the Northern Puffer has not been ascertained, but probably exceeds 5 years. The species is capable of attaining a length of 14 inches and a weight of about 1½ pounds. Approximate lengths for the first 4 years are 5.5, 8.8, 9.1, and 10 inches.

Like all members of the family Tetraodontidae, Northern Puffers have jaws modified to form a beak of four heavy, powerful teeth, two above, and two below. This parrotlike dentition enables Northern Puffers to crush any small animal they capture. Foods identified in the diet are crabs, clams, mussels, shrimps, worms, sea urchins, sponges, sea anemones, and sea squirts. The puffer family includes species that produce tetrodotoxin—a toxic substance that causes puffer poisoning. Found chiefly in the skin, liver, gonad, and intestines, tetrodotoxin may

cause death by suffocation or cardiac paralysis if consumed. Some scientists believe Northern Puffers posses the toxin; others think they do not.

Fishing. The Northern Puffer became an important food fish as a result of meat rationing during World War II. In the 1950s and 1960s the species was abundant in Virginia and North Carolina coastal waters. Today the species is scarce, and is caught incidentally to other finfish by commercial fishermen using otter trawls, pound nets, seines, gill nets, traps, and fyke nets. In Chesapeake Bay, Northern Puffers are caught in the spring in pound nets and in the summer and fall in crab pots. The species is sold on the fresh-fish market as Sea Squab. The recreational fishery consists of hook and line fishing from boats and from the shore. Most Northern Puffers are caught on light spinning and bait-casting tackle.

Preparation. The meat is similar to that of a chicken drumstick in shape and consistency and is excellent battered and fried. As mentioned earlier, the fish should be thoroughly cleaned of all skin and viscera before cooking.

Suggested Readings. 139.

COASTAL
PELAGIC FISHES

LADYFISH
Elops saurus

Ten Pounder, Skipjack, Bigeye Herring

Habits. The Ladyfish is a sport fish in many areas along the southern Atlantic and Gulf coasts of the United States. Although it does not have the reputation of the Tarpon or Bonefish, it does possess surface-skipping and leaping qualities that engender respect among the anglers fortunate enough to hook it. Two species of ladyfish are reported to occur in Florida and perhaps elsewhere in the western Atlantic. One is *Elops saurus*, and the other is as yet undescribed.

Ecologically, Ladyfish are similar to Tarpon. They inhabit warm coastal waters, but also thrive in waters that are brackish or completely fresh. The distribution extends from Massachusetts to Rio de Janeiro. The species is most abundant around Florida and the Antilles.

Ladyfish have long, slender herringlike bodies with a singular, unspined dorsal fin. The mouth is terminal and extends well back of the eye. The coloration is blue-gray along the back, and the sides and belly are bright silver with a tinge of yellow. The fins are pale yellow.

Ladyfish are believed to spawn pelagic eggs offshore in the late winter and early spring. The larval stages are characterized by a metamorphosis through a leptocephalus phase. Ladyfish of all sizes are piscivorous. Menhaden, Mosquitofish, anchovies, Pinfish, and Sheepshead Minnows are most frequently eaten. The species may reach a length of about 36 inches.

Fishing. Although Ladyfish are caught commercially by handlines, gill nets, and seines, most are landed by sport fishermen. The best fishing is from a small boat in tidal creeks or in mangrove stands. Medium-sized artificial surface lures with good action are preferred. Fishermen usually benefit from the rising tide as it allows them easily to pole or slowly motor their boats through the tidal creeks. Lures are cast at the base of mangroves, or near marsh grasses, and are retrieved with short jerks, making them splash on the surface. Ladyfish may also be taken on fly rods using topwater popping bugs. Because the species is considered to be a second-rate food fish, it is used as bait for tunas and billfish or, as in the West Indies, processed into fishmeal.

Preparation. For those who wish to try something new, the fish may be poached. The following recipe may be used for many other species. The ingredients are 3 or 4 pounds of dressed fish, ½ cup of milk, ½ cup of water, 4 slices of lemon, ½ teaspoon of allspice, ½ teaspoon of salt, 1

sprig of parsley, 2 cups of medium white sauce, juice of ½ lemon, and 2 chopped hard-cooked eggs. Place the fish in a frying pan. Add combined milk, water, lemon slices, allspice, salt and parsley. Cover and cook over low heat for 20 minutes or until the fish is tender. Place the fish and mixture on a hot platter. Combine white sauce, lemon juice, and eggs, and pour them over the fish. Serve immediately. Serves 6.

Suggested readings. 15, 46, 134.

TARPON
Megalops atlanticus

Silver King

Habits. The Tarpon is a powerful and active swimmer famous for its spectacular leaps when hooked. Although distributed from Nova Scotia to Brazil, the species is most abundant in south Florida, the West Indies, and Central and South America. The preferred habitat is coastal waters such as lower rivers, passes between islands, and mangrove-lined lagoons. In these waters, the peculiar rolling movements of the fish at the surface are familiar sights to fishermen. Tarpon are blue-gray on the back with silver sides. They are easily identified by their large scales, strongly protruding lower jaws, and small dorsal fins that have an elongated ray. These combined characteristics separate Tarpon from their close relatives, the Ladyfish, *Elops saurus*, and the Bonefish, *Albula vulpes*.

Tarpon reach sexual maturity between their sixth and seventh years, when they are approximately 4 feet long. Spawning occurs over an extended period, from May through September. Although the species spawns over a large geographical area, the Caribbean coast of Mexico is an important spawning ground. After hatching, the larvae are ribbon-shaped and are called leptocephali. The leptocephalus stage lasts for several months before the fish metamorphose into the juvenile form. Tarpon grow rapidly, attain a large size (up to 8 feet and 350 pounds), and may live as long as 15 years. Average lengths for fish aged 1 to 12 years are 12, 20, 27, 34, 41, 45, 51, 56, 58, 59, 63, and 65 inches. Favorite foods are crabs and fishes such as sardines, anchovies, mullets, silversides, Hardhead Catfish, and Atlantic Cutlassfish.

Fishing. As a game fish, the Tarpon has few equals. The fighting quality, characterized by an initial hard strike followed by a series of leaps and runs, is superb. When a Tarpon strikes, there is no doubt what has taken the bait. Sport fishermen use two basic methods to catch Tarpon: casting artificial lures from an anchored or drifting boat and float fishing with live bait. For casting, a 5½-foot rod, level-wind casting reel with star drag, and 150 to 200 yards of 15- to 20-pound test line are standard. Some anglers prefer saltwater spinning tackle or fly rods.

Because Tarpon are temperamental regarding lure type and color, one should have a well-stocked tackle box that includes surface plugs as well as deep-running and slow-sinking lures of all shapes and colors. Given a choice, however, most experienced Tarpon fishermen would probably choose a yellow and silver mirror-sided lure. Most of the fish are caught

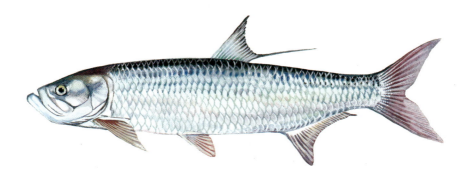

from March through June and in October and November. Anglers usually float fish from bridges, piers, and anchored boats. A lively fish such as a jack or Bluefish is attached to a medium-size hook and suspended from the surface by a plastic float or balloon. This type of fishing is particularly popular north of Florida.

Preparation. The Tarpon is seldom caught by commercial fishermen, and it is not considered a food fish in the United States. The scales are occasionally used to make ornamental flowers or wind chimes and in the manufacture of artificial pearls.

Suggested Readings. 15, 46, 143.

ATLANTIC MENHADEN
Brevoortia tyrannus

Pogy, Bunker, Bughead

Habits. More pounds of Atlantic Menhaden are landed each year by commercial fishermen than any other fish in the United States. A member of the herring family, the Atlantic Menhaden is euryhaline, inhabiting near-fresh to salt waters. It occurs in the Atlantic Ocean and inland tidal areas along the eastern coast of the United States from Nova Scotia to southern Florida. A similar species, the Gulf Menhaden, *Brevoortia patronus*, occurs along the coast of the Gulf of Mexico from Florida to Mexico. Two other species, the Finescale Menhaden, *B. gunteri*, and the Yellowfin Menhaden, *B. smithi*, are much less common in the region.

The body of the Atlantic Menhaden is deep and compressed. The mouth is large with the lower jaw fitting into a notch in the upper. Adipose eyelids give the fish a sleepy look. Menhaden are bluish along the back, with silvery sides that may have a reddish or brassy tint. The fins are pale yellow edged in black. Menhaden also possess a dark spot on the shoulder, usually followed by two or three irregular rows of smaller spots. Dense schooling is a characteristic behavior, with 50 to more than 200 thousand fish in a school. Marked seasonal migrations are made each year: slowly northward as waters warm in April and May and southward in early autumn.

Menhaden spawn during all months of the year, but not in all locations each month. A few individuals mature at age 1 (8 inches long), most are mature by age 2 (10 inches), and all fish are capable of spawning by their third year. Estimates of the number of eggs spawned range from 38 to 631 thousand per female. Peak spawning off the southeastern United States is October to March. The eggs are free floating and hatch at sea, where the young are carried into sounds and bays by landward winds and currents. Young fish spend their first year in these sheltered estuaries. Menhaden feed by straining very small plants and animals out of the water by means of long filaments on the gills. Perhaps the most significant role of the species is as food for larger fishes important to sport and commercial fisheries. Mackerels, Atlantic Bonito, Bluefish, Striped Bass, and seatrouts are only a few of the many fish that eat menhaden.

Fishing. Since the mid-1800s commercial fishermen have caught menhaden by purse seines and pound nets. Purse seines are nets 1,300 to 2,000 feet long and 65 to 85 feet deep. The net is carried in two

purse boats, each about 36 feet long, dispatched by a larger carrier vessel, 65 to 200 feet long. Today spotter planes locate schools of fish and direct the setting of the net. The net encircles a school and is closed—or pursed—along the bottom; the fish are then pumped aboard the carrier ship. A pound net is a weir made of netting hung on poles situated in shallow waters. Only about 4 percent of the menhaden caught come from pound nets. Each year approximately 700 million pounds are landed by the Atlantic fishery. The dried meat is processed into poultry and swine feeds and the oil is used in the production of paints and cosmetics or is exported for making margarine and cooking oil. Another billion pounds are landed in the Gulf of Mexico.

Preparation. The species is not usually considered edible, although the roe may be fried as is done with other herrings. The flesh is occasionally pickled.

Suggested Readings. 124.

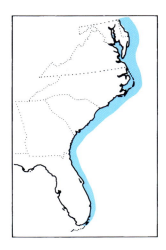

BLUEFISH
Pomatomus saltatrix

Snapper, Blue

Habits. The Bluefish is one of several members of the family Pomatomidae, and is important to saltwater fishermen throughout much of the world. The species occurs in temperate and warm waters of the western Atlantic from Nova Scotia to Uruguay, off the west African shelf, in the Mediterranean and Black Seas, in the Indian Ocean, and off Tasmania and Australia. In the United States there are two major fishing areas, Cape Cod Bay to Cape Lookout and Cape Canaveral to Pompano Beach.

Bluefish are greenish-blue along the back and silver on the sides and belly. The shape of the body is similar to that of the jacks. Like other coastal pelagic fishes, Bluefish school by size and make seasonal migrations, north in spring and south in winter. Large fish tend to congregate in the northern part of the range.

Both sexes are about the same size and may live for 14 years. A 1-year-old fish is approximately 9 inches long and 0.3 pound; a 5-year-old is about 27 inches and 7 pounds; a 10-year-old is about 32 inches and 15 pounds; and a 14-year-old may attain 34 inches and 19 pounds. An average-size female will lay 1 million eggs annually after reaching maturity during the second year of life. There are two spawning groups off the southeastern United States. One spawns at sea during the spring, and the young spend their first year in coastal bays and sounds; the other group spawns at sea in the summer, and the young remain offshore. The Bluefish diet is varied—Butterfish, menhaden, Round Herring, silversides, anchovies, seatrouts, Atlantic Croaker, Spot, shrimps, lobster, crabs, worms, and many other items.

Fishing. When Bluefish are feeding, they will strike almost any object in the water—including swimmers. Anglers fish from boats, piers, bridges, jetties, and the surf, by using cut baits fished on the bottom and by casting and trolling artificial lures. Surf fishing is very popular, particularly in the fall. Typical gear may include a heavy surf rod, 10- to 20-pound test monofilament line, two 6/0 hooks baited with cut fish, and a sliding 5-ounce pyramid sinker. A wire leader, 9 to 18 inches long, is important because Bluefish will bite through nylon and monofilament lines.

For casting, Hopkins lures, Clark Spoons, bright-colored popping lures, Sea Hawks, and lead-headed plastic grubs are preferred. For trolling, one may select spoons or use feather or nylon lures with mullet

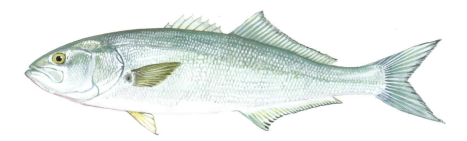

strips. These lures usually catch larger fish. Small Blues may be caught by trolling small jigs and spoons. Best fishing is in the spring, April and May, and in the fall, October and November, although small fish may be caught all year. Commercial fishermen catch the species with trawls, seines, gill nets, and pound nets. The market price is generally low, but Bluefish supplement fishermen's incomes when more desirable species are not available.

Preparation. Bluefish, particularly the larger ones, are oily and therefore are usually broiled or smoked. Smaller fish may be fried. The flesh is gray, and the bones are large and easily discarded.

Suggested Readings. 59, 64, 165.

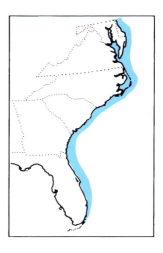

COBIA
Rachycentron canadum

Cabio, Ling, Crab Eater, Lemonfish

Habits. Fishermen often misidentify large Cobia in the water as sharks or sharksuckers. Not only is the species dark brown with a single dorsal fin, but also occasionally tags along with sharks, rays, and turtles, swimming in a slow, deliberate manner. Young Cobia are more active than adults and are colored conspicuously, with alternating black and white horizontal stripes with splotches of bronze, orange, and green. The species has a circumtropical distribution, and in the United States is a seasonal favorite of fishermen from Virginia south and throughout the Gulf of Mexico. In late spring, small schools, or pods, of fish may be seen migrating through coastal waters, including bays and sounds.

Cobia are known to live as long as 10 years, perhaps to 15, and to reach a length of 6 feet and a weight exceeding 100 pounds. Females are slightly larger than males and will grow to 16 inches, or 1 pound, the first year; 49 inches, 36 pounds, by the fifth year; and about 60 inches, 69 pounds, by the eighth. Males reach sexual maturity when they are 2 years old and 24 inches long, and females when they are aged 3 and about 36 inches long. An 8-year-old female may lay between 6 and 7 million eggs at one time. The spawning season extends from late June to mid-August along the southeastern United States and from late summer to early fall in the Gulf of Mexico. Although Cobia eat some fishes, such as mackerels and eels, the bulk of the diet is crustaceans—shrimps and crabs. Thus the common name, Crab Eater.

Fishing. Cobia are rugged fighters when hooked and are considered by some to be one of the finest eating fish. While anglers may cast or troll artificials, most prefer to bottom fish using cut or live bait. Favorite fishing spots are channels and deep holes in bays and sounds, as well as the waters around floating and stationary objects such as buoys, pilings, and wrecks. Inshore buoys and beacons, often bypassed by fishermen, are excellent places to catch Cobia, as well as Greater Amberjack and Tripletail.

A typical outfit includes a 6-foot boat rod and a 3/0 casting reel with 12- to 20-pound monofilament line. Terminal tackle consists of a single 6/0 hook, a 2-foot wire or 80-pound monofilament leader with fish-finding sleeve, and a heavy 6- to 8-ounce sinker. Live menhaden or Pinfish are good bait when they are available, although whole dead fish often produce good results. Best fishing is from late May through June, late in the afternoon and on a rising tide. For an added dimension in

angling enjoyment, try fishing for Cobia with a fly rod. An 8½-foot rod with a 4-inch single-action reel is a good outfit. Use No. 9 saltwater taper floating fly line and 125 yards of 20-pound test braided casting line for backing. Cobia will strike streamer flies and large popping bugs. Commercial fishermen catch Cobia in pound nets, gill nets, and seines. The market price usually stays high because availability seldom exceeds the demand.

Preparation. Cobia flesh is white and flaky. This fish is excellent fried, broiled, baked, or basted over charcoal. Baked fish is delicious dipped in melted butter and lemon juice.

Suggested Readings. 46, 59, 64.

STRIPED MULLET
Mugil cephalus

Jumping Mullet

Habits. There are at least six species of mullets that inhabit Atlantic waters of North America, but only two, the Striped, *Mugil cephalus*, and the White, *M. curema*, are important to fisheries along the southeastern coast. Both species have long cylindrical bodies, small mouths, widely separated dorsal fins, and thick fleshy eyelids that give the fish a sleepy appearance. Striped Mullet differ from White Mullet in having 8, rather than 9 rays in the anal fin, 38 to 42 scales along the sides (White Mullet have 35 to 40), and few scales on the second dorsal and anal fins (these fins are densely scaled on White Mullet). The Striped Mullet has a cosmopolitan distribution in temperate and tropical coastal and estuarine waters. In the western Atlantic it is found from Cape Cod to Brazil and occasionally enters fresh waters. The fish is bluish-gray to green above, shading to white on the belly with six or seven longitudinal dark stripes on the sides.

In the fall, large schools of mature Mullet, those 2 years old and older, emigrate from the inlets and passes into the open sea, where they spawn. The spawning season in the southeast extends from September to February with a peak in the activity in October and November as water temperatures begin to fall. Fecundity varies from about 45 thousand eggs for a fish 13 inches long to more than 4 million for a 22-inch female. Mullet release their sex products indiscriminately, and the fertilized pelagic eggs hatch as they are transported by winds and surface currents. Recently hatched Mullet gradually move inshore to estuarine nursery areas, where they remain for 6 to 8 months. These juveniles provide excellent forage for large piscivorous species and often are used by anglers as bait for flounders, Striped Bass, Bluefish, and trouts.

The Striped Mullet is a moderately long-lived species and may attain a length of about 25 inches. Average lengths for fish aged 1 to 6 years are 8.5, 13.1, 16.9, 20, 22.4, and 24 inches. The species is primarily herbivorous and feeds on small algae and other living organisms as well as on detrital organic matter, which is consumed along with large amounts of sand and mud. Occasionally, Striped Mullet may be seen feeding at the surface on worms and other invertebrates. Only during these times may they be caught on hook and line.

Fishing. Although the diet of the Striped Mullet normally precludes their being caught by recreational fishermen, they are vulnerable to commercial fishing gear such as haul seines, gill nets, pound nets, and trawls.

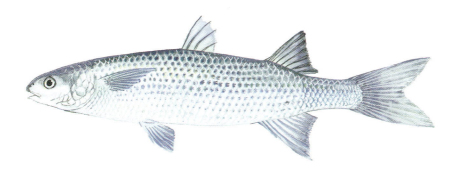

Most are landed by haul seines along the southeastern United States. These nets range from 200 to 1,000 yards in length and are 4 to 20 feet in depth. The bar mesh size is about 1 to 1¼ inches. Fishermen sight schools moving along the beach and set their nets around them. Because the weight of a net full of fish is enormous, tractors and trucks are used to retrieve the nets and beach the catch. Another effective method of harvesting Striped Mullet is by cast netting.

Preparation. The flesh and roe are marketed fresh and salted. The species may be fried, broiled, or smoked. A suggested method of preparation is to dress, lightly salt, and dry mullets before barbecuing them over a charcoal fire. The fish should be headed and eviscerated but not scaled. They are then spread open on a grill and basted with a heated mixture of tomato sauce, Tabasco sauce, Worcestershire sauce, horse-radish, salt, and pepper. A simple mixture of vinegar and catsup may be used instead. The fish are placed on the grill skin side down after they have been basted. As the flesh whitens, baste and turn. Repeat, basting each time until the meat is brown and flakes easily with a fork.

Suggested Readings. 3, 64, 140.

WHITE MULLET
Mugil curema

Silver Mullet

Habits. The White Mullet is a coastal marine species that inhabits western Atlantic estuaries from Massachusetts to Brazil, including Bermuda and the West Indies. It is of minor importance to fisheries except in Florida. Even there, landings of White Mullet are far exceeded by those of Striped Mullet. White Mullet are dark olive to bluish on the back, shading to silver below. A dark spot is often found at the base of the pectoral fins.

Spawning takes place at sea from March to mid-August, with a peak in the activity in May. The pelagic eggs hatch in about 40 hours in waters that are 68°F. The recently hatched larvae spend their first couple of weeks in open ocean waters, sometimes as far from shore as the Gulf Stream. When they are about an inch long, the young White Mullet move into estuarine nursery areas. This immigration extends from late April through August, as schools of juveniles enter the bays and sounds. In the fall, the young White Mullet emigrate from the estuaries and begin to migrate along the beaches. The maximum length of this species, which lives for at least 5 years, is approximately 14 inches. Average lengths for fish aged 1 to 5 years are 8, 11.7, 12.9, 13.6, and 13.9 inches. Feeding habits are similar to those of the Striped Mullet.

Fishing. Even though this species is a sporadic visitor to our coast, it is very vulnerable to commercial fishing gear such as haul seines, gill nets, pound nets, and trawls. Most are landed by haul seines along the southeastern United States. These nets range from 200 to 1,000 yards in length and are 4 to 20 feet in depth. The bar mesh size is about 1 to 1¼ inches. Fishermen sight schools moving along the beach and set their nets around them. Because of the enormous weight of a loaded net, tractors and trucks are usually used to retrieve the nets and beach the catch. Another effective method of harvesting White Mullet is by cast netting.

Preparation. Mullet, as well as other oily fish, are excellent smoked. The ingredients are six dressed mullet, about 1 pound each, 1 cup of salt, 1 gallon of water, and ¼ cup of salad oil. The fish should be prepared by removing the head and viscera and by cutting them along the back so they will spread open and lie flat in one piece. Add the salt to the water and stir until it is dissolved. Pour the brine over the fish and

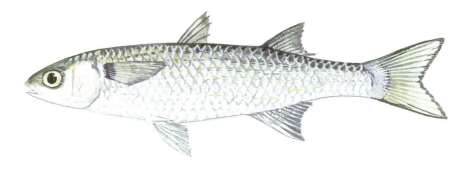

let them soak for about 30 minutes. Remove the fish from the brine and rinse in cold fresh water.

To smoke the fish, use a charcoal fire in a covered grill. Let the fire burn down to a low, even heat. Cover the coals with hickory chips that have been presoaked in water overnight. Place the fish on a well-greased grill, skin side down, about 4 inches above the smoking coals. Add more chips as needed to keep the fire smoking. Brush the fish with the oil, cover, and cook about 15 minutes. Baste the fish again, cover and cook 10 minutes longer or until the meat is lightly browned. Serves 6.

Suggested Readings. 3, 46, 140.

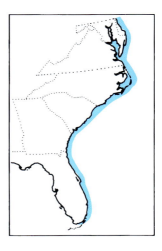

LITTLE TUNNY
Euthynnus alletteratus

False Albacore, Spotted Bonito

Habits. Although one of the most common members of the mackerel and tuna family, the Little Tunny, or False Albacore, is not adequately appreciated as a food fish in the United States. It is found in tropical and subtropical waters on both sides of the Atlantic, including the Mediterranean, Caribbean, and Gulf of Mexico. The Little Tunny, as well as Bluefish and King and Spanish Mackerels, is a schooling species that migrates northward through coastal waters in the spring, and southward in fall and winter. Large, elliptical schools cover up to 2 miles on the long axis.

Fish coloration is metallic overall, being steel-bluish above and silver below. Wavy stripes along the posterior portion of the back, several scattered dark spots below the pectoral fin, and small finlets behind the second dorsal and anal fins are identifying characters. Even with these features, the Little Tunny is one of the fish most frequently misidentified by marine recreational fishermen.

Both sexes are fast-growing, with males attaining larger sizes than females. A fish 1-year-old is approximately 14 inches, and a 4-year-old more than 30 inches long. Little Tunny seldom live longer than 5 years. Females as young as 1 year are capable of spawning. A female 31 inches long and weighing 14 pounds may lay as many as 1.8 million eggs. Off the United States, the species spawns during all months of the year except December. Major spawning areas have been identified in offshore waters that are 100 to 330 feet deep. Little Tunny feed almost exclusively on small crustaceans, Round Herring, Spanish Sardine, Round Scad, and squids.

Fishing. The presence of flocks of diving birds over coastal waters is often indicative of feeding by schools of Little Tunny. Fishermen in charter boats and smaller outboards respond to seasonal visitations and troll baits, cast lures, and float fish with live bait such as Bluefish, Pinfish or Spot. For trolling, fishermen usually select small lures with mullet or Ballyhoo, or use colored feathers that are trolled at slow speeds (2 to 4 knots).

Some anglers cover large areas by trolling fast with feathers or other surface lures until fish are located, and then stop to cast in the school with light spinning tackle and 6- to 10-pound test monofilament line. In these situations, Hopkins Lures or jigs are presented with a fast, jerky retrieval. Most Little Tunny landed are discarded or used as strip bait.

The species is not taken by commercial fishermen in the United States because it is not well regarded as a food fish. It is excellent, however, if handled properly.

Preparation. The fish should be bled and iced immediately after it is caught. One way to prepare Little Tunny is to make Tuna Salad. Fillets are baked, chilled, flaked, and mixed with salad dressing, hard-boiled eggs, celery, sweet pickle cubes, and salt and pepper. These ingredients should be added to taste and to provide the desired consistency. Serve over lettuce with tomato slices. To reduce the naturally fishy flavor, remove the dark strip of meat that extends the length of each fillet.

Suggested Readings. 32, 46, 59, 92, 168.

ATLANTIC BONITO
Sarda sarda

Bonito

Habits. A spring and fall visitor to the coastal waters of the region, the Atlantic Bonito is caught along with other nearshore schooling pelagic fishes such as Bluefish, Little Tunny, and Spanish and King Mackerels. This small, striped scombrid is found on both sides of the temperate and tropical Atlantic, including the Gulf of Mexico, Mediterranean Sea, and Black Sea. In the western Atlantic, it occurs from Nova Scotia to Argentina.

Atlantic Bonito are identified by their color, the conspicuously wavy lateral line, 16 to 22 gill rakers on the first arch, and the three lateral keels on the caudal peduncle. The species has a steel-blue back and upper sides punctuated by 5 to 11 dark, slightly oblique stripes that run forward and downward. The lower sides are silver. The Skipjack Tuna, *Euthynnus pelamis*, is also striped, but the markings are along the lower sides and belly.

Spawning presumably occurs in coastal waters throughout the region from mid-May through July with a June peak in reproductive activity. Females generally spawn for the first time at the end of their second year of life (about 21.5 inches long), and some initially reproduce by the end of the first year, or when they are 17.5 inches long. Each female produces from 450 thousand to over 3 million pelagic eggs, which are concentrated in the upper 16 feet of the water column.

As soon as the young Bonito are able to feed, they waste no time in searching for prey. The species has been described as an insatiable predator that feeds throughout the day, but probably most frequently at dawn and dusk. Larvae feed on other fish larvae, but prefer copepods; juveniles also consume larvae. Adults eat larger fish such as mackerels, anchovies, Alewives, menhaden, and silversides as well as squids and shrimps. Growth is rapid. Approximate lengths for fish aged 1 to 9 years are 13.8, 19.7, 23.6, 25.6, 26.6, 27.6, 28.3, 29.1, and 29.5 inches. The maximum size is about 36 inches in length and a weight of about 27 pounds.

Fishing. Atlantic Bonito are landed commercially throughout their range in the western Atlantic, but primarily in Venezuela, Mexico, Martinique, and Grenada. They are caught by gill nets, trammel nets, purse seines, and beach seines. Many of the fish are misidentified as Little Tunny and are discarded by recreational fishermen in the United States. Sport fishermen, trolling small artificials and casting jigs and Bucktails, take

202

the species throughout the region in the spring and fall. Angling techniques described for Little Tunny and King and Spanish Mackerels also apply for Atlantic Bonito.

Preparation. The flesh is delicious, and is marketed fresh and canned. It is perhaps best prepared by broiling or as tuna salad.

Suggested Readings. 32, 46, 169.

KING MACKEREL
Scomberomorus cavalla
King, Kingfish

Habits. The King Mackerel is the largest mackerel in the western Atlantic, reaching a length of 5½ feet and a weight of 100 pounds. The size led to the species name *cavalla*, derived from the Spanish word for horse.

The body of the fish is iron-gray along the back, and silvery on the sides and belly with pale to dusky fins. Small King Mackerel may have spots along the sides as do Spanish Mackerel; but they may be distinguished from the latter species by the lateral line, which dips sharply, and also by the color of the anterior dorsal fin, which is gray instead of black. King and Spanish Mackerels lack the longitudinal black stripe that is characteristic of the Cero, *Scomberomorus regalis*, a species common only off south Florida. King Mackerel are caught as far north as the Gulf of Maine, but more often from Virginia south to Brazil, including the Caribbean and Gulf of Mexico. Warm waters are preferred, and fish seldom enter water below 68°F. This affinity for warm water and the availability of food result in extensive annual migrations along the southeastern United States, south in the fall and north in the spring.

Although a fish as old as 14 years has been reported, individuals over 7 years old are rare. Females are larger than males. A female in its seventh year is approximately 39 inches long, while a male the same age measures about 32 inches. Spawning occurs from April through November with a peak from late summer to early fall. Males mature between their second and third years, and females between their third and fourth. A large female may release from 1 to 2.5 million eggs during a spawning season. Along the southeast coast, spawning takes place at sea just landward of the Gulf Stream. The inshore boundary is dictated by high turbidity water that the fish avoid. Kings feed mainly on migratory, surface-schooling fishes such as menhaden, Thread Herring, and Spanish and Scaled Sardines. They also consume small quantities of squids and shrimps. Feeding fish often leap out of the water in pursuit of prey.

Fishing. Millions of pounds of King Mackerel are landed annually, generating millions of dollars in revenue. Commercially, fish are caught by trolling lines, gill nets, purse seines, pound nets, and trawls. Gill nets are very effective and are used almost exclusively in Florida. There, nets 400 to 700 yards long may fish 70 feet of water and have 4¾-inch

stretch mesh. The net encircles the schools, and the average set produces 8,000 to 10,000 pounds of fish.

Sport fishermen troll, cast, and float fish for Kings. Most of the larger fish are caught by trolling double 8/0 hook rigs of mullet on feathers, by using spoons, or with live fish trolled slowly in the boat's wake. The typical line is 50-pound Monel wire with 8 feet of No. 7 stainless wire leader and an 8-ounce trolling weight. Another effective bait is a large plain spoon pulled deep by using a planer. The best months for fishing off North Carolina and Virginia are May and October, whereas winter and early spring are best off south Florida.

Preparation. The flesh of King Mackerel is oily and is best broiled or cooked over charcoal. Fillets should be basted with barbecue sauce or with cream of celery or mushroom soup. Large fish may be cut into steaks and basted with butter and lemon juice while being broiled or grilled.

Suggested Readings. 9, 32, 59.

SPANISH MACKEREL
Scomberomorus maculatus

Spaniard

Habits. A beautifully colored fish with a slender, graceful body, the Spanish Mackerel is prized for its table and sporting qualities. It is much smaller than its relative, the King Mackerel, averaging only 2 to 3 pounds in weight. Spanish Mackerel are greenish dorsally with silver sides and belly. Yellow or olive oval spots traverse the body, which is covered with very tiny scales.

The species forms immense, fast-moving surface schools that are distributed from New York to Mexico depending on the temperature of the water, with 68°F being the preferred minimum. Schools occur off North Carolina in April, off Chesapeake Bay in May, and off New York in June. In late summer and early fall, they move slowly southward to spend the winter and early spring along Florida's southern coast. Unlike the King, Spanish Mackerel do not appear to move freely around the Florida Keys. This creates two separate populations, one in the Gulf and the other off the southeastern states.

Spanish Mackerel are fast growing and may attain a length of 12 to 15 inches the first year. Individuals have been aged as old as 8 years, though fish older than age 5 are rare. Over 90 percent of the fish caught are 3 years old or younger. Both sexes are capable of reproducing by the second year. A 2-pound fish may lay 0.5 million eggs, and a 6-pounder 1.5 million. Spawning extends from April through September off North Carolina and Virginia. Thread Herring, menhaden, mullet, anchovies, shrimps, and squids are favorite foods. Feeding Spanish Mackerel are often seen forcing schools of small fish into tight bundles, nearly pushing them out of the water.

Fishing. Almost any small, shiny metal lure may be used to catch Spanish Mackerel. Metal squids, spoons, and diamond rigs are favorites. Feathers, No-Alibi jigs (⅛ to ½ ounce, either hair tails or nylons), and shad darts are also good baits. When fish are plentiful, these lures may be rigged in multiples behind a single line. After the fish have been hooked, boats make tight circles to stay in the schools of fish. Light 6- to 10-pound spinning tackle provides excellent sport. Because Spanish Mackerel migrate close to land, they are caught from small craft as well as from larger boats, piers, bridges, and jetties. Commercial fishermen catch the species with gill nets, hook and line, pound nets, seines, and trawls. Gill nets are very effective and are usually 3⅝-inch stretch mesh, whereas purse seines are ¾-inch, and beach seines 1¼- to 2

¾-inch stretch mesh. Most landings of Spanish Mackerel made along the southeastern United States occur during the summer and early fall. Whole fish are frequently sold as bait for billfishes.

Preparation. Spanish Mackerel are excellent eating fish and are easily filleted. Although suitable for frying, they are perhaps best broiled with lemon juice, paprika, and butter placed on top. Another method of preparing is to barbecue the fillets. The ingredients are 2 pounds of fillets or steaks, 1 cup of commercial barbecue sauce (or substitute by making sauce with catsup, vinegar, syrup, hot sauce, lemon juice, butter, garlic salt, Worcestershire sauce, and salt and pepper), 1 sliced onion, and 2 lemons. Arrange the fillets or steaks in a shallow pan. Squeeze the lemon juice over the steaks. Brush barbecue sauce over the fish and place onion slices on top. Broil, basting several times, until the flesh is easily flaked with a fork. Serves 6.

Suggested Readings. 10, 32, 59.

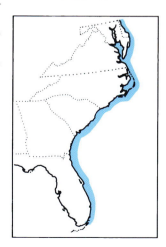

OFFSHORE
REEF FISHES

SILKY SHARK
Carcharhinus falciformis

Habits. The Carcharhinidae is the largest family of sharks and consists of approximately 60 species found throughout the world. Members of this family are often referred to as requiem sharks because many are man-eaters, thus the association with death. One of the most common carcharhinids is the Silky. Its name is derived from the fact that its denticles are so small that the skin feels smooth.

The species is circumtropical in distribution, being found on both sides of the Atlantic as well as in the Indo-Pacific and eastern Pacific. In the western Atlantic, the range extends from Delaware Bay to Brazil, including the Gulf of Mexico and the Caribbean. The Silky Shark inhabits oceanic waters from the continental slope to far beyond it, although it occasionally moves into coastal waters. It usually lives near the surface, but sometimes occurs at considerable depths (to 1,650 feet).

A combination of physical characteristics easily distinguishes this shark from other carcharhinids that occur in the area: long and slender body, distinctive teeth (upper teeth strongly serrated, lower teeth smooth), long pectoral fins, position of the first dorsal fin origin behind the free rear tips of the pectoral fins, presence of a mid-dorsal ridge, and the very small second dorsal fin with a distinctly long trailing lobe. The body is dark gray to bluish-black along the back with a grayish or white belly.

Unfortunately, as is true with many of the more common sharks, very little is known of the life history of the Silky, particularly the age and growth. The species is viviparous and produces from 2 to as many as 11 young at one time. It feeds primarily on fishes, crabs, and squids.

Fishing. The Silky Shark is caught by commercial fishermen using both surface and bottom longlines. It is also taken incidentally in gill nets and purse seines, where it causes considerable damage to the fishing gear. Silky Sharks are caught by sport fishermen who troll baits, or fish natural baits while drifting or while anchored. Heavy reels, strong lines, wire leaders, and stout hooks are required. Chumming from an anchored or drifting boat increases the chance of catching sharks. Angling methods discussed in more detail for other large sharks apply equally well for this species.

Preparation. The flesh of the Silky Shark may be smoked, fried, baked, or broiled. A suggested method of preparation is to make a simplified Shark-Fin Soup. Rinse ½ pound of dried shark fin and soak for 4 hours

210

in 8 cups of warm water. Pour off the water, rinse again and drain. Place the fin in a pot, add 6 cups of warm water, bring to a boil, and simmer for 1 hour. Pour off the water and repeat the process. Drain. Bring lean pork (¾ pound), pork bones, and water (8 cups) to a boil and simmer for 15 minutes. Add a chicken (2½ pounds) and simmer for 30 minutes. Remove the chicken, pork and pork bones. Shred the breast meat of the chicken. Add the shark fin to the stock and simmer for 1 hour. Add the shredded meat, salt, and a mixture of 2 tablespoons of cornstarch and 2 tablespoons of water. Simmer for 5 minutes and serve. If this sounds too fancy, replace pork and chicken with bouillon cubes.

Suggested Readings. 12, 46, 132.

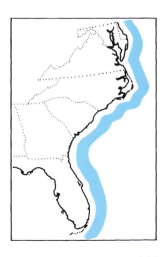

BLACKTIP SHARK
Carcharhinus limbatus

Habits. During the summer months many Blacktips visit the coast along the southeastern United States. They are medium-size sharks that attain a maximum length of about 8 feet. The species is often confused with the Spinner Shark, *Carcharhinus brevipinna*, another member of the family Carcharhinidae that also has conspicuously black-tipped fins. However, the combination of characters such as the moderately long snout, large eye, absence of a mid-dorsal ridge, narrow and finely serrated teeth, and the black markings easily distinguishes the Blacktip from its close relatives.

The species inhabits coastal and offshore waters from New England to southern Brazil. It is one of the most common sharks around the Bahamas and off southern Florida. The body is dark gray, dusky, or ash blue on the back and upper sides, shading to white or yellow-white below. The pectoral fins are prominently tipped with black. In younger fish the dorsals, anal, and lower lobe of the caudal fins are also black-tipped, but these marks usually fade with increased size.

Reproduction is viviparous, and the number of embryos produced by a gravid female ranges from 1 to 10. The young, born in the late spring, are 20 to 24 inches long, a size larger than that of most newly birthed sharks. Blacktip Sharks feed on squids, menhaden, Butterfish, sardines, sharks, stingrays, and many other fishes and invertebrates.

Fishing. Because Blacktips often occur in aggregations of six or more, and readily take a baited hook, they frequently are caught by anglers fishing from charter boats and head boats. The species is reputed to put up a strong fight and may even leap out of the water when hooked. Heavy reels, strong lines, wire leaders, and stout hooks are required. Chumming with oily, cut fish from an anchored or drifting boat will increase the chances of catching sharks. Commercial fishermen catch Blacktips with longlines, and occasionally with trawls, gill nets, and pound nets.

Preparation. The edible flesh is marketed fresh and salted, particularly in the Caribbean. It is also used to produce fishmeal. The meat is reputed to be good smoked, fried, and pickled. Fillets may be used to prepare Shark Marseillaise, and Fish Kabobs. Ingredients for the latter are 1 pound of fillets or steaks, ½ cup of catsup, ½ teaspoon of salt, 1

whole clove, 2 tablespoons of melted butter, cherry tomatoes, fresh mushroom caps, small onions, and bell pepper strips.

Cut the fish in 1-inch cubes. Make a marinade by combining the catsup, salt, and the clove. Soak the fish in the marinade for about 3 hours. Alternate the fish cubes, tomatoes, mushrooms, onions, and bell peppers on skewers. Brush the fish and other ingredients with melted butter, and broil for about 10 minutes, or until tender. Turn frequently and baste while cooking. Serves 4.

Suggested Readings. 12, 46, 132.

SPOTTED MORAY
Gymnothorax moringa

Moray

Habits. Morays are vicious tropical eels that live in holes and crevices in coral reefs and rock outcrops. Large morays have been depicted by the movie industry as being life-threatening dangers to man. This is pure fiction. Morays do not grab divers and pull them into their lairs. However, they are aggressive at times, and may cause serious lacerations with their sharp teeth. Fishermen, divers, and swimmers should approach morays with caution—if at all.

Fishermen in the region catch at least four species: Spotted Moray, Ocellated Moray, *Gymnothorax saxicola,* Reticulate Moray, *Muraena retifera,* and Stout Moray, *M. robusta.* They are difficult to identify to species. All are stocky, powerful eels with very small gill openings and no pectoral fins.

The body coloration of the Spotted Moray is highly variable, but typically consists of numerous irregular brown to purplish-black markings on a yellow-white background. The Ocellated Moray is the smallest of the four, and has white spots scattered over a tan-yellow background. The dorsal fin is margined in black. The Reticulate Moray has a dark blotch over the gill opening, and the body is covered with a rosette pattern, or groups of light spots on a dark brown background. The Stout Moray has a deep, thick head and a dark blotch over the gill opening. The body is very dark overall with large chocolate brown spots or blotches. This pattern is particularly evident on adults.

Spotted Morays are distributed from North Carolina to Brazil, including the Gulf of Mexico, Caribbean, Central America, and northern South American coasts. Along the southeastern United States, the shoreward distribution is limited by the temperature of the water. In more southerly latitudes, the species is found in shallow waters only a few feet deep, whereas off North Carolina and South Carolina it normally occurs in waters deeper than 80 feet (warmed by Gulf Stream currents).

Little is known of the life histories or behavior of morays. They feed on fishes and crustaceans, and they are secretive, and primarily nocturnal. The number of eggs produced by a female each season is believed to be low, perhaps as few as 2 to 3 thousand.

Fishing. Morays are caught with baited fish traps, trawls, and hook and line. Most are caught over reefs by fishermen fishing on the bottom with squid and other cut baits for snappers and groupers. The best time to catch them is at night when they venture from their hiding places to

search for prey. When hooked, morays often wrap themselves around corals or rocks making retrieval almost impossible. Once boated, the strong, squirming eels are difficult to remove from the hook. Fishermen should wear thick cotton or rubber gloves to avoid deliberate bites from the eels' sharp teeth.

Preparation. Morays are marketed fresh and frozen in the West Indies, although the consumption of large eels has resulted in ciguatera poisoning. There is no market for morays in the United States. The flesh is white and has a pleasing texture. It is usually smoked or fried.

Suggested Readings. 17, 46.

SQUIRRELFISH
Holocentrus adscensionis

Habits. Squirrelfish are very spiny reef fish that have large eyes, reddish bodies, and slender, delicate caudal peduncles. Two species are most frequently caught along the southeastern United States: the Squirrelfish, and the Longspine Squirrelfish, *Holocentrus rufus*. The former is the more common of the two. It is recognized by having 45 to 50 lateral line scales, a long lower jaw, and by lacking white markings on the dorsal fin. The Longspine Squirrelfish has a very slender third anal spine, a narrower caudal peduncle, and white triangles or spots near the tip of each dorsal spine. Squirrelfish are red with golden reflections and have alternating red and white longitudinal stripes on the sides. The undersides are white; the dorsal fin is orange anteriorly and greenish posteriorly.

The Squirrelfish is nocturnal and inhabits coral reefs and other reeflike bottom areas from North Carolina to Brazil including the Caribbean and parts of the Gulf of Mexico. In more tropical regions, such as the West Indies and south Florida, the species occurs in shallow water. Off North Carolina, South Carolina, and Georgia, Squirrelfish are generally restricted to habitats ranging from 100 to 250 feet deep, warmed by Gulf Stream currents.

Spawning has been documented off North Carolina in May. Spawning fish were caught at night, during a full moon, in water 150 feet deep. The number of eggs produced by a female in one season is probably only a few thousand. The eggs and larvae are pelagic and are dispersed by the warm currents and winds.

Larvae have been found in the stomachs of surface-feeding pelagic fishes such as Dolphin and tunas. Squirrelfish feed at night over reefs or nearby grass beds. Preferred foods are crabs, shrimps, worms, and snails. During the day, the species usually hides in holes and crevices in the reef.

Fishing. Squirrelfish are seldom caught. Occasionally, a commercial fisherman using handlines, traps, or gill nets will catch one, as will an angler bottom fishing for snappers and groupers. Squirrelfish are popular with divers who are brave enough to venture into tropical waters at night. The fish are colorful, may be encountered in easily accessible shallow reefs, and are not afraid of man.

216

Preparation. Squirrelfish are reported to be good eating, but are seldom found in fish markets. This is because they are small, and possess very sharp scales and numerous spines that make them difficult to clean. Frying is perhaps the best method of cooking.

Suggested Readings. 17, 46, 122.

BANK SEA BASS
Centropristis ocyurus

Yellow Sea Bass

Habits. The Bank Sea Bass is a small serranid that usually is found adjacent to hard bottom, high-relief areas in deep water. To experienced fishermen searching for reef fish, the appearance of Bank Sea Bass in the catch indicates that prime reef habitat has been missed. The species is distributed from Virginia to the Yucatan Banks in waters ranging in depth from 50 to 500 feet. This depth zone is generally deeper than that occupied by either the Black Sea Bass, *Centropristis striata*, or the Rock Sea Bass, *C. philadelphica*.

Bank Sea Bass are best recognized by their large mouths, tapering bodies with trilobed caudal fins, and by their color. Unlike the Black Sea Bass, the Bank Sea Bass is yellow-brown overall, and is marked with large black blotches and small jet black spots. The black markings consist of three longitudinal rows of blotches on the sides in addition to spots on the dorsal and caudal fins. The head, fins, and front portion of the body often have numerous blue and yellow spots and stripes.

The species is hermaphroditic; nearly all individuals begin life as females and change to males as they grow larger (older). While fish aged 1 and 2 years are predominantly females, those aged 3 to 6 are usually males. Collections of ripe females in March and April, combined with the appearance of young fish in late April, suggest that the species spawns offshore in spring. At least some females have the potential to spawn after only 1 year of life, although most spawn for the first time when they are 2 or 3 years old. A 4-inch fish is capable of spawning over 4 thousand pelagic eggs during a season, and a fish 8 inches in length may lay about 30 thousand.

Bank Sea Bass are known to live for at least 7 years. Approximate average lengths for fish aged 1 to 7 years are 4.9, 7, 8.3, 9.2, 9.6, 10.2, and 10.7 inches. The Bank Sea Bass is an opportunistic carnivore that uses its large mouth to swallow crabs, shrimps, brittle stars, calico scallops, and small fishes.

Fishing. Bank Sea Bass are not sought by fishermen. The species does appear as an incidental catch to commercial fishermen using traps, trawls, and hook and line. Bank Sea Bass are usually caught by commercial fishermen and anglers using two-hook bottom rigs weighted with a heavy lead sinker and baited with cut squid or fish. The species offers little resistance when hooked, and is met with a total lack of enthusiasm once boated. Because the fish are small, and people are not

218

familiar with them, the market price is very low, even though the flesh is similar in flavor to that of the Black Sea Bass.

Preparation. This species, which has lean, flaky meat, makes an excellent fish salad, and may also be pan fried.

Suggested Readings. 80.

219

BLACK SEA BASS
Centropristis striata

Sea Bass, Blackfish

Habits. The Black Sea Bass is a temperate marine species that inhabits irregular hard-bottom areas such as wrecks, reefs, and rock outcroppings from Cape Cod to Cape Canaveral. There are believed to be two populations, one north of Cape Hatteras and the other south of Cape Hatteras. The two populations spawn at different times of the year and have slightly different rates of growth. Black Sea Bass in the South Atlantic Bight generally occur inshore of the more tropical reef fishes—snappers, groupers, porgies, and grunts—which also prefer hard-bottom habitats.

The species is easily identified by body shape, fin characteristics, and color. Overall, the color is black for the larger individuals and dusky brown for the smaller. The exposed parts of scales are paler than the margins, giving the fish the appearance of being barred with a series of longitudinal pale dots. The belly is only slightly lighter than the sides, and is never white. The fins are dark, and the dorsal is marked with a series of white spots and bands. The upper portion of the caudal fin generally ends as a filament. During the spawning season, large males have a conspicuous blue nuchal hump.

Black Sea Bass are protogynous hermaphrodites. Large fish are males. Females reach reproductive condition for the first time during their second year, when they are about 7.5 inches long. Males become sexually mature when they are 3 years old and 9 inches long. The spawning season is protracted, extending from June through October in the Mid-Atlantic Bight, and from February through May in the South Atlantic Bight. The number of eggs produced in a season ranges from about 30 thousand for a small female to more than 500 thousand for a large fish.

Although Black Sea Bass are reported to live as long as 20 years, fish older than 9 years are rare. The maximum size attained is approximately 24 inches and 6 pounds. Sea Bass grow slowly. A 1-year-old fish is only 5 inches long; a 5-year-old is 12 inches; and one 8 years of age is only 15 inches long. Black Sea Bass are opportunistic feeders, eating whatever is available. They are particularly fond of crabs, shrimps, worms, clams, and small fishes. Bass caught in deep water and then quickly retrieved to the surface, often regurgitate their food, thus attracting more fish.

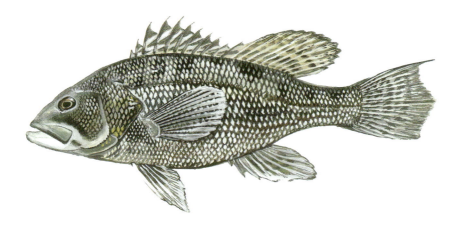

Fishing. Fishing for Black Sea Bass takes place all along the East Coast from Massachusetts to Florida. Commercially, Bass are landed by otter trawls, handlines, pound nets, and traps. Fishing operations move with the fish, inshore in summer and offshore in winter. Fishing distance from the shore, therefore, varies seasonally. Trawling is conducted in water 50-feet deep in the Middle Atlantic Bight. Traps, baited with fish, are usually set in water 65 to 100 feet deep. Echo sounders, or depth recorders, are used to locate rough bottoms where Bass congregate. Sport fishermen use medium-weight boat rods and reels with 15- to 20-pound test line. The typical bottom rig consists of two 4/0 to 6/0 hooks baited with squid, and an 8- to 10-ounce sinker. In shallower waters, anglers occasionally use light spinning tackle with spoons and jigs.

Preparation. Black Sea Bass flesh spoils very quickly. Fish should be iced and then cleaned as soon as possible. Whole fish and fillets are usually fried. Some believe that no tastier saltwater fish can be brought to the table than Black Sea Bass prepared in this manner.

Suggested Readings. 74, 80, 101.

SAND PERCH
Diplectrum formosum

Habits. Related to the seabasses and groupers, the Sand Perch is a small, slender fish that populates the edges of low-lying reefs at moderate depths along the continental shelf. It is the only member of the family Serranidae that has two bony preopercular lobes, each with numerous spines. The coloration is also distinctive. The body is light tan with a complex of dark, wedge-shaped vertical bars, and seven to eight narrow blue horizontal stripes. A series of four or five bright blue-green lines cross the snout and cheeks, and the eyes are emerald bordered with golden rings. The dorsal fin has two or three horizontal blue lines, each bordered with bright orange.

Sand Perch are distributed from Virginia to Uruguay, including the Gulf of Mexico and the Caribbean in waters 25 to 165 feet deep. Along the Atlantic coast of the United States, the northern range and inshore distribution are limited by the temperature of the water. Sand Perch are seldom found in waters less than 55°F. During extremely cold weather, fish move offshore, where the water is warmed by Gulf Stream currents. The preferred habitats are edges of rock, limestone, or coral reefs, and along the upper edges of depressions on the ocean floor. In shallow water Sand Perch are found near jetties, wrecks, and artificial reefs. Sand Perch generally hover 6 to 12 inches above the bottom or rest on the bottom propped up by their pelvic fins. Small fish frequently excavate shallow hiding places in the sand next to a rock, coral head, or sponge.

The Sand Perch is a synchronous hermaphrodite; both sperm and eggs occur simultaneously in mature fish, or those larger than 7.5 inches long. Scientists believe that a fish functions as either a male or a female at any given time, and mates with another Sand Perch that functions as the opposite sex. The spawning season occurs in late spring and summer. Gonad development begins in March and April, reaching a peak in May. Spawning may continue through September.

A moderate life span of about 7 years and a slow growth rate typify the age and growth characteristics of the Sand Perch. Approximate average lengths for fish aged 1 to 6 years are 2, 3.9, 6.7, 8.8, 9.8, and 10.4 inches. Sand Perch are aggressive and voracious predators that feed on small animals living on or near the bottom. Favorite foods are shrimps, crabs, amphipods, brittle stars, worms, and small fishes such as blennies, gobies, and searobins.

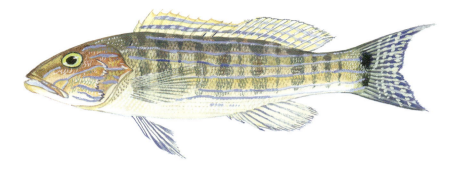

Fishing. Sand Perch are caught by anglers fishing on the bottom with squid or cut fish and by commercial fishermen using handlines, traps, and trawls. The species is caught incidentally to other reef fish and is of little commercial or recreational importance in the United States. Catching Sand Perch usually indicates that prime reef fish habitat is close by. For angling techniques and equipment, see the discussions on fishing for Red Porgy and Black Sea Bass.

Preparation. Because of the small size, there is little market value. The flesh is edible however, and may be prepared in a variety of ways.

Suggested Readings. 18, 46.

SPECKLED HIND
Epinephelus drummondhayi

Strawberry Grouper, Kitty Mitchell, Calico Grouper

Habits. One of the most beautifully colored groupers caught off the southeastern United States is *Epinephelus drummondhayi*. The common names stem from the profusion of tiny white spots that cover the deep reddish-brown head, body, and fins. The name Kitty Mitchell reportedly associates the fish's coloration with a red-haired, freckle-faced lady of the evening who was an acquaintance of Gulf Coast comercial snapper fishermen during the last century. In addition to the normal color pattern, some juveniles undergo a xanthic phase, where white spots cover a light yellow background.

Speckled Hind inhabit warm, moderately deep waters from North Carolina to Cuba, including Bermuda, the Bahamas, and the Gulf of Mexico. The preferred habitat is high- and low-profile hard bottom in depths ranging from 150 to 330 feet, where temperatures are 60° to 85°F. Off the Carolinas, the species is usually found inshore of deep-water reef fish (tilefish and Snowy, Warsaw, and Yellowedge Groupers), and offshore of the Black Sea Bass fishing grounds.

Like other reef fish studied in the South Atlantic Bight, Speckled Hind seem to display a fish size - water depth relationship; smaller fish occur inshore, whereas larger individuals are found in deeper water. Most of the fish caught are in the 5-pound size class, although the species grows much larger. The world record is a 64-pound Speckled Hind caught off North Carolina. Strawberry Grouper are never very common in sport or commercial landings, a fact that has hampered research on the species. Subsequently, little is known about its life history.

Like other epThis inepheline groupers, Speckled Hind are protogynous hermaphrodites. Most of the larger, older fish are males. Females reach sexual maturity probably as 4- or 5-year-olds (about 19 to 21 inches long). Spawning takes place offshore from July through September. The fertilized eggs, which may number up to 2 million for a large female, are pelagic. The recently hatched young are also found on the water's surface before they migrate to the bottom.

Growth is rapid for the first 3 years, and then levels off for the life of the fish, which may be 15 years. Average lengths for fish aged 1 to 15 years are 7.3, 12.5, 16.1, 18.7, 20.8, 22.5, 24.1, 25.4, 26.7, 27.9, 29.1, 30.5, 31.6, 33, and 33.9 inches. Speckled Hind generally engulf their prey whole. The fish opens its mouth and extends the gill covers rapidly to draw in a current of water, thus inhaling the food. Groupers

are also known to pursue their prey and strike it. Items in the diet include fishes, crabs, shrimps, and mollusks that inhabit hard bottom.

Fishing. Although fishermen regard the Speckled Hind highly, they are unable to fish specifically for them. When a fisherman's line goes overboard, the chance is remote indeed that a Speckled Hind will take the bait. This is not necessarily the case with deep-water groupers and tilefish that may be fairly accurately pinpointed by depth and bottom topography. Strawberry Grouper are caught almost exclusively by hook and line; a few are caught by traps and trawls. The same methods described for fishing for Snowy Grouper apply for Speckled Hind.

Preparation. The Speckled Hind is easily filleted and is delicious when prepared by broiling, baking, or frying. A suggested method of cooking is to charcoal the fillets, basting them with melted butter seasoned with garlic and onion salts. Because the scales are so small and deeply embedded, the fish are usually skinned.

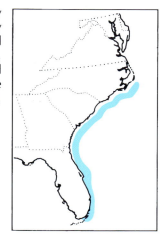

Suggested Readings. 46, 97, 148.

YELLOWEDGE GROUPER
Epinephelus flavolimbatus

Grouper

Habits. The Yellowedge is a large, sturdy-bodied grouper that inhabits deep water of the western Atlantic from North Carolina to Brazil, including the Caribbean and Gulf of Mexico. Fishermen in the region usually catch Yellowedge along with Snowy Grouper and tilefish at the continental shelf break, where the bottom is characterized by a series of troughs and terraces and by precipitous dropoffs.

The species is best identified by its size and color. The body is light tan to grayish brown along the back and upper sides; the lower sides and belly are whitish. The dorsal, pectorals, and occasionally the caudal fins are trimmed in bright yellow. Juveniles are usually speckled with white spots and possess a black blotch on the caudal peduncle, which does not reach below the lateral line. A similar spot is found on young Snowy Grouper, but it is positioned lower.

Like most of the inhabitants of the deep-reef community, the Yellowedge has not been studied extensively, owing to the difficulty of obtaining samples. However, some information is available on reproduction and feeding. The species is a protogynous hermaphrodite. Most of the fish smaller than 30 inches are females, whereas those larger are generally males. Spawning occurs offshore from April through October, with a peak of activity in September. The eggs and larvae are pelagic.

Food studies on the species have been hampered because fish retrieved from deep water often evert their stomachs, voiding them of contents. Identified food items, however, indicate the Yellowedge is an aggressive predator that feeds on large, bottom-dwelling animals. Selected foods include squids, octopuses, crabs, eels, lizardfish, seahorses, scorpionfish, and searobins. These and other foods are swallowed whole. Yellowedge may live 20 years or longer and attain a length of approximately 45 inches.

Fishing. Yellowedge are caught infrequently throughout their range by commercial and recreational fishermen. Most are landed from waters 450 to 850 feet deep, where the bottom is very irregular. Depth recorders and lorans are required to locate good fishing grounds. Yellowedge caught off the Carolinas range from 12 to 42 inches in length (average about 31 inches), and weigh from 1 pound to more than 30 pounds. As is true with fishing for other deep-water reef fish, the bait (cut fish or squid) must be fished directly on the bottom. Heavy sinkers are required to negate the effects of strong offshore currents.

226

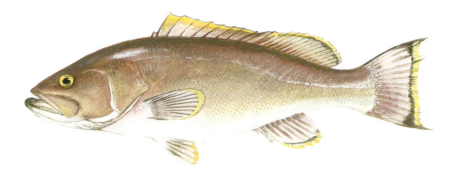

Preparation. Yellowedge are excellent food fish. The white flaky fillets may be baked, broiled, basted over charcoal, or prepared in a fish chowder. The bones are large and easily discarded. A suggested dish is Baked Fish in Sour Cream. The ingredients are 2 to 3 pounds of fish fillets, 1 cup of sour cream, 2 tablespoons of chopped dill pickle, 2 tablespoons of chopped green pepper, 2 tablespoons of chopped onion, 1 tablespoon of parsley flakes, ¼ teaspoon of dry mustard, and ¼ teaspoon of sweet basil. Mix the ingredients together and pour them over the fillets in a buttered pan. Bake at 375°F for 20 to 25 minutes. Serves 4 to 6.

Suggested Readings. 46, 148.

RED HIND
Epinephelus guttatus

Strawberry Grouper

Habits. Besides the Speckled Hind, there are two other groupers that are referred to as hinds and are caught in the region. Both the Red Hind and the Rock Hind, *Epinephelus adscensionis*, have numerous dark spots on a lighter background. This color feature alone distinguishes the two from the Speckled Hind. They are typical serranids with robust bodies and large mouths. Red Hind have pale pink bodies with uniform red spots. The back and sides lack the large black blotches or saddles that are seen on Rock Hind, and the soft-rayed portions of the dorsal and anal fins as well as the caudal fin are margined in black. The species is found in tropical and subtropical waters as deep as 400 feet from North Carolina to Brazil, including the southern part of the Gulf of Mexico and the Caribbean. It is most abundant off Bermuda and in the West Indies.

Red Hind are protogynous hermaphrodites. Most of the fish larger than 12 inches are males. Spawning takes place over an extended period of time, March through July, in waters 68° to 82°F, which are usually 100 to 130 feet deep. During the spawning season, sexually mature fish, or those 3 years old and older, form large aggregations over irregular bottoms. The eggs are pelagic and range in number from about 90 thousand for a 10-inch female to more than 3 million for a fish that is 18 inches long.

The species is long lived, living up to 17 years, or possibly longer, and attaining a size of 23 inches and 10 pounds. Approximate average lengths for fish aged 1, 2, 5, 10, and 17 years are 4.8, 7.4, 12.6, 17, and 19 inches. Like other medium-sized groupers, Red Hind feed on various animals that are found on or near the bottom. Favorite foods are small fishes, crabs, shrimps, and squids. Prey are captured from ambush as the Red Hind hides in holes and crevices, or they are consumed after a short chase.

Fishing. Red Hind are captured throughout their range by commercial fishermen using hook and line, traps, seines, and occasionally trawls. Recreational fishermen catch the species bottom fishing with cut fish or squid as bait. Fishing is best inshore over irregular bottom in water 80 to 180 feet deep, and along the shelf break where the depth ranges from 240 to 350 feet. Sturdy boat rods and electrically or manually operated reels with 80-pound monofilament line are used by sport fishermen. Terminal tackle usually consists of a heavy sinker and two 4/0 to 6/0

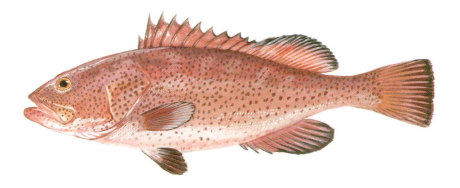

hooks baited with squid or cut fish rigged on a 200-pound test monofilament leader.

Preparation. The flesh is white and flaky; it is considered to be of excellent quality. Usually marketed fresh, it may be prepared in fish salads and chowders, or by baking or broiling.

Suggested Readings. 21, 46.

RED GROUPER
Epinephelus morio

Grouper

Habits. A large, robust fish, the Red Grouper is distributed from North Carolina to Brazil, including the Gulf of Mexico and the Caribbean. The species is most abundant along Florida's east and west coasts, and throughout the Gulf of Mexico. It inhabits ledges, crevices, and caverns of rocky limestone reefs, and also lower-profile, live-bottom areas in waters 10 to 400 feet deep.

Red Grouper are easily recognized by their color and by the sloped, straight-line appearance of the spiny dorsal fin. The fin has a long second spine and an unnotched interspine membrane. Most epinepheline groupers have a notched dorsal spine membrane and a third spine longer than the second. The body is deep brownish-red overall, with occasional white spots on the sides. Tiny black specks dot the cheeks and operculum. The Red Grouper is most closely related to the Nassau Grouper, *Epinephelus striatus*, a fish marked by vertical bars and blotches, and one that is somewhat more restricted to coral reefs such as those found in the West Indies.

Red Grouper are protogynous hermaphrodites, and many females transform into males when they are 18 to 26 inches long. Some females are capable of reproducing for the first time when they are 4 years old; all are sexually mature by age 7. Spawning takes place from March through July, with a peak of activity in April and May. The pelagic eggs are usually released in waters 63° to 70°F and 80 to 300 feet deep. Ripe females spawn an average of 1.5 million eggs during a season. Fecundity varies from about 300 thousand to more than 5.7 million, depending on fish size. The larval Groupers remain at the surface for 30 to 40 days before settling to the bottom.

As is typical of other protogynous animals, the males of the species live longer and grow to greater sizes than females. The maximum age is at least 25 years. The average sizes for fish aged 1, 2, 3, 4, 5, 10, 15, and 18 years are 8.5 (about 0.33 pound), 12, 15.3 (2.2 pounds), 17.6 (3.3 pounds), 19.4, 26.1, 28.8, and 32.5 (25 pounds) inches. Like other large serranids, Red Grouper generally ambush their prey and swallow it whole. Favorite foods are crabs, shrimps, lobsters, octopuses, squids, and fishes that live close to reefs.

Fishing. Red Grouper are highly esteemed as food and game fish throughout their geographical range. Most are caught on hook and line in Florida, where the Red Grouper and Red Snapper fisheries have been

230

closely related. As Red Snapper became less plentiful, market prices for Red Grouper increased, and today this Grouper forms the bulk of Florida's commercial reef fish landings. Navigational and fishing equipment described in previous discussions for other reef fishes also apply for the Red Grouper.

Preparation. The flesh is white and firm. Marketed fresh and frozen, it is excellent prepared by all the generally popular methods.

Suggested Readings. 46, 105.

WARSAW GROUPER
Epinephelus nigritus

Grouper

Habits. There are two species of very large groupers caught by fishermen in the region: the Jewfish, *Epinephelus itajara*, weighing up to 750 pounds, and the Warsaw, which may weigh over 300 pounds. The Warsaw has a wider distribution along the southeastern United States and is caught more frequently than the Jewfish. Warsaw range from North Carolina to the Florida Keys and throughout much of the Caribbean and Gulf of Mexico to the northern coast of South America.

The species is the only member of the genus *Epinephelus* that has 10 dorsal spines, the second of which is much longer than the third. The color is a grayish brown to dark red-brown background with numerous small, irregular white blotches on the sides. The color appears much lighter around the nape and along the posterior margin of the operculum. All of the fins are dark brown, excepting the white-splotched spiny portion of the dorsal. In death, Warsaw are uniformly dark brown.

The species inhabits irregular bottom—notches, valleys, and dropoffs —of the continental shelf break in waters 350 to 650 feet deep. This habitat occurs 40 to 50 miles off the coast of North Carolina and about 12 to 20 miles off the east coast of Florida. Other important species of reef fish that are found in this productive deep-water zone are Snowy and Yellowedge Groupers, tilefish, and Silk Snappers.

Very little is known about the reproduction of Warsaw; however, the eggs and larvae are presumed to be pelagic. Like other *Epinephelus* groupers, the Warsaw is long-lived and has a slow rate of growth. Longevity is thought to be 25 to 30 years, and the maximum length attained is about 6½ feet. Average lengths for fish aged 1, 5, 10, 15, 20, and 24 years are 13, 36, 47, 51, 55, and 58 inches. The Warsaw's huge mouth enables it to engulf prey whole after capturing it from ambush, or after a short chase. Crabs, shrimps, and fishes are major foods.

Fishing. Commercial fishermen as well as recreational anglers catch Warsaw with hook and line. The species is considered a trophy game fish by sport fishermen, but contributes less than 1 percent to the commercial landings of groupers in the Southeast. Although caught in small numbers, giant-sized Warsaw attract anglers to the offshore fishing grounds. The chance of catching a fish weighing 200 to 300 pounds is enough to entice some fishermen to endure the long boat rides and occasionally rough seas.

Several pieces of equipment are essential for locating and catching the species: loran, depth recorder, and heavy tackle. Good fishing locations are the key to success, and off the Carolinas these are the notches and precipitous dropoffs on the bottom in waters 360 to 420 feet deep. Once located, Warsaw are caught on electric or hydraulic reels with 60- to 100-pound test line and bottom rigs consisting of two 7/0 to 9/0 hooks, strong leader, and a 1- to 3-pound sinker. Preferred baits are whole squid, cut amberjack, or a live Red Porgy or Vermilion Snapper. Warsaw usually bite a free-spooled or slack line best. The strike, a strong, slow tug, may be misinterpreted as a hangup on the bottom. Like most other fishes caught from the bottom in deep water, Warsaw suffer from embolism because gases expand within the body as they near the surface. Therefore, once the fish are more than 33 feet off the bottom they begin to rise naturally, and the fight subsides.

Preparation. Because the fillets are large, they are best prepared like a piece of beef or pork—baked or basted over charcoal. The white flaky meat also makes excellent fish chowders.

Suggested Readings. 46, 90, 148.

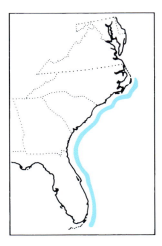

SNOWY GROUPER
Epinephelus niveatus

Snowflake

Habits. The outer continental shelf of the South Atlantic Bight, characterized by ridges, terraces, and precipitous cliffs bathed by warm Gulf Stream currents, provides an ideal habitat for fishes associated with deep-water reefs. Snappers, tilefish, porgies, and groupers support offshore commercial and sport fisheries from North Carolina to Florida. The most frequently caught deep-water grouper is the Snowy.

The species is distributed in the western Atlantic from Massachusetts, occasionally as juveniles, to Brazil, including the Gulf of Mexico, the Lesser Antilles, and the northern coast of Cuba. It also occurs in the Pacific from Baja California to Panama. Adults inhabit waters 200 to 860 feet deep, where bottom water temperatures fluctuate from about 60° to 84°F. Most of the fish are concentrated in a narrow zone extending from 300 to 420 feet deep, approximately 50 miles off the coasts of North Carolina and South Carolina.

The coloration of the species varies with fish size. Smaller fish are dark brown overall, punctuated with coin-size pearly white spots on the sides. A distinctive black, saddle-shaped blotch occurs on the caudal peduncle and extends down below the lateral line. Larger fish usually lose the white spots and caudal saddle and become dark brown with a slight coppery tint. The spiny portion of the dorsal fin has a black margin.

Snowy Grouper are protogynous hermaphrodites, changing from females to males as fish attain larger sizes. Fish are first able to reproduce when they are 4 or 5 years old, about 18 to 20 inches long. Females may lay more than 2 million eggs during the spawning season, which extends from May through July. The larvae are pelagic, drifting with the currents and winds, before settling to the bottom to populate favorable habitat.

The species may live for at least 17 years and reach a weight of 70 pounds. Average lengths for ages 1 to 17 years are 8.3, 12.9, 15.9, 18.2, 20.2, 22.1, 23.8, 25.5, 27, 28.4, 30, 31.4, 32.8, 34.4, 35.4, 36.4, and 37.7 inches. Like other large groupers, the Snowy Grouper is territorial, occupies a specific area and waits to ambush its prey. Probable foods are fishes such as snappers, Round Scad, and porgies, and crustaceans.

Fishing. To overcome the problems of distance from land and deep water, fishermen must have specialized equipment to catch Snowy

Grouper. Seaworthy boats with radar, loran, and depth finders are necessary to reach the fishing grounds safely and to locate good bottom having concentrations of fish.

Most fishermen use electrically or hydraulically powered 6/0 to 9/0 reels to retrieve fish from the deep waters. Some commercial fishermen still rely on bicycle reels that are operated manually. Tackle normally consists of 80-pound test monofilament or Dacron line with a terminal rig made of 200-pound test monofilament leader, two 6/0 to 9/0 hooks baited with squid or cut fish and weighted with 8-ounce to 3-pound lead sinkers.

Snowy Grouper fight hard initially before the changes in pressure cause the air bladder to expand, forcing the fish to the surface. The key to good fishing is finding favorable bottom—usually sharp dropoffs or notches—and being able to make slow drifts with the baits on the bottom. Anchoring is very difficult because of the depths and currents.

Preparation. Size, eating quality, and market price make the species popular with fishermen. The flesh is white and flaky; fillets are excellent broiled, charcoaled, baked, stewed, or fried.

Suggested Readings. 46, 97, 148.

GAG
Mycteroperca microlepis
Charcoal Belly

Habits. Two genera of groupers are caught along the continental shelf of the South Atlantic Bight: *Mycteroperca* and *Epinephelus*. *Mycteroperca* groupers, such as the Gag, have long, compressed bodies and 11 to 14 rays in their anal fins. *Epinephelus* groupers are more robust, and have only seven to nine anal rays. The Gag is the most widely distributed grouper in the region. Adults occur from North Carolina to Brazil over low- and high-profile hard bottom in waters 60 to 250 feet deep. The species is found throughout the Gulf of Mexico but not in the West Indies. Young Gag inhabit estuaries from Massachusetts to Cape Canaveral, but it is not known whether the species uses estuaries as primary nursery grounds.

The coloration is highly variable and changes with the size of the fish. Large Gag are dark brownish-gray above, and paler below, with traces of dark wavy markings on the sides. Small fish are much lighter and have numerous dark brown or charcoal kiss-like marks along the sides. The Scamp, *M. phenax*, and Black Grouper, *M. bonaci*, closely resemble the Gag and often occur in the same habitat. Gag have deeply notched preopercles, and are thus distinguished from Black Grouper, and do not have the extended caudal rays that are characteristic of Scamp. Black Grouper also have numerous bronze spots on the head and side of the body.

Spawning takes place in February off the Carolinas and January through March in the Gulf of Mexico. Sexual maturity is attained at age 5 or 6, when fish are 27 to 30 inches long. Gag are protogynous hermaphrodites. Sexual transition usually occurs between 10 and 11 years. Very little is known about egg production; however, one 37-inch female contained 1.5 million eggs that were considered pelagic.

Gag are capable of living for at least 15 years, and may reach a weight of 55 pounds (about 51 inches in length). Average lengths for fish aged 1 to 13 years are 11, 16, 21, 24, 27, 30, 32, 34, 36, 37, 39, 40, and 43 inches. Gag congregate around rocky ledges. Divers often see them in small groups, slowly swimming along crests or peeking out from under overhangs. Favorite foods are Round Scad, sardines, porgies, snappers, grunts, crabs, shrimps, and squids.

Fishing. Bottom fishing with hook and line is the most effective method of catching Gag. Some are caught by bottom longlines, trawls, and traps. The rugged bottom limits the use of longlines and trawls, and

236

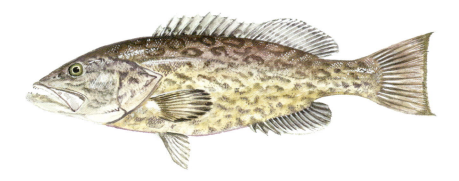

most traps used in the region are selective for smaller fish. Fishermen use boats equipped with loran and depth recorders to help them locate good bottom and concentrations of fish. Gag do not usually mark on the recorders, but fishing at the right depth over irregular bottom can produce good results. A ridge with 6 to 12 feet of relief in 100 to 200 feet of water is almost certain to have grouper around it.

Sturdy rods with electrically or manually powered reels and 80-pound line are standard. Terminal tackle consists of heavy leader, 6- to 32-ounce lead sinkers and two 6/0 to 9/0 hooks baited with squid or cut fish. The most effective way to catch large Gag is from an anchored boat. Fish the bottom with a whole Spanish Sardine on a 7/0 hook attached to a 10- to 12-foot monofilament leader and an 8- to 16-ounce sliding lead sinker.

Preparation. The flesh is white, flaky, and excellent to eat. Like other groupers, Gag have deeply embedded scales that make scaling the fish virtually impossible. The fillets are easily skinned however, and may be fried, baked in the oven, or broiled and basted over charcoal.

Suggested Readings. 46, 84, 148.

SCAMP
Mycteroperca phenax

Habits. The Scamp is a medium-sized serranid related to the Gag and other slender-bodied groupers of the genus *Mycteroperca*. It inhabits continental shelf waters from the Campeche Banks, in the Gulf of Mexico, to Florida, and northward along the East Coast to North Carolina. Juveniles have been collected off Massachusetts, but these fish do not indicate that established populations exist in the more northern latitudes. Although the species occasionally congregates over high-profile bottom, such as wrecks and rock outcroppings, the preferred habitat is low-profile, live-bottom areas in waters 75 to 300 feet deep from Cape Fear, North Carolina, southward along the South Carolina coast. These areas are characterized by profuse growths of soft corals and sponges populated by Red Grouper, White Grunt, Red Porgy, and numerous species of small, tropical reef fish.

Scamp are similar in appearance to Yellowmouth Grouper, *M. interstitialis*, a species with which it occurs, particularly on the Campeche Banks and in the northern Gulf of Mexico. The Scamp may be distinguished from the Yellowmouth by the pronounced anal and soft dorsal ray extensions, a more concave profile of the head, and the color. Scamp have a tan to grayish-brown body covered with sharply defined, well-separated dark spots, which are approximately an eighth of an inch in diameter. Yellowmouth have either a uniformly gray-brown color or a pattern of very close-set spots separated by narrow lines. The mouths of both species are yellow tinted.

In April and May, sexually mature Scamp, those at least 3 years old and larger than 16 inches, spawn thousands of pelagic eggs in offshore waters. Recently hatched larvae are also pelagic, and continue this surface-associated existence for days before settling to the bottom to populate favorable habitats.

Scamp have been aged as old as 21 years, but they probably live for 25 to 30 years based on their projected maximum size of about 43 inches in length and 36 pounds in weight. Average lengths (and weights) for fish aged 1, 2, 3, 4, 5, 10, 15, 20, and 21 years are 8.5 (0.33 pound), 13.2 (1.2 pounds), 16.3 (2.2), 18.5 (3.1), 20.3 (4.1), 26.1 (8.6), 30.3 (13.2), 34.8 (19.7), and 35.2 (20.5) inches. During low-light periods of the day, Scamp are aggressive predators, capturing crabs, shrimps, and fishes and swallowing them whole.

Fishing. The Scamp is considered to be a seafood delicacy by many fishermen and restauranteurs. It is caught primarily by hook and line throughout its range. Seaworthy boats, equipped with loran and depth recorders, locate concentrations of fish and productive-looking bottom.

Anglers use electric, hydraulic, or manual reels mounted on stiff boat rods to fish on the bottom. Terminal rigs consist of two 6/0 to 9/0 hooks baited with live fish, cut fish, or squid and weighted with an 8-ounce to 3-pound lead sinker. Best fishing is from an anchored boat, or if drifting, with free-spooled line, late in the afternoon or early in the morning.

Preparation. Scamp are excellent baked or broiled. However, the flesh is perhaps best cut in finger- sized slices and deep fried. A Santee-Cooper Batter is suggested: to season 2 pounds of fillets, combine 1 pint of buttermilk, ¾ tablespoon of Tabasco sauce, 1 cup of flour, 1 cup of white cornmeal, 1 tablespoon of cumin, and salt and pepper to taste. This batter may be used to fry any fish.

Suggested Readings. 46, 98, 148.

BLUELINE TILEFISH
Caulolatilus microps

Gray Tilefish, Tilefish

Habits. The Blueline Tilefish is a bottom-dwelling marine species found in water ranging in depth from 240 to 780 feet from Virginia to the Campeche Banks, Mexico. It frequently inhabits the same areas as deep-water groupers and snappers. The preferred habitat is irregular bottom, characterized by a series of troughs and terraces intermingled with sand, mud, and shell hash, paralleling the continental shelf break. Bottom water temperatures usually range from 59° to 73°F. The species has recently been found to inhabit cone-shaped burrows, which it enters head first.

The fish is a dull olive-gray overall with white below. The lack of a fleshy protuberance behind the head distinguishes it from the commercially important Tilefish, *Lopholatilus chamaeleonticeps*, of the mid-Atlantic and Gulf of Mexico. Another close relative, the Goldface Tilefish, *Caulolatilus chrysops*, resembles the Blueline Tilefish except the former has bright yellow streaks below the eyes.

The Blueline Tilefish is long-lived, up to 15 years. It grows approximately 6 inches the first year, and may eventually attain a length of 32 inches. Average lengths for fish aged 1 to 15 years are 6.5, 11.2, 14.1, 16.3, 18.3, 19.9, 21.4, 22.7, 23.9, 24.9, 25.8, 26.6, 27.3, 27.9, and 28.6 inches.

Some females are sexually mature the first year of life; most are mature by their fifth. Spawning extends from May through October with a peak during the summer. A large female may lay more than 4 million free-floating eggs. Evidence suggests that the species may be hermaphroditic, with the females changing to males at larger sizes. Blueline Tilefish feed on the bottom, browsing on small fishes, crabs, shrimps, worms, snails, and sea urchins.

Fishing. Since Blueline Tilefish occur in deep water, usually far offshore, large seaworthy boats are required to reach the fishing grounds safely. Vessels, such as charter boats and head boats, equipped with loran and depth recorders, carry anglers to places good for fishing on the bottom.

Fiber glass rods 5 to 6 feet long with 6/0 to 9/0 electric or manually operated reels are preferred. The line, usually 80- to 120-pound test, must be strong enough to resist wear on the rugged bottom and also to support the weight of fish and heavy lead sinkers. Bottom rigs generally consist of 200-pound test monofilament line with two 6/0 to 9/0 hooks baited with squid or cut fish such as Greater Amberjack. Sinkers vary

from 6 to 28 ounces depending on the depth and conditions of the current. Boats usually drift over good fishing spots, although some anchor after locating promising bottom or concentrations of fish. Blueline Tilefish are also harvested by commercial fishermen using the same methods as sport fishermen. In addition, horizontal longlines and vertical Kali poles with many baited hooks are sometimes set on the bottom overnight.

Preparation. The flesh is white and flaky, excellent for chowders and fish salads. It may also be baked, fried, or broiled.

Suggested Readings. 46, 128, 148.

TILEFISH
Lopholatilus chamaeleonticeps
Golden Tilefish, Rainbow Tilefish

Habits. Golden Tilefish, the largest of the American tilefishes, are caught regularly by sport fishermen in water deeper than any other demersal fish off the United States. Tilefish are easily distinguished from other members of the family Malacanthidae by the large adipose flap, or crest, on the head. The species is beautifully colored. The back is blue-green and iridescent, with numerous spots of bright yellow and gold. The belly is white and the head is rosy, with blue under the eyes. The cheeks are fawn-colored; pectoral fins are sepia-colored, and the margin of the anal fin is a purplish blue.

Tilefish inhabit the outer continental shelf and upper continental slope along the entire east coast of the United States and the Gulf of Mexico south to Venezuela. The habitat is a relatively narrow band, less than 20 miles wide, in waters from 250 to 1,500 feet deep, where bottom temperatures range from 49° to 58°F. Individuals live in cone-shaped burrows. They venture from the burrows to feed, and retreat to them when frightened. Although schooling is not characteristic of the family, Tilefish concentrate in small groups, or pods.

Females are smaller than males, presenting the possibility that the species is a protogynous hermaphrodite. Sexual maturity is reached when fish are about 27 inches long and weigh about 9 pounds. Spawning occurs from March through September. Reproductive activity peaks in July in the Mid-Atlantic Bight. Females lay from 2 to 8 million pelagic eggs, which hatch in 40 to 70 hours depending on water temperature.

Tilefish feed during the day on the bottom on crustaceans, clams, snails, worms, fishes, sea urchins, anemones, and sea cucumbers. Growth is slow. Fish are only about 4 inches long at the end of their first year. Approximate sizes for fish aged 5, 10, 15, 20, 25, and 30 years are 13.5, 22, 28, 32, 36, and 38 inches.

Fishing. Tilefish were unknown until May 1879, when a Cod fisherman caught several off Nantucket Shoals in water 900 feet deep. The next two summers proved Tilefish were plentiful enough to support a fishery, and the fish were popular in the market. Then disaster struck. News of a large fish kill came in March 1882 as ship after ship reported multitudes of dead fish. Estimates totaled at least 1.5 million sighted. It is believed that cold water flooded the bottom where the fish lived. Tilefish were watched for the next 17 years, and in 1915 they seemed numerous

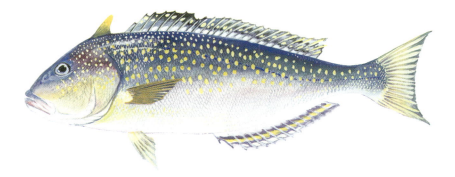

enough for a commercial fishery. Market development was slow, although 11 million pounds were landed in 1917. The demand did not hold up, and the catches dwindled to about 500 thousand pounds annually.

The same gear, longlines, used in the early 1900s is still used today. Longlines are coiled in large tubs aboard fishing vessels. Each tub contains about half a mile of line. Every 15 feet or so, branch lines, or snoods, are tied to the mainline. Each snood is approximately 18 inches long and has a 7/0 to 9/0 hook baited with squid or cut fish. The longlines are set on the bottom and are buoyed at both ends. In addition to longlines, commercial fishermen use otter trawls and electric snapper reels.

Sport fishermen catch the species through-out its range. Electric reels are used to raise and lower terminal tackle, which consists of strong leader, two large hooks, and a heavy sinker. Most Golden Tilefish caught range from 10 to 24 pounds but fish as large as 60 pounds are not uncommon.

Preparation. The flesh is white, flaky, and easily filleted. Fish are excellent baked and broiled. Some believe the taste resembles that of a crab or lobster, and the meat is delicious dipped in melted butter.

Suggested Readings. 52.

GREATER AMBERJACK
Seriola dumerili

Amberjack

Habits. There are many species in the family Carangidae that are important to fisheries. The Florida Pompano is perhaps the most popular, but other carangids such as the Greater Amberjack, Almaco Jack, *Seriola rivoliana*, Banded Rudderfish, *S. zonata*, Lesser Amberjack, *S. fasciata*, Blue Runner, *Caranx crysos*, Crevalle Jack, *C. hippos*, Bar Jack, *C. ruber*, Permit, *Trachinotus falcatus*, and African Pompano, *Alectis ciliaris*, are all excellent game fish. The members of the genus *Seriola* are the largest jacks, some weighing nearly 200 pounds.

Greater Amberjack are found in the Mediterranean Sea and the Atlantic, Pacific, and Indian Oceans. In the western Atlantic, they are distributed from Nova Scotia to Brazil, including the Gulf of Mexico and the Caribbean, where they concentrate around reefs, rock outcrops, and wrecks.

The coloration is characterized by a dark stripe on the head, which extends from the origin of the first dorsal fin through the eye. The back is blue or olivaceous; the sides and belly are silvery-white. Occasionally, there is an amber, even pinkish, cast to the body. Juveniles have five or six dark vertical bars along the sides.

The four species of *Seriola* are similar in appearance, but may be distinguished by the length of the anal fin base, number of gill rakers, and numbers of spines and rays in the dorsal fins. Banded Rudderfish have a short anal fin base, 12 to 16 gill rakers, 8 dorsal spines, and 34 to 39 dorsal rays. Greater Amberjack have a long anal fin base, 11 to 19 gill rakers, 7 dorsal spines, and 30 to 34 dorsal rays. Almaco Jack have a long anal fin base, 21 to 26 gill rakers, 7 dorsal spines, and 28 to 31 dorsal fin rays. Lesser Amberjack have a long anal fin base, 21 to 24 gill rakers, 8 dorsal spines, and 29 to 32 dorsal fin rays.

Greater Amberjack spawn from March through July with a peak in May or June for much of the region. Some females are first able to reproduce between their third and fourth years, or when they are about 33.5 inches long; all are sexually mature by age 5. Greater Amberjack have been aged to 10 years; they reach a weight of at least 190 pounds and a length of 6 feet. Approximate average lengths for fish aged 1 to 10 years are 16.4, 24.7, 31.5, 37.2, 40.2, 43.3, 46, 49.9, 52.8, and 55 inches. Amberjacks are voracious predators that forage over reefs and wrecks in small groups. To scuba divers, Amberjacks are almost constant companions that frolic over and around submerged objects. The diet

consists of crabs, squids, Round Herring, Round Scad, filefish, Little Tunny, and other fishes.

Fishing. The Greater Amberjack is a powerful fish that will test angler and tackle with its strong, deep-running fight. Embolism, which proves fatal to most deep-water species, does not reduce the endurance of Amberjacks. Once hooked, they constantly struggle to escape. Although some are caught by commercial fishermen using longlines, pound nets, gill nets, traps, and trawls, most are landed by recreational fishermen.

Anglers catch Amberjacks by still fishing with live or cut baits and by trolling with spoons and other deep-running artificial lures.

Preparation. Except in local, Hispanic communities, Amberjacks are seldom eaten in the United States. This rejection is partially due to the frequent occurrence of tapeworms, which encyst in the caudal musculature. In the Caribbean, the species also has been associated with ciguatera poisoning. Fish caught off the southeastern United States and properly cleaned are excellent charcoal broiled, basted with butter, and garlic and onion salts.

Suggested Readings. 17, 20, 46, 122.

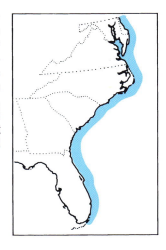

ALMACO JACK
Seriola rivoliana

Amberjack

Habits. Saltwater fishermen along the southeastern United States catch Almaco Jack less frequently than they do Greater Amberjack. This probably happens because the species usually occurs deeper than Greater Amberjack, and is reported to be more oceanic in its habits. Almaco Jack are similar in appearance to Greater Amberjack, but have conspicuously long lobes on the second dorsal and anal fins. The species is found in warm waters on both sides of the Atlantic. In the western Atlantic, the range extends from Massachusetts to Brazil, although fish are rarely caught north of North Carolina. The body and fins are generally a uniform dark brown or dark bluish-green. The lower sides and belly are lighter, sometimes with a lavender or brassy tint.

The species is large, attaining a maximum length of about 38 inches and a weight of 55 pounds. No information is available on its life history. One would expect the Almaco Jack's reproductive, growth, and feeding characteristics to closely resemble those described for the Greater Amberjack.

Fishing. Almaco Jack are caught almost exclusively by hook and line. The species is caught by recreational fishermen trolling deep-running artificial lures or fishing on the bottom with cut bait as well as by commercial snapper fishermen. Almaco are excellent sport fish, making very strong, deep runs when hooked. They are usually caught around buoys, wrecks, or natural reefs.

Preparation. The flesh is edible, but often contains tapeworms, which are encysted in the caudal peduncle musculature. This problem is easily resolved because the parasitized flesh can be cut away. Although associated with ciguatera poisoning in the Caribbean, the species may be safely consumed if caught off the southeastern United States. Suggested methods of preparation are to broil in the oven or baste with melted butter on the charcoal grill.

The following recipe is often used with tuna, but other fishes including amberjack, may substitute. The ingredients are 3 cups of cooked, flaked fish, 2½ cups of drained, chopped canned pineapple, 2 cups of green pepper strips, 2 tablespoons of butter, ⅔ cup of pineapple syrup, 1 chicken bouillon cube, 1 cup of boiling water, 2 tablespoons of cornstarch, 2 tablespoons of soy sauce, 2 tablespoons of

vinegar, ⅓ cup of sugar, ½ teaspoon of salt, dash of pepper, and 2 cans of chow-mein noodles.

The Sweet and Sour Fish is prepared by cooking the pineapple in butter for about 3 minutes. Add ⅓ cup of the pineapple syrup and green peppers. Cover and simmer for 10 minutes. Dissolve the bouillon cube in boiling water. Add it to the pineapple, and mix in the cornstarch with the remaining syrup. Stir. Add soy sauce, vinegar, and sugar. Cook, stirring constantly, until the ingredients are thick. Add fish, salt and pepper, and heat for 5 to 10 minutes. Serve over chow-mein noodles. Serves 6 to 8.

Suggested Readings. 17, 46, 85.

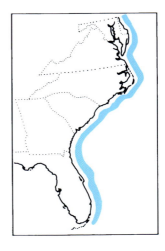

RED SNAPPER
Lutjanus campechanus
American Red Snapper

Habits. The Red Snapper is the most valuable of the snappers to commerce and recreation. Anglers consider the species to be the prize catch of all the reef fishes, and it consistently ranks near the top in value per pound of all fish on the market. The species is distributed throughout the Gulf of Mexico and up the Atlantic coast of the United States to North Carolina, occasionally to Massachusetts.

The back and upper sides are scarlet to brick red, and the lower sides and belly are lighter. Small Red Snapper, up to 10 inches, have a dark spot on the upper sides just below the soft dorsal fin. Adult Red Snapper are easily distinguished from other red-colored snappers. They are much deeper bodied than the Vermilion Snapper and not as streamlined. Red Snapper have a bright red iris, whereas the Silk Snapper has a yellow iris. Red Snapper lack the prominent black spot at the base of the pectoral fin, which is characteristic of another lutjanid, the Blackfin Snapper, *Lutjanus buccanella.* The Mutton Snapper, *L. analis,* is seldom caught north of Cape Canaveral.

Off the southeastern United States, Red Snapper occur in depths of 150 to 300 feet over both low- and high-relief hard bottom. They are opportunistic bottom feeders that consume a variety of invertebrates and small fishes. Fish are eaten more as the Red Snapper grow larger.

Spawning extends through the warmer months, beginning as early as April off North Carolina. Females as small as 10 inches and males as small as 9 inches are capable of spawning. The free-floating eggs have been hatched in the laboratory in 24 to 27 hours, and the larvae start to feed 3 days after hatching.

As with other reef fish, growth of this species is slow. Fish are about 9 inches and weigh half a pound at the end of their first year; 23 inches and 7 pounds at age 5; 33 inches and 22 pounds at age 10; and approximately 37 inches and 30 pounds when they are 14 years old. Although the maximum age is at least 16 years, most of those caught are 5 and 6 years old.

Fishing. The species is caught commercially throughout the range, primarily by handlines. Large electrically and manually powered snapper reels are used with multiple-hook rigs.

Whether fishing for pleasure or profit, consistently catching Red Snapper by hook and line is an art. Not only must one know where the best fishing grounds are located, but also the bait must be presented in a

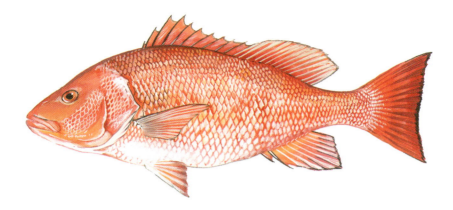

manner to entice the Snapper to bite. A fathometer and loran are necessary to pioneer new bottom as well as to relocate proven grounds and concentrations of fish. While multiple-hook rigs similar to those used for other reef fish are effective, a favorite rig for large Red Snapper is a single 7/0 hook. The hook is fastened to a 4- to 5-foot dropper off the main leader, which ends with an 8- to 16-ounce sinker. Selection of bait is critical. Squid heads with long tentacles, whole medium-size fish, and fresh bloody strips of Little Tunny or Greater Amberjack catch the big Red Snapper. The fish seem to prefer a still or very slowly moving bait. Fishing from an anchored boat is productive, but when drifting, one might free spool the line for a few minutes before slowly retrieving the slack.

Preparation. The white flesh of Red Snapper is rated the very best. It may be prepared in a variety of ways, but frying should be considered a misdemeanor crime. Baked stuffed Red Snapper smothered with cream sauce is a delightful dish made famous in New Orleans and Charleston.

Suggested Readings. 46, 57, 112.

GRAY SNAPPER
Lutjanus griseus

Mangrove Snapper

Habits. The Gray Snapper, also known as the Mangrove Snapper, is a tropical marine reef fish that commonly occurs in the western Atlantic from the northern coast of Florida to Rio de Janeiro. Young fish are occasionally found as far north as Massachusetts, but these do not indicate the presence of established local populations. The habitat is highly variable and includes irregular bottom areas offshore, such as coral reefs, rock outcroppings, and shipwrecks, to a depth of about 300 feet. Inshore, the species is found over smooth bottom, usually near pilings, rock piles, seagrass meadows, and mangrove thickets. Large fish are generally found offshore, and smaller ones in shallow water.

The Gray Snapper resembles other members of the genus *Lutjanus*, except it does not have a distinct spot on the sides, characteristic of some species, and it has a rounded, rather than a pointed, anal fin. The species is most often confused with the Cubera Snapper, *L. cyanopterus*, perhaps because of the body shape and the presence of large canine teeth. The two species may be distinguished, however, by the shape of the tooth patch on the roof of the mouth. The Cubera Snapper has a triangular-shaped patch, whereas that of the Gray Snapper is anchor-shaped. The body coloration of the Gray Snapper is highly variable. The back and upper sides are dark gray to gray-green. The lower sides and belly are grayish with a reddish tinge.

Spawning takes place in the summer, in shallow water, and usually at dusk during the time of a full moon. Ripe fish have been collected in June, July, and August. Fish 3 years old and older, or larger than about 9 inches, take part in the spawning act, which is characterized by one female being courted by one to several males. The eggs are released, fertilized, and are reported to settle unattended to the bottom. The Gray Snapper may live for as long as 21 years and grow to a length of 35 inches and a weight of 25 pounds. Average lengths of fish aged from 1 to 19 years are 3.7, 7.8, 10.9, 13.2, 15, 16.7, 18.3, 19.8, 21.1, 22.3, 23.5, 24.6, 25.4, 26.4, 27.2, 28.4, 29, 29.8, and 30.4 inches.

The diet consists primarily of crustaceans and fishes and changes as the fish grow larger. Juveniles feed on copepods, amphipods, and palaemonid shrimps. Adults eat fishes, crabs, and penaeid shrimps. Like other large lutjanids, adult Gray Snapper may leave their resident reef to feed on nearby grass flats late in the afternoon and at night.

250

Fishing. The Gray Snapper is important to recreational and commercial fisheries because it is a game fighter on sporting tackle and is excellent to eat. The species is very popular in Florida and around the Antilles, where it is caught by hook and line (rod and reel, handlines, and longlines), beach and boat seines, and traps. Anglers fish for reef fish, including the Gray Snapper, from head boats and smaller private boats using manual and electric reels, sturdy boat rods, heavy monofilament line, and two-hook bottom rigs baited with squid and cut fish. Depth recorders are useful in locating good bottom and concentrations of fish. In addition to fishing offshore, anglers also catch Gray Snapper in mangrove - and seagrass - dominated estuaries using shrimps, clams, bloodworms, and occasionally artificial lures.

Preparation. Like other commercially important snappers, the Gray has white, flaky,
easily filleted flesh. Usually marketed fresh,
it is prepared by baking or broiling.

Suggested Readings. 46, 93, 149.

LANE SNAPPER
Lutjanus synagris

Habits. The Lane Snapper is a small, vividly colored lutjanid found in the extreme southern portion of the region. Although reported from North Carolina to Brazil, including the Caribbean and Gulf of Mexico, it is seldom caught north of Florida.

The species is rose with a faint greenish tint on the back and upper sides, which reveal several obscure, vertical dark bars. A series of 8 to 10 horizontal yellow stripes traverse the lower sides, and a dark lateral spot, larger than the eye, is located below the soft dorsal fin, just above the lateral line. The position and size of this mark, in addition to an anchor-shaped tooth patch on the roof of the mouth, 18 to 22 gill rakers on the first arch, and a rounder anal fin, separate the species from its close relatives. The Mahogany Snapper, *Lutjanus mahogoni*, is similar in appearance and also has 12 soft dorsal rays, but the lateral spot is smaller and is lower on the body.

The Lane Snapper is known to occur in a variety of habitats ranging from coral reefs in clear water to grass flats and mangrove-bordered estuaries where the waters are brackish and murky.

The spawning season is extended, beginning as early as March and lasting through September. A peak in activity takes place from June through August. Both sexes are capable of reproducing for the first time when they are 1 year old and as small as 6 to 7 inches long. Depending on her size, a female may lay 300 thousand to more than 1 million pelagic eggs during a season. The juveniles immigrate to estuarine nursery areas and remain hidden in grass beds for several months before migrating to offshore reefs when they are 5 or 6 inches long.

The largest Lane Snapper ever recorded was 23 inches, weighed 5 pounds, and was probably older than 10 years. Average lengths for fish caught along Florida's east coast aged 1 to 10 years are 6.1, 8, 9.3, 10.5, 11.1, 11.9, 13.2, 15.2, 15.5, and 16 inches. These sizes for given ages agree closely with those of fish collected off Cuba.

Like other small snappers, Lane Snappers are opportunistic carnivores and feed on many different types of animals that live on or near the bottom. Adults presumably move off reefs late in the day to feed over grass beds on anchovies, scad, crabs, shrimps, worms, and mollusks. The species is fast enough to pursue and capture its prey, but it also methodically picks food from the substrate.

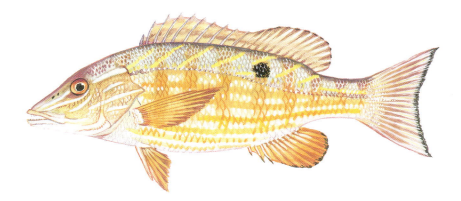

Fishing. Because it is small and occurs in shallow water, the Lane Snapper is caught by baited traps and in beach seines as well as by hook and line. It is a fierce fighter on light tackle. Fishing techniques discussed for other reef fishes also apply for this species.

Preparation. The Lane Snapper is highly regarded as a food fish. The species is caught commercially throughout its range; the flesh is marketed fresh and frozen. Small fish are usually fried; large fish are baked or broiled.

Suggested Readings. 46, 88, 148, 149.

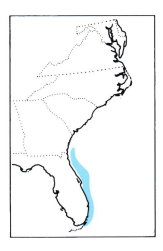

SILK SNAPPER
Lutjanus vivanus

Yelloweye Snapper

Habits. The Silk Snapper is known as Yelloweye in the Carolinas and other locations along the eastern coast of the United States, and as the Day Snapper, Day Red Snapper, Longfin Snapper, Pargo de la Alto, and West Indian Snapper in more southerly latitudes. It makes an important contribution to reef fish landings in the Southeast and appears in catches as frequently as the Red Snapper.

The yellow iris easily identifies the Silk Snapper from its close relatives, the Red Snapper and the Blackfin Snapper, *Lutjanus buccanella*, each of which possesses a red iris. The Blackfin also has a very distinct black spot at the base of the pectoral fin. Another red-colored snapper, the Vermilion, may be distinguished from the Silk Snapper by its more streamlined body and deeply forked tail. The body of the Silk Snapper is red overall, darker above and lighter below with fine, wavy longitudinal yellow lines. The caudal fin has a dusky margin.

The species commonly occurs in the western Atlantic from northern South America to North Carolina. It is found in the Gulf of Mexico and Caribbean as well as around Bermuda. The Silk Snapper generally occurs in waters somewhat deeper than those frequented by either the Red or the Vermilion Snappers. Off Bermuda the species is common at depths of 400 to 500 feet during the day, but occurs in shallower waters at night. In the Bahamas it is caught at the edge of the Gulf Stream in waters 500 to 800 feet deep, and from rough bottom 200 to 450 feet deep off the Carolinas.

Spawning occurs from late spring through summer. Earlier work off North Carolina suggests that Silk Snappers spawn from late May to late June in deep water. Recently, ripe females were collected off North Carolina in June, July, and August. The smallest Silk Snappers in spawning condition were a 9-inch female and an 11-inch male.

No information is available on age and growth. This phase of the life history is currently under investigation. Like other lutjanids, the Silk Snapper feeds on a variety of fishes and invertebrates. Some of the foods in the diet are crabs, shovel-nose lobsters, and fishes. Silk Snapper from off the Virgin Islands feed primarily on fishes, crabs, and shrimps.

Fishing. The species is caught on hook and line by recreational and commercial fishermen throughout the southeastern United States, Gulf of Mexico, and Caribbean. Fish and squid are the preferred baits, fished on the bottom in waters 200 to 800 feet deep. Seaworthy vessels, loran,

depth recorder, and electric reels are used to catch this deep-water fish. Although they may attain a length of 3 feet and a weight of 40 pounds, the average Silk Snapper landed off the Carolinas weighs between 10 and 11 pounds and is approximately 26 inches long. The species is generally smaller in other areas of its range. Silk Snapper can be caught year-round off the southeastern United States by methods previously described for other deep-water reef fish.

Preparation. This excellent food fish is usually marketed fresh. The methods of preparation described for the Red Snapper apply equally well for this species.

Suggested Readings. 46, 57, 148.

YELLOWTAIL SNAPPER
Ocyurus chrysurus

Habits. The Yellowtail Snapper is a colorful tropical reef fish with a streamlined body and a deeply forked tail. The species is distributed from North Carolina to southeastern Brazil, but is most abundant in the Bahamas, off south Florida, and in the Caribbean. It appears to have the same role in the tropical reef fish community that the Vermilion Snapper has with reef fish assemblages in the more northerly latitudes in the region. Both species form schools and are found above the bottom over hard substrates in waters 60 to 300 feet deep.

The scientific name roughly translates to "swift-swimming golden fish." The coloration is characterized by a prominent lateral yellow stripe originating on the snout, widening posteriorly, and finally covering the caudal fin. The back and upper sides are olive to bluish with yellow irregular spots. The belly and lower sides have narrow longitudinal stripes that are pale red to yellow, and the fins are yellowish.

Spawning takes place from April through August, with a peak in June and July. Some females are sexually mature as 2-year-olds; most are mature by 3; and all are capable of reproducing when they are 4. The number of pelagic eggs spawned varies from about 11 thousand for a 9-inch fish to more than 1.5 million for a female 23 inches long. Research in south Florida indicates that mature fish migrate offshore to deeper water to spawn.

Yellowtail Snappers have been aged as old as 14 years; they may attain a maximum length of about 28 inches and a weight of 7 pounds. Most of those caught are only 2 to 5 years old, and range from ½ to 1½ pounds. The size at a given age for males and females is similar for fish younger than 5 years, but older females may be larger than males of the same age. Approximate lengths for ages 1 to 14 are 6, 10.6, 13.1, 15, 16.4, 17.8, 18.5, 20.1, 20.5, 21.1, 21.6, 22.2, 22.6, and 22.8 inches.

The shape of the body and tail and the size of the mouth and eye suggest that Yellowtail Snappers feed differently from most lutjanids. The majority of the animals making up the diet live off the bottom. By contrast, most western Atlantic snappers feed predominantly on benthic fish and large invertebrates. Yellowtails eat small pelagic crustaceans, pelagic worms, gastropods, ctenophores, salps, and tunicates. Usually, fish that feed on plankton do so at night.

Fishing. Fishermen have the highest respect for the Yellowtail Snapper as a sport fish and also regard it as a quality food fish. Commercially, the

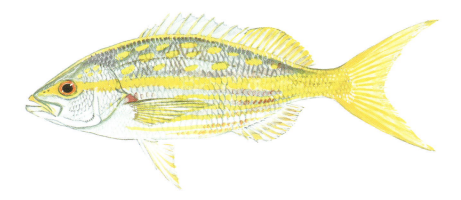

species is caught by hook and line, baited trap, trammel net, and beach seine. Most are landed and marketed fresh in Cuba, Mexico, the United States, and Venezuela. Anglers use cut fish and squid to catch Yellowtails inshore by fishing on the bottom from bridges and piers, and catch them offshore by fishing over reefs from small private boats and larger head boats. Some fishermen attract schools by baiting burlap bags with finely chopped meat and then lowering and raising the bag to bring the fish to the boat. Tackle described for Vermilion Snapper and Red Porgy apply for this species. Like Vermilion Snappers, Yellowtails may be difficult to hook because their mouths are small, and because they are not as agressive as other snappers and groupers in taking the bait.

Preparation. Fried Yellowtail Snappers are a specialty in many fine Cuban restaurants. The flesh is also highly esteemed baked, broiled, and cooked over charcoal. It is one of the most preferred eating fishes in the region.

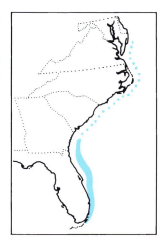

Suggested Readings. 17, 46, 70.

VERMILION SNAPPER
Rhomboplites aurorubens

Beeliner, Night Snapper

Habits. The Vermilion Snapper is the most frequently caught snapper along the southeastern United States, and is also one of the smallest, attaining a length of 25 inches and a weight of only 6 pounds. The species is found in tropical and warm temperate waters of the western Atlantic from Cape Hatteras to southeastern Brazil, including Bermuda, the West Indies, and the Gulf of Mexico. Off the United States the preferred habitat is irregular reeflike bottom in waters ranging in depth from 80 to 350 feet. In some tropical areas of the Atlantic, the species is replaced by its close relative, the Yellowtail Snapper, *Ocyurus chrysurus*, which occupies the same type of habitat and feeds on similar foods.

Vermilions are beautifully colored and have streamlined bodies. The species name, *aurorubens*, means "golden red," and for good reason. The body is vermilion above and pale to silver white below. Narrow yellow-gold streaks, some horizontal and others oblique, occur below the lateral line. The dorsal fin is rosy colored with a yellow margin. The caudal fin is red, but has a faint black margin.

Some females reach sexual maturity during the third year, when they are 10 to 12 inches long. Most do not mature until their fourth year, when they are 14 to 16 inches long. Multiple spawning is characteristic of the species, and free-floating eggs are released offshore from late April through September. A small female, 10 inches long, lays approximately 8 thousand eggs, and a fish 22 inches long may lay 1.8 million. Females, which grow larger and live longer than males, may reach an age of 10 years. Most of the fish caught, however, are 4 to 5 years old. A 1-year-old fish is about 5 inches long; a 5-year-old is about 16; and a Vermilion Snapper 10 years of age is about 24 inches long.

Unlike most snappers, which feed on large fishes and crustaceans on the bottom, Vermilion Snappers forage on small animals high in the water column. Favorite foods are small crustaceans (copepods, amphipods, stomatopods, crabs, and shrimps), squids, small fishes, and fish eggs. This midwater feeding behavior enables fishermen to chum Vermilion Snapper to the surface by filling bags with bait, lowering them to the bottom, and then slowly raising the bags to the boat.

Fishing. Although the species is relatively sedentary, and occurs off the southeastern United States year-round, most Vermilion Snappers are caught from April through November. Bad weather usually reduces offshore fishing during winter and early spring. Two pieces of naviga-

tional equipment are very important: loran to relocate good fishing grounds, and a recording fathometer to find promising bottom and aggregations of fish. Vermilion Snapper schools are easy to mark, and appear as fine, V-shaped traces on the recorder. Fishing is best inshore over irregular bottom in water 80 to 180 feet deep and along the shelf break where the depth ranges from 240 to 350 feet. Like other reef fishes, Vermilions bite best at sunrise and just before dark. However, on moonlight nights good catches may be made from about 8 to 10 pm. Sturdy boat rods and electrically or manually operated reels with 80-pound monofilament line are used by sport fishermen. Terminal tackle usually consists of a heavy sinker and two 4/0 to 6/0 hooks baited with squid or cut fish rigged on a 200-pound test monofilament leader. Commercially, the species is harvested by hook and line, traps, and trawls. The market price is good, often approaching that of Red Snapper.

Preparation. Vermilion Snapper are delicious fried, baked, and broiled. The roe is excellent pan fried in butter or broiled.

Suggested Readings. 56, 57, 148.

TOMTATE
Haemulon aurolineatum

Habits. One of the smallest of the grunts, the Tomtate is distributed in the Atlantic from Cape Hatteras to Brazil, including the Gulf of Mexico, the Central American coast, and the Caribbean. Preferred habitat is rough bottom areas, which are scattered over the otherwise smooth plain of the continental shelf. Tomtates are seldom found in waters less than 54°F.

Because of their small size, they are not highly regarded by fishermen. The species is important, however, as food for large fish-eating reef fishes. Tomtates are colorful inhabitants of natural and artificial reefs. Often seen by recreational divers, they are easily approached and may be fed by hand. Large schools frequently accompany divers and serve as a warning when large fish—sharks and amberjacks—are near. The fish react by tightening their schools and moving closer to the bottom and away from the direction of the predator's approach.

They are silver white overall with a yellow-brown stripe running the length of the body and ending as a black blotch at the base of the caudal fin. This spot is also evident on most juvenile grunts. The mark may become lost in older, larger fish. The species name, *aurolineatum*, comes from the Latin, meaning "marked with gold lines." The inside of the mouth is bright red.

Females may mature when as small as 5.5 inches and males when as small as 6.5 inches. About half of all fish 3 to 5 years old are sexually mature, and all those older than age 5 are capable of reproducing. The spawning season is in the spring, with a peak of activity in April along the southeastern United States. The number of eggs produced by a female ranges from a few thousand to more than 70 thousand.

Tomtates may live as long as 9 years, reaching a length of 12 inches and a weight of 1 pound. Length at ages 1, 2, 5, and 9 are 5, 6.5, 9, and 11 inches. Like other members of the family Haemulidae, Tomtates feed on the bottom on small invertebrates such as worms, snails, clams, crabs, shrimps, and amphipods. Schools have been seen migrating short distances from reefs to grass beds to feed late in the afternoon and at night. Tomtates in turn serve as food for snappers, groupers, and mackerels.

Fishing. In the United States, Tomtates are caught by handlines, traps, and trawls. Because of their small size and low market price, the species is usually discarded at sea or used as bait for other fish. A live Tomtate

fished on the bottom is an excellent bait for large groupers and snappers. They also may be used to catch mackerels and other pelagic species by suspending them near the surface. Fishing techniques discussed for other inshore reef fish apply equally well for this species.

Preparation. Tomtates seldom wind up on the table. Although small and bony, they are good fried.

Suggested Readings. 37, 46, 83.

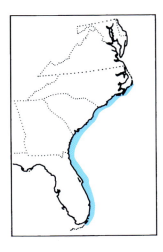

WHITE GRUNT
Haemulon plumieri

Grunt, Redmouth

Habits. French naturalist Father Plumier first sketched the White Grunt in Martinique in the nineteenth century, and was rewarded for his efforts by having the species named for him. The genus name, *Haemulon*, comes from the Greek words *haimia*, meaning "blood," and *oulon*, meaning "mouth," because the interior of the mouth is bright red.

The White Grunt is a tropical and warm-temperate water species that inhabits irregular bottom areas of the continental shelf from Virginia to Brazil, including Bermuda, the Caribbean, and the Gulf of Mexico. Although catches of White Grunt are made along most of the southeastern United States, the species is infrequently caught off northeastern Florida.

One of the more colorful members of the family Haemulidae, the White Grunt is silver gray, with numerous blue and yellow stripes on the head and body. On some individuals the scales are tipped with bronze. The pectoral fins are chalky and the other fins are gray. The lining of the body cavity, or peritoneum, is black.

White Grunt are generalized carnivores that feed on bottom-dwelling invertebrates by rooting around in sand and shell hash between rocky ledges and at the bases of coral formations. Preferred foods are worms—sipunculids and annelids—crabs, shrimps, mollusks, and small fishes. Fish become sexually active for the first time during their third year, when they are about 10 inches long. Off the southeastern United States, spawning occurs in late spring and summer, or from May through July. A small female spawning for the first time may lay 62 thousand eggs, whereas a large fish is capable of producing more than 1 million ova during a spawning season.

The species is reported to live as long as 13 years, attaining a length of 25 inches and a weight of 8 pounds. Like other reef fishes, White Grunts grow slowly. By the end of the first year, fish are approximately 7 inches long; at age 5 they measure 13 inches; and by age 13 White Grunt are about 21 inches long.

Fishing. Handlines, traps, seines, and trawls are used by commercial fishermen to catch White Grunt. However, the market price is low, and White Grunt are seldom targeted by commercial fisheries in the United States. Sport fishermen on charter boats and head boats use manually and electrically powered reels to catch the species over natural and artificial reefs. After locating concentrations of fish, boats either anchor

or drift over good fishing spots. Scamp, porgies, triggerfish, Vermilion Snapper, and White Grunt often are caught at the same sites. Small hooks, baited with squid, and medium-weight sinkers are the standard bottom rigs.

Preparation. Because the fish are small and bony, they are usually fried. Restaurants in the Florida Keys often include grits and fried grunt on breakfast menus.

Suggested Readings. 17, 37, 46, 121.

263

SPOTTAIL PINFISH
Diplodus holbrooki

Spottail Bream

Habits. The Spottail Pinfish is a medium-sized member of the porgy family (Sparidae), attaining a maximum length of approximately 17 inches and a weight of 3 pounds. It is one of the reef fishes most frequently observed by divers exploring irregular bottom areas along the southeastern United States coast.

The distribution extends from Chesapeake Bay to the Florida Keys and includes the northeastern portion of the Gulf of Mexico. Spottail Pinfish typically inhabit two different habitats in the South Atlantic Bight. Young fish are found in high-salinity inshore waters on sparsely vegetated sand-mud bottom, as well as around pilings and jetties in bays and harbors. Adults populate irregular bottoms such as rock piles, reefs, and wrecks to a depth of about 100 feet.

Spottail Pinfish have a dusky to metallic blue back, silvery sides and a large, dark blotch or saddle that covers the sides of the caudal peduncle. Juveniles often have a series of narrow dark bands on the sides. The genus *Diplodus* is easily distinguished from other porgies because of the black spot, deep rounded body, long pectoral fins, and the well-developed incisor-shaped teeth in the front of the mouth.

Two other similarly shaped sparids, the Sea Bream, *Archosargus rhomboidalis*, and the Silver Porgy, *Diplodus argenteus*, are found in the extreme southern part of the region. They are easily distinguished from the Spottail Pinfish. The Sea Bream lacks the spot on the caudal peduncle, and although the Silver Porgy possesses the spot, it is smaller, and is located above the lateral line.

Spawning is believed to take place in the late winter and early spring when ripe females release their pelagic eggs in offshore waters. Compared with most species of reef fishes, Spottail Pinfish grow rapidly and are short-lived. Average lengths for fish aged 1 to 10 years are 4.8, 6.9, 8.4, 9.4, 10.2, 10.8, 11.5, 12, 12.8, and 14.4 inches.

The strong molars and incisorlike teeth enable the species to feed on a variety of small fishes and invertebrates such as crabs, barnacles, sea urchins, worms, and snails. Food items are picked from the substrate, and are crushed by the powerful teeth.

Fishing. The species is taken incidentally to other reef fishes throughout its range by hook and line, trawls, traps, seines, and gill nets. The small mouth size usually prevents large numbers of the species from being captured by recreational fishermen.

264

Preparation. Although the flesh is of good quality, it is seldom marketed. This is because the fish are relatively small, and are not caught in large numbers. Trawls, which might otherwise be effective, are unable to fish the rough bottom. Like other sparids, Spottail Pinfish may be prepared by frying, baking, and broiling.

Suggested Readings. 46, 154.

WHITEBONE PORGY
Calamus leucosteus

Chocolate Porgy

Habits. The Whitebone Porgy is the most commonly caught member of the genus *Calamus* in the South Atlantic Bight from Cape Hatteras to Cape Canaveral. It also occurs to the Florida Keys, along with a multitude of other tropical porgies, and throughout the Gulf of Mexico. The preferred habitat is high- and low-profile reef-like bottom in water ranging from 100 to 240 feet in depth.

The body is silvery overall, with regular brown markings of varying intensity on the sides, more like splotches than spots. Brown markings also occur on the fins, and occasionally the sides bear brown crossbars. The species can be distinguished from two other frequently caught deepwater porgies, the Red Porgy, *Pagrus pagrus*, and Knobbed Porgy, *Calamus nodosus*. The former is predominantly pink; the latter has a very steep sloping forehead and cheeks that are speckled with bright blue and yellow. Although most members of the genus have 14 to 15 pectoral rays, the Whitebone has 16.

Very little was known about the life history of the species until recently. Like other members of the family Sparidae, Whitebone Porgies feed on the bottom, picking up crabs, shrimps, snails, worms, and sea urchins that hide among the rocks, sponges, and corals. Strong teeth enable porgies to crush heavy-shelled animals, and they are fast enough to capture fish. The species is known to live as long as 12 years, reaching a length of 18 inches and a weight of 5 pounds. The Whitebone Porgy not only attains a relatively small size but also grows at a slow rate. Approximate lengths for ages 1, 2, 5, 10, and 12 years are 6, 9, 12, 13, and 14 inches.

Both sexes apparently mature early, between their first and second years of life. Spawning extends from April through August, with a peak in the activity during May. Females may lay between 30 thousand and 1 million pelagic eggs during a season. Whitebone Porgies are protogynous hermaphrodites; most females change sex as they grow older. Large fish are almost always males.

Fishing. Whitebone Porgy represent only a small fraction of the commercial landings of reef fish along the southeastern United States. The species is never very plentiful at any fishing location. Porgies are caught incidentally to groupers, snappers, and Black Sea Bass by handlines, traps, and trawls. Recreational fishermen on charter boats and head boats catch the species throughout the range. The same

266

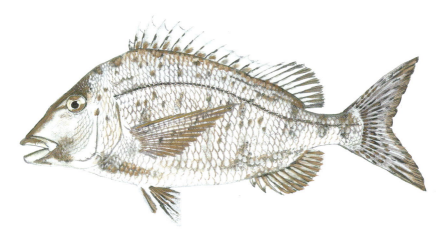

equipment used to fish for other reef fishes—loran, depth recorder, electric-powered reels, sturdy boat rods, and heavy sinkers—is used to catch Whitebone Porgy.

Preparation. The flesh is white and flaky, although somewhat bony. Porgies may be baked or broiled, but are best fried. It is alleged that Whitebone Porgies as well as other reef fishes have been served in restaurants as groupers or snappers.

Suggested Readings. 163.

KNOBBED PORGY

Calamus nodosus

Key West Porgy

Habits. The Knobbed Porgy is a beautifully colored, deep-bodied sparid that has a conspicuously steep forehead and bony protrusions just in front of the eyes. The body is iridescent silvery blue, and the head is purplish with numerous yellow-bronze spots and blue streaks under the eyes.

The species inhabits hard-bottom areas—coral reefs, rock outcroppings, and wrecks—in waters 90 to 300 feet deep from North Carolina to the Florida Keys and throughout much of the Gulf of Mexico. Knobbed Porgy are generally caught with other reef species such as Red Porgy, Whitebone Porgy, White Grunt, Gag, Scamp, and Red Grouper along the southeastern United States.

Spawning occurs at sea in May and June. Like other porgies studied in the region, Knobbed Porgy probably attain sexual maturity when they are 4 or 5 years old and lay thousands of pelagic eggs. The species is long-lived and slow growing, reaching a maximum size of about 20 inches and having a known life span of at least 17 years. Average length for fish aged 1 to 17 years are 7.6, 9.9, 11.5, 12.9, 13.9, 14.6, 15.1, 15.9, 16.4, 16.7, 16.9, 17.4, 18, 18.4, 19.1, 19.5, and 19.8 inches.

Because they have large incisors and strong molars, Knobbed Porgy are able to crush and consume hard-bodied animals such as clams, snails, crabs, sea urchins, starfish, and barnacles. They are fast enough to capture small fishes, but these appear less frequently than invertebrates in the diet.

Fishing. The species is captured almost exclusively by hook and line throughout its range. Occasionally, individuals are caught by traps and trawls. Although prized by both commercial and recreational fishermen, Knobbed Porgy are seldom landed in large numbers. Boats, fishing, tackle and electronic fish-finding gear described for Red Porgy and other inshore reef fishes are also needed to catch this species.

Preparation. The meat is marketed fresh, is white and flaky, and has an excellent flavor. It is easily filleted and may be fried, baked or broiled. A suggested method of preparing is Fish Stuffed with Shrimp. This recipe may be used with any marine fish that has lean, flaky meat.

The ingredients are 1 cup of boiled shrimp, 2 pounds of fish fillets, 1 cup of cooked wild rice, ½ teaspoon of curry powder, ½ teaspoon salt, ½ cup of melted butter, and paprika. To prepare, combine the shrimp,

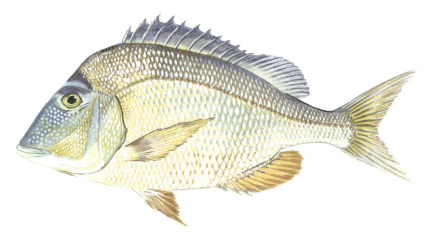

rice, curry powder, salt, and half of the butter. Spread between the fillets and fasten them together with toothpicks. Pour remaining butter over the fish, sprinkle paprika on top, and bake in the oven at 350°F for 30 to 40 minutes. Serves 4.

Suggested Readings. 67, 148.

RED PORGY

Pagrus pagrus

Pink Porgy, Silver Snapper

Habits. Anglers fishing from charter boats and head boats for reef fish along the southeastern United States often catch Red Porgy. The species ranks second only to Black Sea Bass as the fish most frequently caught while bottom fishing offshore from Cape Hatteras to Cape Canaveral.

Red Porgy occur in deep warm-water zones of continental shelves on both sides of the Atlantic. They are found in the eastern Atlantic from the British Isles south to Angola off the southwest coast of Africa. In the western Atlantic, the species occurs from North Carolina to Argentina, but has not been reported from the Caribbean or Central America. Preferred habitat along the southeastern United States is rough bottom at depths ranging from 90 to 350 feet, bathed by warm Gulf Stream waters, 59° to 73°F.

Fish color is reddish above and silver white below, highlighted by rows of small blue spots along the upper body and by two blue streaks, one above and the other below the eye. The dentition is pronounced, and the back teeth are molarlike.

Red Porgy are protogynous hermaphrodites, changing sex from female to male with increased size. Most fish longer than 18 inches are males. Approximately 37 percent of the females are mature at age 2, 81 percent by age 3, and all are capable of reproducing by the fourth year. A female 12 inches long may lay 49 thousand eggs and an exceptionally large female 20 inches long may lay 489 thousand at one time. Spawning takes place at sea from January through April. The eggs and young are pelagic before settling to the bottom.

Although fish have been aged to 15 years, most caught are 4 to 7 years old. The average Red Porgy landed off the Carolinas is about 16.5 inches long and weighs 2¼ pounds. Growth is rapid for the first 4 years of life. Average lengths for both sexes aged 1 to 15 years are 7, 10, 12.4, 14.5, 16.2, 17.2, 18.2, 19.1, 19.8, 20.7, 21.7, 22.5, 23.6, 24.4, and 25.2 inches. Red Porgy feed on the bottom, browsing on worms, snails, crabs, and sea urchins, which are crushed by the strong teeth. They occasionally feed on small fishes such as Round Scad and Tomtate.

Fishing. Bottom trawls, traps, and hook and line are used to capture Red Porgy throughout most of the range. Off the southeastern United States the species is taken almost exclusively by hook and line by both sport and commercial fisherman. Tackle used must be sturdy enough to resist hangups on the bottom and also to land large fish.

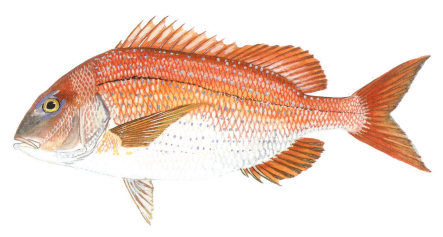

A typical outfit may include a 6/0 to 9/0 electric powered reel and a 5- to 6-foot boat rod with 80- to 120-pound line with two 4/0 to 7/0 hooks baited with squid or cut fish. A single sinker is used and varies in weight from 8 to 28 ounces depending on the depth and current velocity. Depth recorders locate promising bottom and concentrations of fish. When they are biting, Red Porgy are very easy to catch.

Preparation. The white, flaky flesh resembles that of snappers and may be baked, broiled, fried, or basted over charcoal.

Suggested Readings. 82, 86.

ATLANTIC SPADEFISH
Chaetodipterus faber

Angelfish

Habits. The Atlantic Spadefish is a medium-size marine fish commonly found schooling near coastal reefs, rocky ledges, wrecks, and pilings from New England to southern Brazil, including the Caribbean and the Gulf of Mexico. Spadefish are easily identified by their deep and laterally compressed bodies, small mouths, blunt heads, and pointed soft dorsal and anal fins.

Adults are silver gray with three to six prominent black vertical bars along the sides. The first bar passes through the eye, and the last is on the caudal peduncle. Juvenile Spadefish are usually black and are frequently misidentified. Because the species prefers warm water, it typically occurs in deep water during the winter in temperate areas, and moves inshore in the summer. Temperature and salinity extremes have been reported as 50° to 92°F and 4 to 43 ppt.

Spawning takes place in open water, at the surface during the summer when water temperatures range from about 75° to 85°F. Large spawning aggregations are usually seen near buoys or anchored boats on calm, warm, sunny days. From a distance it is difficult to tell whether the gently rolling fish are feeding or spawning. However, a closer observation reveals mated pairs in their courtship displays. During a spawning period lasting 10 to 30 minutes, a female may lay a million eggs. The eggs are buoyant and hatch in about 24 hours in water 81°F.

The Atlantic Spadefish has been described as one of the most generalized reef fish in its food habits. The species not only lurks in reef crevices, picking up animals and plants from the substrate, but also feeds on very small animals that are found off the bottom, at mid-depths, and near the surface. The diet is diverse and includes sponges, polychaetes, tunicates, soft corals, algae, amphipods, sea cucumbers, feather stars, sea anemones, sabellid worms, and crab and lobster larvae. No information is available on the size of Atlantic Spadefish at a given age.

Fishing. Atlantic Spadefish are caught by commercial fishermen incidental to other species in traps, seines, and trawls. The species is very difficult to catch on hook and line because of the small mouth size, and because most types of food in the diet are not usually used as bait. Some Spadefish are landed by anglers using tiny hooks baited with pieces of shrimp and by divers using spearguns. In addition, fishermen occasion-

272

ally snag them with unbaited treble hooks from around the pilings of ocean fishing piers.

Preparation. Sold fresh in Caribbean and Central American fish markets, the flesh is reported to have an excellent taste. It does, however, have an unusual, rather tough texture.

Suggested Readings. 29, 46, 71, 121.

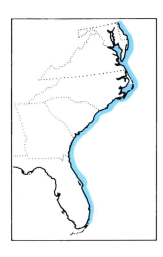

HOGFISH
Lachnolaimus maximus

Habits. The Hogfish, not to be confused by its name with the Pigfish, is an unusually large member of the family Labridae, or wrasses. Whereas most wrasses are small reef fish such as the brilliant yellow-and-red Spanish Hogfish, *Bodianus rufus*, and the Spotfin Hogfish, *B. pulchellus*, the Hogfish reaches a weight of about 25 pounds. The species has a long, piglike snout, protrusible jaws with thick lips and strong canine teeth. The first three spines of the dorsal fin, as well as the upper and lower tips of the caudal fin, are extended into long filaments.

Color is highly variable, changing with fish size. Adults vary from pink to deep wine red. The scales on the back are often edged in yellow, and a dark spot is at the rear base of the dorsal fin. This spot disappears with age. Males possess a dark oblique band that covers the top portion of the head, extending to the tip of the snout. Juveniles are much lighter overall, being pink and gray with white mottling along the sides.

Distributed from North Carolina and Bermuda to the northern coast of South America, the Hogfish is common throughout the Caribbean. It inhabits hard bottom areas—coral reefs, rocky ledges, and wrecks —and occasionally ventures over adjacent open sand. The species usually forms loose aggregations of 5 to 20 fish.

The Hogfish is a protogynous hermaphrodite that spawns from September to April off the coast of Florida. A peak in activity occurs in February and March. The time of spawning for other areas in the region is unknown. The smallest size at which females are capable of reproducing is about 8 inches. Most mature at larger sizes. Depending on their size, females release from 41 thousand to 147 thousand eggs.

Information on age and growth is not very conclusive. Only females have been aged and these do not exceed 4 years. Approximate lengths for fish aged 1 to 4 years are 10.6, 12.7, 15, and 16.8 inches. Like most species of reef fish, Hogfish are opportunistic, thus nonselective, in their feeding habits. They really do not care what the food is, as long as they can get it in their mouths. Hogfish generally feed on sessile or slow-moving animals such as clams, snails, crabs, and sea urchins. These invertebrates are crushed with the strong teeth.

Fishing. Although an excellent food fish, the species is of little commercial value since so few are caught. It is prized by anglers in the region, particularly in Florida where it is the fish most frequently speared by divers.

Preparation. The white, flaky meat, which is reported to taste like a combination of lobster and grouper, is marketed fresh and frozen. It is delicious baked or cooked over charcoal and then dipped in melted butter.

Suggested Readings. 17, 39, 46.

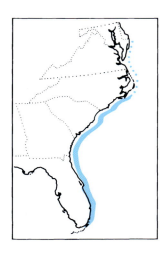

GREAT BARRACUDA
Sphyraena barracuda

Barracuda

Habits. A flashy and aggressive fighter, the Great Barracuda is often called the Tiger of the Sea. The species has gained a reputation not only as an excellent game fish but also as a threat to swimmers and divers. Although attacks on humans rarely result in death, severe lacerations have been authenticated on numerous occasions by the unmistakable tooth marks. Cleaver-like bites of two nearly parallel rows of punctures are distinguishable from those produced by sharks. The Great Barracuda is found in all tropical seas except the eastern Pacific. In the western Atlantic, they occur from Massachusetts to Brazil, including the Caribbean and the Gulf of Mexico. The preferred habitat is high-profile bottom such as reefs and wrecks in waters that are 68°F or warmer.

Barracuda are pike-like fishes, elongated and slender with long jaws and protruding, razor-sharp teeth. The body is colored silver overall, with dark green to gray along the back. Blotches on the lower sides are variable in number, size, and position. The species reaches a length of 6 feet and a weight slightly greater than 100 pounds. Other members of the family Sphyraenidae, the sennets (the Northern Sennet, *Sphyraena borealis*, and the Southern Sennet, *S. picudilla*), are often mistakenly identified as Barracudas. Sennets not only are much smaller (only 10 to 20 inches long) but also have more scales along the lateral line; they have nine anal rays, whereas Great Barracuda have seven or eight.

Barracuda mature early in life: males when they are aged 2 (18 inches) or 3 (20 inches) years and females when they are 3 or 4 years old (26 inches long). The spawning season extends from April through September. A female 35 inches long may lay 0.5 million eggs during a spawning season. While the species is known to live as long as 14 years, most of the fish caught are 4 to 6 years old. The average Barracuda is about 11 inches long at the end of the first year's growth, 30 inches long by the end of the fifth year, and 41 inches by the tenth. Great Barracuda are piscivorous and feed on many species of fish. Favorite foods are jacks, needlefish, silversides, parrotfish, and filefish.

Fishing. The species has little commercial value because the market price is low. In the more southern part of the range, the flesh, particularly of larger fish, is considered toxic, being associated with fish poisoning, or ciguatera. Most anglers catch Barracuda by trolling spoons, feathered jigs with strips of fish, Bucktails, or brightly colored

rubber tubing, which are eel-like and spin as they move through the water.

The trick to catching the species seems to be lure action as much as anything else. Trolling or retrieval speed must be rapid and the lure action should be erratic to excite the fish into biting. Some fishermen use spinning and bait-casting tackle to cast topwater plugs. For shallow-water casting, the ideal lure is a plug about 4 inches long. It should be made of wood or very durable plastic so it won't be destroyed by the Great Barracuda's teeth. Wire leaders are essential regardless of the type of tackle used.

Preparation. In the more northern areas of their range, Barracuda are safe to eat. Fillets are excellent basted and cooked over a charcoal fire.

Suggested Readings. 41, 46.

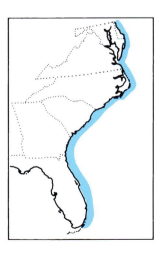

GRAY TRIGGERFISH
Balistes capriscus

Triggerfish

Habits. The Gray Triggerfish is a strange-looking fish with large incisor teeth and a deep, laterally compressed body covered with tough, sandpaper-like skin. Unlike their cousins, the filefish, Triggerfish have more than one dorsal spine. It is the action of these spines which gives the fish its common name. The first spine is large; when erect, it remains so until the smaller second spine is deflexed, triggering the first. The Gray Triggerfish is easily recognized by its drab color from the more vividly colored Queen Triggerfish, *Balistes vetula*. A similar-shaped species of the same family, the Planehead Filefish, *Monacanthus hispidus*, has a longer snout, only one dorsal spine, and a long filament on the dorsal and anal fins. The body of the Gray Triggerfish is grayish overall with darker mottling. The fins are usually spotted or barred.

The species is found on both sides of the tropical and temperate Atlantic from Massachusetts to Brazil, and from England southward along the west coast of Africa. Along the southeastern United States, it typically inhabits hard bottom areas such as wrecks, rock outcroppings, and coral reefs in waters 80- to 300-feet deep. Fishes occurring in the same habitat include Red Porgy, Vermilion Snapper, White Grunt, Red Snapper, Gag, and Scamp.

Triggerfish probably reach sexual maturity when they are 3 years old (about 12 inches long). Spawning occurs offshore during the spring and summer. Unlike most reef fish, Triggerfish have demersal eggs that are deposited in guarded nests. Fecundity has been estimated as 49 thousand for a 12-inch female; 66 thousand for a 16-inch fish; and more than 90 thousand for a fish 22 inches long. Age and growth studies indicate that females live longer and attain larger sizes than males. Approximate average lengths for fish aged 1, 2, 3, 4, 5, 10, and 12 years are 4.3, 8.9, 11.9 (1.3 pounds), 14, 15.9 (3.2 pounds), 21.5, and 22 inches.

Triggerfish use undulating motions of their dorsal and anal fins to ascend and descend vertically and to hover over the bottom searching for food. The species relies on its powerful teeth to dislodge and crush shelled animals such as sea urchins, barnacles, and mussels. It also feeds on very small planktonic crustaceans and larval fishes, which are often ingested whole.

Fishing. Although some Triggerfish are taken in trawls, traps, and seines, most are caught on hook and line by commercial and recreational

fishermen. Triggerfish are difficult to hook because they nibble the bait with their small mouths. Once hooked, however, they put up a fierce fight and are brought to the surface spiraling in large circles. The bottom-fishing gear discussed for Red Porgy and Vermilion Snapper apply equally well for the Triggerfish, which is usually caught by those fishing for the more popular reef fishes.

Preparation. The firm and white flesh is excellent baked, broiled, and fried. It is also delicious prepared in a New England-style milk-base fish chowder with bacon drippings, sautéed onions, butter, salt, pepper, diced potatoes, celery, frozen mixed vegetables, thyme, bay leaves, and parsley.

Suggested Readings. 17, 46, 121.

PORCUPINEFISH
Diodon hystrix
Spiny Puffer

Habits. The family Diodontidae includes inflatable fishes that are like the puffers, but they have longer and more numerous spines covering the body. Three species are occasionally encountered by fishermen: Porcupinefish, Balloonfish, *Diodon holocanthus*, and Striped Burrfish, *Chilomycterus schoepfi*. The last has three-rooted, stout spines, or burrs that are fixed erect, as well as curved stripes and several large, dark blotches on the body. The other two species have slender spines that can fold back, and bodies that are covered with many small black-brown spots. The Porcupinefish may be distinguished from the Balloonfish by its larger spots, and by the spines on the forehead, which are shorter than those behind the pectoral fins. This identification is difficult, and many fishermen and scientists confuse the two species.

Porcupinefish have pale tan to white bodies, with a light greenish tinge, especially along the back. The fins are covered with numerous brown or black spots, and the cheeks have two dusky, vertical bars.

The species is distributed in the western Atlantic from Massachusetts to Brazil, including the Caribbean and the Gulf of Mexico. It usually inhabits warm waters, often over reefs, and is rarely seen north of Cape Hatteras. When inhabiting reefs, Porcupinefish usually occur singly, and may be seen nibbling foods from the corals, rocks, and plants that cover the bottom. Porcupinefish also concentrate around floating *Sargassum* in the Gulf Stream. They use rapid movements of their pectoral fins to swim from one patch of algae to the next to feed on crabs and shrimps that they seize with their strong, parrot-like beaks.

Porcupinefish must be constantly wary of the predators that roam the adjacent waters. Even with their ability to inflate into a spiny ball, Porcupinefish fall prey to large gamefishes such as Dolphin, Wahoo, and tunas. Little is known about the life history of the species, probably because it is scarce and is not important to fisheries. Although the maximum size is reported to be 3 feet, most fish are less than 10 inches long.

Fishing. Commercial fishermen only occasionally catch the species in trawls, seines, and pound nets. Porcupinefish are of no direct value to recreational fisheries.

Preparation. The species is not marketed in the United States. It is beyond comprehension that anyone, no matter how hungry, would even

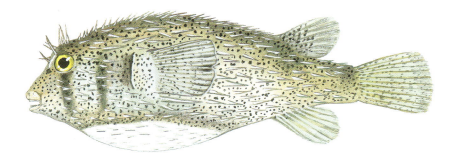

try to eat this spiny creature. Dried and varnished Porcupinefish are sometimes sold in gift shops as curios.

Suggested Readings. 46, 64, 162.

OCEANIC
PELAGIC FISHES

SHORTFIN MAKO
Isurus oxyrinchus

Mako

Habits. The mackerel sharks, makos, white sharks, and porbeagles, all of which belong to the family Lamnidae, are important to the world's shark fisheries. Of this group, the Shortfin Mako is a frequently caught species. It is large, exceeding 1,000 pounds in weight and 13 feet in length. The body is slender with a long pointed snout, a well-developed lateral keel on the caudal peduncle, and a tail with upper and lower lobes of almost equal length. The Longfin Mako, *Isurus paucus*, has a blunter snout and much longer pectoral fins by comparison. The Shortfin Mako is blue-gray to deep blue along the back and upper sides and the belly is white.

At least two other members of the family, the Basking Shark, *Cetorhinus maximus*, and the White Shark, *Carcharodon carcharias*, are found in the region. The Basking Shark is a large, dark brown-black shark that is seen at the surface straining small foods from the water. The White Shark is the much feared maneater. It may reach a very large size, and usually has a black spot at the base of the pectoral fin. The Shortfin Mako is oceanic and is distributed in the western Atlantic from Cape Cod to Argentina. The species is very common in the Caribbean, but is rarely caught off Bermuda.

Makos are ovoviviparous and produce 1 to 10 young in the late spring. The age at sexual maturity varies with sex. Females are not capable of reproducing until they are 6 or 7 years old, whereas males are mature at only 2 or 3 years. Young Makos are approximately 2 feet long at birth. Growth is rapid compared to most sharks. For instance, the species grows at nearly twice the rate of the Porbeagle, *Lamna nasus*, a close relative. Average lengths for Shortfin Mako aged 1 to 11 years are 4.1, 5.5, 6.5, 7.1, 7.6, 8.2, 8.8, 9.1, 10.1, 10.4, and 11.1 feet. These data are of questionable accuracy because hard structures such as scales, otoliths, opercular bones, and vertebrae normally used to age fish are not available. Sharks do not have bones, but are cartilaginous. Makos feed on squids and pelagic fishes such as mackerels and herrings.

Fishing. The Shortfin Mako is one of the most active and strongest swimming sharks. It has tremendous stamina and often makes spectacular leaps when it is hooked. Most recreational anglers prefer to fish for Makos from an open cockpit boat and to fight the fish from a standing position with the aid of a gimbel belt. The standard gear is 50- to 130-pound monofilament line on a 4/0 to 6/0 reel with a single-piece

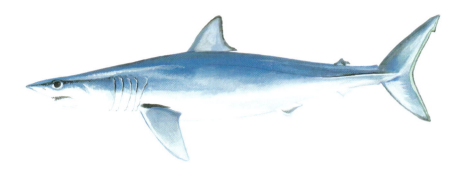

fiber glass rod. The terminal tackle may consist of a 15-foot single-strand wire leader with an 8/0 to 10/0 hook baited with live or dead whole mackerel, Bluefish, menhaden, herring or shad. An oily fish is best.

Sharks are attracted by ladling out pieces of cut fish, which drift past the set lines. Sharks are most efficiently located by fishing several baits, one at a depth of 30 to 40 feet (depending on the depth of the water), another at 18 feet, and the third just below the surface. When fishing for large sharks, anglers should always carry a 5-inch flying gaff and a conventional long-handled gaff. The species is caught commercially by longlines and is marketed fresh or dry-salted.

Preparation. Just as any shark is prepared for the table, the Mako should be cleaned as soon as possible after it is caught. This reduces the uric acid content in the flesh. The fish is cleaned by removing the head, tail, and fins before skinning, and then filleting. The flesh is considered to be of good quality; it may be broiled or barbecued after soaking overnight in brine.

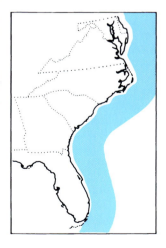

Suggested Readings. 12, 46, 132.

SPINNER SHARK
Carcharhinus brevipinna
Large Blacktip Shark

Habits. The Spinner is a seldom recognized shark, and is frequently confused with the Blacktip, *Carcharhinus limbatus*. Some fishermen know it by its slender shape, long pointed snout, and small eyes. To the trained observer, the two species may be separated by the position of the first dorsal fin and by the shape of the lower jaw. The dorsal fin of the Spinner originates above and behind the pectoral fin, whereas that of the Blacktip is positioned in front of it. The trailing edge of the mandible of the Spinner is straight, but it is distinctively notched in the Blacktip. The Spinner is gray on the back and white below with a conspicuous white band along the sides. The anal fin is tipped in black; that of the Blacktip lacks this pigmentation.

The Spinner is found on both sides of the Atlantic, in the Mediterranean Sea, and in the Indian and western Pacific Oceans. In the western Atlantic, it ranges from North Carolina to Florida, and has been collected off the Bahamas, in the northern Gulf of Mexico, and off Cuba, Puerto Rico, and Brazil. Records tend to be spotty due to the identification problem, which has also hindered research on the life history.

The Spinner, which may attain lengths of 9 to 10 feet, is viviparous and produces 6 to 15 embryos at one time. The young are large, ranging from approximately 20 to 29 inches at birth. Like other large sharks, the Spinner feeds on schooling fishes, squids, skates, rays, and sharks.

Fishing. Although caught primarily on floating longlines by commercial fishermen, the species is also taken on hook and line by anglers trolling baits and by still fishing. It is an active, fast-swimming shark that has developed a reputation for making spinning vertical leaps when it is hooked.

Drifting and chumming is perhaps the best method for catching large open ocean sharks. Good chum material and proper types of hooks, leaders, lines, reels, and floats are important to this type of angling. The chum should consist of cut oily fish, such as herrings, that create a slick on the surface of the water. Wire leader is a must. Fifteen to eighteen feet of No. 9 wire—104-pound test stainless and 114-pound test piano wire—should handle most sharks. Hooks may range in size from 6/0 (for fish up to 100 pounds) to 16/0 for the larger ones. The hooks may be rigged fixed, for dead bait, or swinging, for live bait. Three lines should be set at various depths. Most fishermen use 250 to 300 yards of 50- to

80-pound test line spooled on reels ranging in size from 4/0 to 12/0 depending on the size of the quarry. Lines should be suspended from the surface by cork or plastic floats.

Preparation. For those who eat sharks, the flesh of the Spinner is recognized as among the best. It may be prepared in a variety of ways; a suggested dish is Shark *Sauté Meuniere*. The meat is cut into ½-inch slices, seasoned with salt and pepper, rolled in flour, and pan fried in butter. Remove the meat from the pan, place it on a hot platter, and squeeze a lemon over it. Heat more butter in the pan until it is light brown, and then pour it over the cooked meat. The shark should be served very hot, sprinkled with parsley, and garnished with lemon wedges.

Suggested Readings. 12, 46, 132.

DUSKY SHARK
Carcharhinus obscurus
Shovelnose

Habits. One of the most abundant sharks in the region south of Cape Hatteras, the Dusky is a semi-pelagic species that occurs from estuarine waters to the outer continental shelf. It is found on both sides of the Atlantic, in the western Indian Ocean, and in the Pacific. In the western Atlantic, the Dusky occurs from April through November; it emigrates as water temperatures decline.

The Dusky Shark belongs to the family Carcharhinidae, one of the largest groups of sharks, whose members have two unequally sized dorsal fins and a caudal fin that is strongly asymmetrical. The upper lobe is much longer than the lower and has a subterminal notch. The Dusky may be identified from other carcharhinids by its moderately long snout—the distance from the mouth to the tip of the snout is less than the width of the mouth—and by the clearly triangular dorsal fin. The color is blue-gray to lead-gray along the back and upper sides, and white below. The fins are often dusky in the young, but plain in adults.

Young sharks, numbering 1 to 14 in a brood, are born viviparously and are about 3 feet long. Information pertaining to the size for sexual maturity and throughout life is not reliable. The maximum size attained by the species is about 12 feet. Duskies are piscivorous and feed on other sharks, groupers, lizardfish, eels, goatfish, and many other fishes.

Fishing. Although occasionally caught by anglers fishing in the surf or from piers, most Dusky Sharks are landed from drifting or anchored boats. Large reels capable of storing heavy line strong enough to handle the powerful sharks are required. Fishermen also should remember to use steel wire (stainless or Monel) because Duskies are able to bite through monofilament or braided lines. When fishing for Duskies and other open ocean sharks, one should fish over deep water, even though most are hooked directly on, or just below, the surface. Also, since the sharks are attracted by smell, a floating chum pot or freely ladled cut fish will concentrate them. Once the sharks are visible, anglers may merely cast their rigged baits over the side. Some of the gamest of the oceanic species, including the Dusky, may be caught on large streamer flies, thus adding a new dimension to the sport. In general the fishing techniques described for Shortfin Mako apply equally well for this species. Harvested commercially, particularly in the Caribbean and the Gulf of Mexico, it is marketed fresh and salted.

Preparation. Like other sharks, Duskies should be cleaned as soon as possible after they are caught. Immediately cut a ring around the caudal peduncle so that the shark will bleed freely. This will greatly improve the flavor of the flesh later when it is prepared for the table. Broiling is a suggested cooking method. The meat may also be prepared in Fish Cakes. The ingredients are 1 cup of cooked, flaked fish, 1 teaspoon of diced onion (add more to taste), 1 teaspoon of lemon juice, ¼ teaspoon of salt, dash of pepper, 1 egg, 1 cup of cold mashed potatoes, 2 tablespoons of flour, and ¼ cup of cooking oil. Combine the fish, onion, lemon juice, seasonings, egg, and potatoes. Mold the mixture into cakes. Roll the cakes in flour and sauté in a frying pan of hot oil.

Suggested Readings. 12, 46, 132.

DOLPHIN

Coryphaena hippurus

Common Dolphin

Habits. The Dolphin is perhaps the most beautifully colored of all saltwater fishes. Unfortunately, the bright turquoise, green, and yellow patterns fade almost immediately upon death. The species is an inhabitant of warm seas and prefers to remain where the water temperature is 68°F or warmer, such as in the Gulf Stream, Caribbean and Gulf of Mexico. A similar species, the Pompano Dolphin, *Coryphaena equisetis*, occasionally occurs with the Common Dolphin, but may be distinguished by having only 48 to 55 dorsal fin rays (Dolphin have 55 to 66), and a very wide and square tooth patch on the tongue.

Dolphin seem to be attracted to floating objects, and off the southeastern United States they frequently congregate around *Sargassum*, a brown alga, which serves as a hiding place and a source of food. Many of the foods eaten by Dolphin such as small fishes, crabs, and shrimps are found in floating mats of *Sargassum*. Feeding characteristics of Dolphin vary greatly. At times the Dolphin is a voracious predator that pursues and captures fast swimming fish such as flyingfish, mackerels, and juvenile Dolphin. On other occasions it seems content merely to nibble on small crustaceans and insects that float on the surface in the weed lines. In addition to foods, a variety of items discarded at sea by man are consumed by Dolphin. Small light bulbs, pieces of plastic wrappers, rope, and string have been removed from Dolphin stomachs.

Like most other pelagic fish, Dolphin are fast growing and do not live very long (only 5 years). Average fork lengths for males and females aged 1 to 4 years are 34.2, 43.6, 50, and 55.5 inches. Males grow faster and live longer than females. The spawning season is extended and varies with the latitude. Dolphin collected in the Florida Current spawned from November through July, whereas those from the Gulf Stream off North Carolina were reproductively active during June and July. A small female, 20 inches in length, may lay 240 thousand pelagic eggs and a fish larger than 43 inches may spawn several million.

Fishing. Sport fishermen trolling lures from large boats are most effective at catching Dolphin. Anglers prefer vividly colored Man-O-Wars, feathers, skirts, and other lead-headed lures rigged with 6/0 to 9/0 hooks baited with squid or mullet strips. Favorite lures are green and yellow feathers, red artificial squid, and purple Jelly Bellies. Standard boat rods and reels with 30- to 80-pound test line are used. For best results, baits are trolled

at about 4 to 6 knots adjacent to weed lines. Adventuresome anglers may fish for Dolphin with saltwater fly rods and streamer flies.

Preparation. Both flesh and roe are excellent to eat. A suggested method of preparation is to place the fillets and roe over charcoal and baste them with melted butter containing garlic and onion salts. Dolphin are also delicious in a fish salad. To prepare, 3 cups of broiled or baked fish are flaked. Add ½ cup of chopped green pepper, ½ cup of chopped sweet pickles, ¾ cup of mayonnaise, 2 tablespoons of lemon juice, 2 tablespoons of seafood seasoning, 12 chopped green olives, and 1 teaspoon of prepared mustard. Add salt, pepper, and red pepper to taste. Mix all of the ingredients lightly, but thoroughly. Chill and serve on a bed of lettuce with tomato wedges. Serves 6 to 8.

Suggested Readings. 59, 91, 116.

WAHOO
Acanthocybium solanderi

Habits. The Wahoo, also known as Ocean Barracuda, Tigerfish, and Pride of Bermuda, is a superb game fish more often mounted as a trophy than any other saltwater species. It occurs in tropical and subtropical waters of the Atlantic, Pacific, and Indian Oceans including the Caribbean and the Gulf of Mexico. The color of the fish is steel blue above and pale blue below, with a series of 25 to 30 irregular blackish-blue vertical bars on the sides. A distinguishing characteristic is that protrusions on the gills, gill rakers, are absent.

Wahoo are short lived and grow rapidly. Approximate lengths (and weights) of fish aged 1 to 4 years are 44.3 inches (16½ pounds), 50.4 (27½), 55.4 (36), and 60.1 inches (45 pounds). Both males and females reach sexual maturity during the first year of life. Males mature as small as 34 inches (7½ pounds), and females as small as 40 inches (12 pounds). Spawning along the southeastern United States takes place in June, July, and August. Fecundity estimates range from approximately 560 thousand eggs for a 13½-pound female to more than 45 million for a fish that weighs 87 pounds.

Wahoo are fast, voracious predators that feed primarily on fishes such as Frigate Mackerel, Butterfish, Porcupinefish, and Round Herring. Pear-shaped parasites, digenetic trematodes, are found in the stomachs of more than 90 percent of the fish caught. These parasites are harmless to man and are discarded when the fish are cleaned.

Fishing. Trolling for Wahoo has long been a favorite sport in the Caribbean, off Bermuda, and in the Gulf of Mexico. However, only since the mid-1960s has this form of fishing become popular along the southeastern coast of the United States. Boats troll at high speeds (6 to 10 knots) over water 240- to 300-feet deep during the summer and early fall. Productive fishing areas are often in the vicinity of floating *Sargassum*. Lines of 80- to 130-pound test pulled close to the boat are rigged with a variety of artificial lures. Bright yellow or red plastic skirts with strips of mullet, Greater Amberjack, or Little Tunny are fastened to 7/0 to 9/0 hooks. Other lures used are Japanese feathers, spoons, brightly colored rubber tubing, and skip baits with whole mullet, Ballyhoo, eel, or flyingfish.

Hawaiians make their own lures from broom handles and chrome pipes. These lures are 6 to 8 inches long with a lead head on one end and on the other plastic strips that flutter in the boat's wake. Experts

differ on whether Wahoo are solitary rovers, as once believed, or aggregate in small schools. Most agree that lures should be trolled near the surface, at high speeds, and in a straight line so that Wahoo in their high speed attack may better predict the path of the bait.

Preparation. The flesh is somewhat oily and is best prepared by boiling, baking, broiling, or charcoaling. After cooking, the fish may be served hot, or chopped and chilled and served as fish salad. The flesh has excellent freezing qualities and may also be smoked. Hors d'oeuvres made from Wahoo are considered a delicacy.

Suggested Readings. 32, 46, 66, 87.

SKIPJACK TUNA
Euthynnus pelamis

Albacore, Oceanic Bonito

Habits. The Skipjack Tuna is a highly migratory, oceanic pelagic fish that inhabits tropical and subtropical seas. The species is found in waters with surface temperatures ranging from 63° to 86°F, but prefers waters that are 68° to 82°F. In the western Atlantic, Skipjack Tuna range from Cape Cod (in the summer) to Argentina, and form large schools often mixed with Blackfin Tuna, *Thunnus atlanticus*. Like other tunas, Skipjack Tuna are built for speed, as evidenced by their sleek, fusiform bodies and powerful, deeply forked tails.

The back and upper sides are dark purplish-blue and the lower sides are silvery with four to six horizontal black stripes. The Skipjack Tuna and Atlantic Bonito, *Sarda sarda*, are the only western Atlantic tunas that have longitudinal stripes. These markings do not present an identification problem, however, because the Atlantic Bonito's stripes occur on the back instead of the belly.

Spawning takes place throughout the year near the equator, and from late spring to early fall in the more subtropical regions. Off the Carolinas, peak spawning occurs in June and July. Although a few fish are sexually mature when they are only 1 year old (about 16 to 18 inches long and 3 to 4 pounds), most reproduce for the first time during their second year. Spawning behavior has been observed by divers, who report paired fish swimming side by side, tilted inward at about 30° angles with their bellies almost touching. Upon release, the pelagic eggs are immediately fertilized by the male. The number of ova produced ranges from about 141 thousand for a 5-pound fish to approximately 1.2 million for a fish weighing 18 pounds.

Skipjack Tuna are fast-growing and live for only a few years. Fish size for a given age is highly variable, which may reflect natural differences in growth or inadequacies of aging studies for this species. Ranges in lengths for ages 1 to 3 are 16 to 18, 19 to 26, and 22 to 31 inches. Skipjack Tuna are voracious predators that feed on fishes and squids found near the surface. A 3-pound Tuna can eat up to 31 percent of its weight per day in food. Peak feeding occurs early in the morning and again late in the afternoon. While feeding, the species displays dark vertical bands on the sides, which brighten and fade with feeding intensity. Favorite foods are Round Herring, flyingfish, squids, Frigate Mackerel, mantis shrimp, amphipods, and larval crabs.

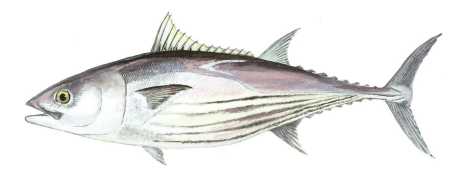

Fishing. Western Atlantic fisheries for Skipjack Tuna are minuscule compared with those operating in the Pacific. There, large pole and line and purse-seine fleets pursue Skipjack Tuna, as well as other species of tunas. Off the southeastern United States, most of the fish are caught by sport fishermen trolling artificial lures from charter boats. Feather and nylon lures, plastic skirts, and strip baits are trolled at the surface at 8 to 10 knots. Boats fishing out of Oregon Inlet and Hatteras catch many Skipjack by trolling baits around *Sargassum* in water 250 to 500 feet deep.

Preparation. The flesh of the Skipjack Tuna is marketed frozen, canned, or salted. The freshly cleaned meat is very bloody, but when baked or broiled turns gray-white. It is eaten raw, broiled, and prepared as tuna salad.

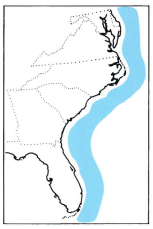

Suggested Readings. 32, 46, 49.

ALBACORE
Thunnus alalunga

Tuna

Habits. A large, cosmopolitan pelagic species, the Albacore is distributed from New England to southern Brazil in the western Atlantic. Although widespread in the Caribbean and off the coast of Venezuela, it is conspicuously absent from the Gulf of Mexico. Albacore are a welcomed, but infrequent, catch of fishermen along the southeastern United States, and are caught primarily by trolling artificial lures, miles from land.

Like other tunas, Albacore have muscular, torpedo-shaped bodies with strong concave tails. They are dissimilar from other species, however, in having very long pectoral fins. This feature makes the identification of the species easy. The back is dark metallic blue; the lower sides, belly, and posterior margin of the caudal fin are white. The first dorsal fin is deep yellow, the second dorsal fin is light yellow, and the finlets are dusky. The species is highly migratory. Schools up to 20 miles wide of similar-size individuals make extensive north-south and transoceanic migrations, usually staying in waters that are 54° to 77°F. They often mix with schools of Blackfin Tuna and Yellowfin Tuna.

Since the species is of far greater importance to fisheries in the Pacific than the Atlantic, most of the research has been conducted on Pacific populations. However, reproductive, feeding, and age and growth characteristics probably are similar for Albacore inhabiting both oceans. Albacore attain sexual maturity when they are 5 years old, or about 35 inches long. Mature fish form large spawning aggregations and release their sex products without selecting a mate. The pelagic eggs are thus fertilized at random. Spawning takes place throughout the year and a female may lay 0.8 million to 2.6 million eggs, depending on her size.

Although Albacore are capable of reaching a length of 4½ to 5 feet and of living for as long as 10 years, most fish caught are 3 to 6 years old and only 24 to 37 inches long. Males live longer and grow larger than females, although growth rates vary from one geographical area to another. Average lengths for fish aged 1 to 10 years from the western Atlantic are 17.3, 21.6, 25.2, 29.5, 34.2, 37.4, 39.4, 40.9, 42.5, and 44.1 inches. The species feeds by sight, thus during daylight hours, on a variety of animals including larval crustaceans, squids, and fishes. Albacore typically feed near the surface, but may consume prey as deep as 1,250 feet below the surface.

Fishing. Albacore are caught in the western Atlantic by recreational fishermen trolling artificial lures from charter boats or large private boats. Anglers use silver or vividly colored lures, which are trolled near the surface at high speeds. Most of the fish are caught by international commercial fishermen using purse seines, longlines, and hook and line baited with live fish. Fishing methods described for Yellowfin Tuna apply for Albacore.

Preparation. The flesh is highly regarded throughout the world, and is marketed canned or frozen. It may be smoked, broiled, made into tuna salad, or basted over charcoal.

Suggested Readings. 8, 32, 46, 48.

YELLOWFIN TUNA
Thunnus albacares

Allison Tuna, Longfin Tuna

Habits. Yellowfin Tuna are beautifully colored, torpedo-shaped fish that inhabit warm waters of the Atlantic, Pacific, and Indian Oceans and all warm seas except the Mediterranean. In the western Atlantic, the species is found from Massachusetts to Brazil, including the Gulf of Mexico and the Caribbean. Yellowfin are popular because they are large (up to 400 pounds), fight hard, and are excellent eating.

They are metallic dark blue on the back and upper sides, changing through yellow to silver on the belly. The dorsal and anal fins, and finlets are bright yellow. Tunas are difficult to identify to species. Bigeye, Blackfin, Albacore, and Yellowfin Tunas are similar in shape and are caught together. Characteristics that distinguish the Yellowfin Tuna from these species are: elongated anal and dorsal fins on large fish, moderately smooth nonstriated ventral surface of the liver, and 26 to 34 gill rakers on the first arch.

Most research on the life history has been done in the Pacific, but information on these populations probably applies to Atlantic stocks. Spawning is at sea in spring and summer, where water temperatures are at least 78°F. A few fish mature during their first year, but most do not reproduce until they are 2 or 3 years old. Yellowfin Tuna have tremendous reproductive potential. A 20-inch female may lay 319 thousand eggs; a 50-inch female may lay 4 million; and a 65-inch fish is capable of laying 8 million ova. Fish may spawn two or three times a year, releasing pelagic eggs in short, sporadic bursts.

Like other scombrids, Yellowfin Tuna are short-lived and have explosive rates of growth (2 inches in the first 4 weeks). Average lengths for ages 1 to 7 are 20, 38.3, 51.2, 58.9, 63.4, 66, and 67.7 inches. Yellowfin feed in open ocean surface waters on fishes and invertebrates associated with *Sargassum*. Foods include larval crabs and shrimps, squids, Paper Nautilus, filefish, triggerfish, and jacks.

Fishing. Commercial fishermen use purse seines, poles and lines, gill nets, longlines, and surface handlines to land the species. In the Pacific pole and line fishery, large boats with live-bait wells pursue schools of Yellowfin Tuna. When a school is sighted, live bait is thrown overboard to attract the tuna, which are hoisted aboard with long fiber glass poles, heavy monofilament lines, and barbless hooks or jigs. The longline fishery is practiced worldwide. Fishing units, called baskets, are composed of a horizontal mainline, buoyed at the surface between two

floats, and four to six branch lines, each with a hook. A single longline may consist of 400 baskets with a total of 2,000 hooks.

Purse seines are popular in the Pacific and are set from one or two purse boats launched from a tender vessel. The net is set around a school and retrieved, forcing the fish into a small area of the net. The Tuna are then pumped aboard the vessel. Sport fishermen catch Yellowfin Tuna by trolling brightly-colored lures at high speeds. A yellow and red plastic skirt trolled at the surface at 10 to 12 knots is an effective bait. When hooked, Yellowfin fight hard and often dive. The species is found near floating objects, so anglers look for logs, grass, and other debris and troll by them.

Preparation. The flesh commands a high price, and is sold fresh, frozen, and canned. Yellowfin Tuna may be prepared as tuna salad (see Little Tunny) or served in two Japanese dishes: sashimi or oshushi. Sashimi is raw tuna strips dipped in soy, vinegar, or hot mustard sauce. Oshushi is raw tuna strips served over rice balls.

Suggested Readings. 31, 32, 46, 89, 99.

BLACKFIN TUNA
Thunnus atlanticus

Tuna

Habits. A small but popular species of tuna, the Blackfin is found only in the western Atlantic, within a range extending from Massachusetts to Brazil. Typically a warmwater fish preferring temperatures above 68°F, it occurs in the more northerly latitudes only in the summer.

The species may be identified by a combination of characteristics: coloration, number of gill rakers on the first arch, and texture of its liver. The body is dark metallic blue above, with silvery lower sides and a white belly. Freshly caught fish have a distinctive wide golden band along the lateral line and finlets that are dusky with a hint of yellow. There are only 19 to 25 gill rakers on the first arch. These characters, in addition to a nonstriated liver, may be used to identify the Blackfin.

From the collection of ripe females and distribution of larvae, it appears that the species spawns offshore in the warm, clear waters of the Gulf Stream along the southeastern United States as well as in the Caribbean and western and northern sections of the Gulf of Mexico. Ripe fish have been collected off North Carolina in June, August, and September. Both sexes are believed to reach sexual maturity when they are 2 years old, as small as 6 pounds for females compared with 4½ pounds for males. The eggs and larvae are pelagic. Contrary to popular belief, Blackfin Tuna are not primarily piscivorous, but actually feed extensively on a wide variety of very small crustaceans as well as on larger prey such as fishes and squids. The modes of feeding include straining food items from the water column and chasing and engulfing them. Major foods of Blackfin Tuna caught off North Carolina are stomatopod larvae, numerous species of crab and shrimp larvae, juvenile fishes, and squids.

Like most other oceanic pelagic fishes, Blackfin Tuna are fast growing and short-lived. The maximum size is about 37 inches in length with a weight of approximately 35 pounds. A fish this size would probably be older than 5 years, although most of those caught along the southeastern United States are 1 to 5 years of age.

Fishing. The Blackfin Tuna contributes to important longline, handline, and pole and line commercial fisheries off Cuba, Haiti, and South America. In the United States, the species is sought primarily by anglers who troll strip baits, spoons, feathers, and jigs in offshore waters at high speeds. Off North Carolina, Blackfin are caught from April through November, though mostly in June and September. The average fish is

approximately 25 inches long and weighs about 8 pounds. In Florida, the sport fishing season occurs all year, with peaks in the fall and spring.

Preparation. The meat is marketed fresh, frozen, and canned. Highly esteemed for its texture and flavor, it is excellent broiled, prepared as tuna salad, or served uncooked as sashimi.

Suggested Readings. 32, 46, 89.

BIGEYE TUNA
Thunnus obesus

Tuna

Habits. Like other tunas, the Bigeye Tuna is a large, fast-swimming species with a metallic-colored, streamlined body. This migratory oceanic pelagic species is found in the warm waters of the Atlantic, Pacific, and Indian Oceans, where water temperatures range from 55° to 84°F (optimum is 63° to 72°F). In the western Atlantic, Bigeye Tuna occur from Massachusetts to Argentina, including the Caribbean and the Gulf of Mexico.

The fish is dark metallic blue on the back and upper sides with white lower sides and belly. The first dorsal fin is deep yellow, the second dorsal and anal fins are pale yellow, and the finlets are bright yellow edged with black. Although the different species of Atlantic tunas are very difficult to tell apart, Bigeye Tuna may be recognized by a combination of several characteristics: the coloration of the finlets, the 23 to 31 gill rakers on the first arch, a prominent lateral keel on the caudal peduncle located between two smaller ones, and a liver with a striated ventral surface.

Spawning takes place throughout the year for Pacific populations, with a peak in activity from April through September. A similar spawning cycle probably occurs for Atlantic stocks. Bigeyes are sexually mature when they are 3 years old, as small as 37 inches for males and 43 inches for females. Schools of spawning fish release their sex products indiscriminantly, and fertilization is random. A female may spawn twice during a year, laying from 2.9 million to more than 6 million ova, depending on her size. The pelagic eggs hatch in about 21 hours.

Although Bigeyes may live longer than 9 years, nearly 70 percent of the fish caught in the Pacific are 3 to 5 years old. Average lengths for tuna aged 1 to 5 years are 20, 37, 51, 61, and 65 inches. The maximum size attained by the species is about 73 inches. Bigeyes feed at night and during the day on fishes, squids, and crustaceans found from the surface to a depth of approximately 500 feet. Mackerel, small tuna, flyingfish, Snake Mackerel, pomfret, squids, larval crabs, and shrimps are favorite foods.

Fishing. In the Atlantic, Bigeye Tuna are caught by international commercial fishermen using surface longlines and by sport fishermen trolling artificial lures. Pacific populations are exploited by anglers and by commercial fishermen using longlines, purse seines, and pole and line gear. Longlines are typically stored in units called baskets, each

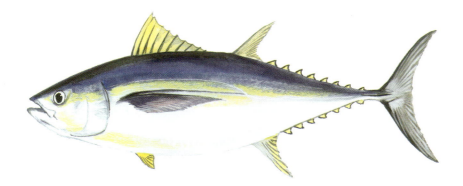

consisting of a mainline of about 1,000 feet, and many branch lines, each with a baited hook. A set usually consists of 1,500 to 2,000 hooks and many miles of line buoyed at both ends.

Purse seines, 3,600 to 4,600 feet in length and 330 to 490 feet deep, are set around schools of tuna. The seines are pursed inward, forcing the fish into an area of net that is decreasing in size. Once confined, the tuna are removed from the net to a large ship. The commercial pole and line fishery uses live fish to attract schools of tuna, which are then caught with hooks baited with live fish or with feathered lures.

Preparation. Bigeye are excellent to eat and may be prepared similarly to Yellowfin Tuna.

Suggested Readings. 25, 32, 46.

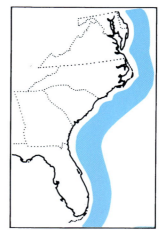

BLUEFIN TUNA
Thunnus thynnus

Tuna

Habits. The Bluefin Tuna is a large pelagic species with a torpedo-shaped body that is nearly circular in cross section. Because it is a fierce fighter, reaches a length of 10 to 11 feet, a weight of 1,390 pounds and has high-quality flesh, it is valued by fishermen. The species is distributed from Argentina and South Africa north to Labrador and northern Scandinavia in the Atlantic Ocean, including the Gulf of Mexico and the Caribbean. Populations in the western and eastern Atlantic are considered separate, although there are occasional transatlantic migrations.

Bluefin Tuna are seasonal inhabitants of the outer continental shelf waters of the United States from the Gulf of Maine to southern Florida. They migrate out of the Caribbean and Gulf of Mexico in the spring, arriving off New York and southern New England in June and July. Larger individuals travel farther north than do smaller fish. Major wintering areas in the western Atlantic are the Caribbean, the Gulf of Mexico, and from the Lesser Antilles to Argentina.

Bluefin Tuna are dark blue-black on the back, and white on the lower sides and belly. Colorless transverse lines, alternating with rows of colorless spots on the lower sides, are present on live fish. The second dorsal fin is reddish-brown. The color of this fin, number of gill rakers on the first arch (34 to 43), and the very short pectoral fins may separate the species from other members of the genus *Thunnus*.

Bluefin 6 years old or older spawn throughout much of the western Atlantic during the warmer months. Females larger than 270 pounds spawn from April through June, primarily in the Caribbean and Gulf of Mexico. Smaller Bluefin Tuna spawn along the shoreward edge of the Gulf Stream in the Mid-Atlantic Bight in June and July. Growth is rapid. Approximate lengths for fish aged 1 to 10 years are 1.5, 2.3, 3, 3.8, 4.6, 5.2, 5.8, 6.3, 6.6, and 7.2 feet. The species may live more than 20 years. Like other tunas, Bluefin feed on animals that are found on the ocean surface. Herrings, mackerels, hakes, and squids are prey of this voracious carnivore.

Fishing. The species is subjected to a relentless international commercial longline fishery throughout its range. In the western Atlantic, at least seven countries are involved in the fishery. During 1978 and 1979, 243 foreign vessels received permits to fish in United States waters and set approximately 7.5 million hooks.

A typical tuna longline consists of a horizontal mainline from which branch lines with baited hooks (as many as 2,000 per set) are hung vertically. The mainline is attached to buoys and may stretch 60 to 75 miles. The hooks are distributed from near the surface to about 500 feet. The lines are hauled every 24 hours. Sport fishermen catch Bluefin Tuna by trolling and float fishing. Aided by high spotter towers on their boats to locate fish, anglers frequently troll two lines, each with a single large squid or mullet on 12/0 to 14/0 hooks. A favorite rig is the daisy chain with six or seven fish, usually mackerel, strung along a wire leader. The end fish is impaled or sewn on the large hook. In the Mid-Atlantic Bight, anglers anchor their boats, chum, and then float fish for giant Bluefin Tuna. Large (14/0 or 16/0) reels, sturdy rods, and 130- to 180-pound test lines are used to catch the Tuna, which pass like freight trains below the boats. Fishermen often stagger their baits (fish or lobster) at 30-foot intervals to locate the fish.

Preparation. Bluefin Tuna flesh is excellent baked, broiled, or prepared as tuna salad.

Suggested Readings. 6, 32, 99, 113.

SWORDFISH
Xiphias gladius

Broadbill

Habits. Swordfish are the most widely distributed billfish, occurring worldwide in all temperate, subtropical, and tropical seas. In the western Atlantic, the species ranges from Newfoundland to Argentina. Confined to waters associated with the Gulf Stream in winter, it inhabits a much broader area in summer.

Swordfish are large, aggressive fish (up to 14 feet long and a weight of 1,200 pounds) with rounded bodies and long flattened snouts. The scientific name comes from Greek and Latin meaning "sword." They have been reported to attack men, boats, whales, and submersibles. Identifying characteristics are the lack of pelvic fins and gill rakers, and the presence of a single lateral keel located on each side of the caudal peduncle. Marlins, spearfish, and Sailfish have two keels. Swordfish are brownish-black on the back and upper sides, fading to a pale brown on the lower sides and belly.

Spawning takes place in tropical waters where temperatures are warmer than 68°F. Fish 5 to 6 years old and older spawn throughout the year in the Caribbean, Gulf of Mexico, and off the coasts of Florida. Data on fecundity are limited; however, one 150-pound fish contained approximately 16 million ova. The recently hatched larvae are pelagic and remain in surface waters with temperatures ranging from 76° to 84°F. Although some individuals may live for 9 years, most caught by recreational fishermen in the Atlantic are 3 to 5 years old. Females grow faster, larger, and live longer than males. Average weights for females aged 1 to 5 years are 9, 33, 88, 154, and 242 pounds.

Swordfish are opportunistic feeders that forage from the bottom to the surface over great depths and distances. Adults often feed on the bottom in shallow water, but rise to the surface to feed at night. Larvae usually feed on zooplankton and larval fish; adults eat mackerel, squids, Barracuda, hake, redfish, lanternfish, and filefish.

Fishing. The species is caught by commercial and recreational fishermen in the Atlantic. Commercial fishermen take Swordfish with longlines and harpoons. The harpoon was the major commercial gear in North America for many years, dating back to colonial times. Small boats with 2 to 4 man crews were sent out from larger vessels when a fish was spotted. A man positioned in the bow struck the Swordfish with a harpoon, which was attached to a buoy. The fish was retrieved when it tired.

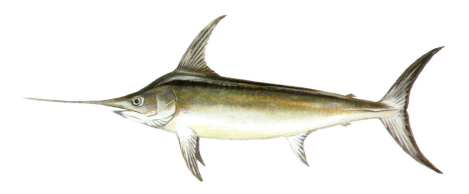

Until recently, sport fishermen caught Swordfish by trolling baits during daylight. Trolling involves sighting a fish and then maneuvering the bait in its path. Fishermen have discovered that drift fishing, particularly at night, is productive for catching Broadbill. The idea is to fish whole baits, such as squid, mullet, or mackerel, at staggered depths using several different rigs, each illuminated with a chemical light. A rig may consist of an 8-foot, 300-pound test monofilament leader with two 12/0 to 14/0 hooks. The chemical light, capable of burning several hours, is attached above the bait. When fishing water 1,000 to 1,400 feet deep, one line may be set 30 to 60 feet down, one at 90 to 120 feet, and another at 200 to 400 feet below the surface. Fishermen also cast live bait at a fish sighted basking at the surface. In these instances, 3/0 to 6/0 reels with 30- to 80-pound test line are used. It takes great skill to cast heavy bait on tackle strong enough to hold a Swordfish.

Preparation. The flesh is marketed fresh or frozen. Swordfish steaks are excellent broiled or basted over charcoal.

Suggested Readings. 115.

SAILFISH
Istiophorus platypterus

Habits. The Sailfish is a very popular billfish with marine gamefish anglers. It is distributed worldwide in tropical and temperate waters and throughout the western Atlantic from the Gulf of Maine south to Brazil, including the Caribbean and the Gulf of Mexico. Compared with marlins and Swordfish, the Sailfish is a nearshore species, with most adults occurring near land where water depth ranges from 120 to 300 feet and temperatures range from 77° to 82°F. Sailfish are dark blue along the upper half of the body, fading to brownish-blue on the lower sides to silver white on the belly. The first dorsal fin is high, sail-like, blue-black, and covered with many small black spots. All related billfishes have a high dorsal fin as juveniles, but only the Sailfish retains the high fin throughout life. The other fins are silver-blue. On the sides are 15 to 20 vertical bars consisting of several small blue spots.

Not much is known about the age and growth of the species, although it is believed to live as long as 10 years and reach a weight of 110 pounds. Most fish caught off the southeastern United States are no more than 3 to 4 years old. Like other pelagic fish, Sailfish grow rapidly. A 1-year-old is about 72 inches in length and weighs 20 pounds. Spawning occurs throughout much of the western Atlantic during the warmer months. A major spawning area is along the lower east coast of Florida, where fish move inshore to spawn from mid-May through September. Pairing, or prespawning behavior, has been observed when a female and one to three males, rise to the surface to spawn. Although a 74-pound female was found to contain 4 million eggs, most produce from 0.8 to 1.6 million ova.

Like other billfish, Sailfish feed primarily during daylight hours on fishes and squids. Favorite foods are tunas, mackerels, halfbeaks, jacks, needlefish, herring, and other surface-swimming species. The feeding behavior of Sailfish is unique. Divers have filmed pods of Sailfish encircling schools of fish, using their high fins to form a wall to keep the prey confined. One by one, the Sailfish dart in to feed, and then return to the outer circle to await their next opportunity.

Fishing. Sailfish are landed off the southeastern United States from May through September by sport fishermen trolling artificial and natural baits. Baits are trolled within 3 feet of the surface at speeds varying from 3 to 8 knots. Sometimes a single bait is pulled, but more often two to four lines are trolled. Sailfish generally are sighted before they are fished for, and

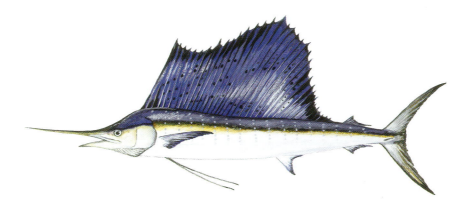

they strike a bait only when it is clearly visible. Fishermen look for fish that are tailing, that is swimming with the upper part of the tail fin and dorsal above the surface. Artificial lures, fish, and squid are used as bait. As with other types of fishing, a controversy exists between anglers over which bait is the best. Mullet, Spanish Mackerel, Bonito, and Ballyhoo are among the most widely used. Outriggers and teasers, which are described for marlin fishing, are important, but not critical for catching Sailfish. Commercial longliners, especially the Japanese, also catch Sailfish in the western Atlantic. These fishermen seek tunas, but their catch of billfish probably causes a decline in local availability and average landings of marlin and Sailfish. Since 1962, the Japanese have averaged 9,000 Sailfish per year while fishing over 1 million square miles of the western Atlantic.

Preparation. Sailfish are not usually eaten in this country, although they may be cut into steaks and then baked, broiled, smoked, or cooked over charcoal.

Suggested Readings. 46, 137, 138.

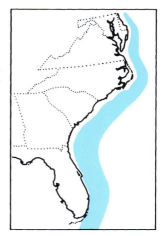

BLUE MARLIN
Makaira nigricans
Marlin

Habits. The Blue Marlin is one of the largest game fishes caught in the Atlantic Ocean. Individuals may exceed 13 feet and weigh over 1,300 pounds. The species is found throughout much of the western Atlantic, seasonally ranging in latitude from about 45°N to 35°S. There appear to be two seasonal concentrations, one from January through April in the southwestern Atlantic between latitudes 5° and 30°S, and the other from June through October, in the northwestern Atlantic between latitudes 10° and 35°N. Blue Marlin are most frequently caught off North Carolina, in the Gulf of Mexico, in the Caribbean Sea, and off Brazil.

The body is dark blue to chocolate brown along the back and upper sides, changing to silvery white on the belly. On the sides there are approximately 15 pale blue vertical bars. Blue Marlin may be distinguished from White Marlin, *Tetrapturus albidus*, by the dorsal and anal fins, and by the fish's size. The dorsal and anal fins of Blue Marlin are pointed, whereas White Marlin have rounded fins. The first dorsal fin of the Blue Marlin is much shorter relative to the body depth when compared to that of the White Marlin. Any marlin caught off the southeastern United States weighing over 150 pounds is almost certainly a Blue Marlin.

Life history information on the species is scarce. Some generalities, however, may be made. Sexual maturity for males is attained when fish weigh about 76 pounds, 103 to 135 pounds for females. Blue Marlin spawn in the North Atlantic from July through September, and in the South Atlantic in February and March. The eggs and larvae are free floating. Longevity probably exceeds 15 years, although most fish caught are less than 10 years old. Age and size data are not available, but we do know that a Blue Marlin 4 feet long weighs about 44 pounds, one 8 feet long weighs about 319 pounds, and a fish 13 feet long weighs around 817 pounds.

Blue Marlin feed on squids and a variety of pelagic fishes such as Dolphin, tunas, mackerels, and flyingfish. Scientists argue whether the bill is used in feeding. However, divers have reported seeing marlins not only stun prey with their bills but also use them to spear fish. Impaled fish were dislodged by the marlin violently shaking its head, and then were swallowed.

Fishing. Commercial fishermen land Blue Marlin with longlines. These consist of a long floating line with many baited hooks. The lines are set and left fishing overnight, and are retrieved the following morning. Many sport fishermen's organizations worldwide oppose the commercial harvesting of billfishes, including Blue Marlin.

Sport fishermen catch the species by trolling artificial and natural baits, and by float fishing with live fish as bait. When trolling, boats pull four lines at speeds ranging from 4 to 8 knots. Two of the lines are pulled close to the boat on the surface and are called flatlines. The other two are attached to outriggers, long whiplike poles that allow the billfish to charge the bait in an effort to stun it, before the strike is made by the angler. An artificial, hookless teaser is pulled in the wake to attract marlin to the surface. Heavy rods and reels with 40- to 150-pound monofilament line are used to fish for Blue Marlin. Artificial lures, squid, Spanish Mackerel, mullet, and Ballyhoo are all good baits, usually rigged with 9/0 to 16/0 hooks.

Preparation. Blue Marlin are seldom eaten in the United States. The flesh is good charcoaled and basted, smoked, broiled, or made into fish salad.

Suggested Readings. 46, 137, 138, 159.

WHITE MARLIN
Tetrapturus albidus

Marlin

Habits. The White Marlin is the most frequently caught marlin along the east coast of the United States. This oceanic, migratory species is a popular trophy fish that occurs in the Atlantic from Nova Scotia to Argentina, including the Caribbean and the Gulf of Mexico. Major fishing areas along the East Coast are Ocean City in Maryland, Oregon Inlet and Cape Hatteras in North Carolina, and Florida. White Marlin inhabit warm waters where temperatures are greater than 66°F (optimum temperature is about 75°F). The species makes extensive seasonal migrations, moving northward off the United States from May through October, and southward from November through April. During migrations, White Marlin are solitary, or form groups of 5 to 12 fish.

The body is dark blue to chocolate along the upper half and brownish to silvery white along the lower sides and belly. The first dorsal fin is blue-black and covered with many small black spots. The other fins are brown-black. Unlike the Blue Marlin, the White Marlin usually has no spots or bars on the sides. The White Marlin has rounded anal and dorsal fins, and a clearly visible lateral line. The Blue Marlin has pointed fins, and the lateral line is not evident.

White Marlin inhabit the upper 40 to 100 feet of the water column and feed near the surface during daylight hours. Foods include a variety of fishes: jacks, mackerels, herrings, Doctorfish, triggerfish, filefish, Dolphin, and flyingfish, as well as squids and crabs. Like other billfishes, White Marlin probably use their spears to stun prey. Little is known about the age and growth; however, White Marlin are fast growing and live at least 6 years. They may reach a length of 9 feet and a weight of 165 pounds. Approximate weights for fish 70, 90, 100, and 110 inches long are 23, 62, 93, and 135 pounds.

Spawning occurs in the spring and both sexes mature when they are about 51 inches long. A female weighing 59 pounds may lay 4 million pelagic eggs, whereas a fish weighing 82 pounds is capable of laying 11 million ova.

Fishing. White Marlin are caught with rod and reel, handlines, and surface longlines. In the past, anglers used linen lines of 27- to 54-pound test, sturdy rods with 6- to 12-ounce split bamboo tips, star drag 4/0 to 6/0 reels, 7/0 to 9/0 hooks, and natural baits. Today, fishermen prefer lighter tackle: 20- to 30-pound test monofilament line, 2/0 to 6/0 reels, fiber glass rods, and a variety of artificial and natural

baits. Whole squid or fish and strip bait are trolled at the surface. Favorite artificials are plastic squids, lures with feather or nylon tails, and spoons.

Two long fiber glass or aluminum poles called outriggers are used to catch billfish. These are permanently mounted on the boat and are lowered to about 45° in use. After the bait has been let out to the desired distance, the line is set in a clip, which is hauled up to the end of the outrigger. This not only provides attractive bait action, but also gives the bait a drop-back effect when the initial strike pulls the line free of the clip. The marlin believes the fish has been stunned and quickly strikes again. Commercial fishermen take White Marlin with hook and line. Small boats and handlines are used in the Caribbean, and larger vessels and surface longlines are used by foreign fleets throughout much of the range.

Preparation. White marlin may be steaked and broiled, baked, or smoked. Regulations concerning mercury levels in the flesh have at times precluded the marketing of meat in this country.

Suggested Readings. 46, 137, 138, 159.

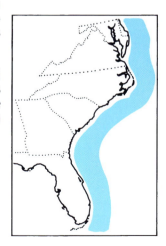

LONGBILL SPEARFISH
Tetrapturus pfluegeri

Spearfish, Hatchet Marlin

Habits. The Longbill Spearfish is a large, oceanic pelagic species that has its upper jaw prolonged into a slender spear much like that of a marlin or a Sailfish. The species is infrequently caught on both sides of the Atlantic Ocean by commercial longliners and by recreational fishermen trolling topwater lines. Longbill Spearfish are distributed from the Cape Verde Islands to South Africa in the eastern Atlantic and from Maryland to Brazil in the western Atlantic. The species is most abundant in the mid- and south Atlantic latitudes. A close relative, the Shortbill Spearfish, *Tetrapturus angustirostris*, occurs in the Pacific and Indian Oceans.

The Longbill, which attains a length of about 6½ feet, may be distinguished from the more common White and Blue Marlins by the slender body, the number of rays in the two dorsal fins (44 to 50; and 6 or 7), and the close proximity of the anus to the origin of the first anal fin. The body is dark blue dorsally, brownish-white along the sides, and silvery on the belly; overall it lacks conspicuous vertical bars. The first dorsal fin is blue-black and unspotted.

Because of its low popularity and infrequent occurrence in fish landings, Longbill Spearfish have not been studied extensively. Limited information is available on reproduction, age and growth, and feeding behavior. Spawning by sexually mature fish, those 2 years old and older, occurs offshore from late November to early May, with a peak in late winter. The ovaries are unequal in size, the left being approximately twice as large as the right. As is true with most other large pelagic game fish, Spearfish are short-lived and grow rapidly. Approximate lengths (and weights) for fish aged 1 to 3 years are 35.4 (4 to 6 pounds), 65 (38 to 41), and 70.9 (60 to 80) inches. Considering the maximum attainable size of 6½ feet, the species is probably capable of living somewhat longer than 3 years.

Longbill Spearfish feed on small- to medium-size fishes and cephalopods that are most abundant near the surface of the water. Feeding takes place during daylight and darkness. It is not known to what extent the fish use their bills to feed.

Fishing. No one specifically fishes for Spearfish, although the species is caught by fishermen angling for tunas and other billfish. Commercial longlining vessels also land Spearfish along with marlins, Swordfish,

sharks, and tunas. Techniques described for the marlins and Yellowfin Tuna may be referred to for this species.

Preparation. Spearfish are occasionally marketed, and the flesh is prepared as sashimi or fish cakes.

Suggested Readings. 46, 138.

BIBLIOGRAPHY

Following are the references used in the preparation of this book. Each is numbered and may be referred to in the text after the discussion for a given species. Those most suitable for the general reader are marked with an asterisk.

1. Ager, L. A., D. E. Hammond, and F. Ware. 1976. Artificial spawning of snook. Proceedings of the 30th Annual Conference of the Southeastern Association of Fish and Wildlife Agencies, p. 158-166.

2. Aggus, L. R. 1972. Food of angler harvested largemouth, spotted and smallmouth bass in Bull Shoals Reservoir. Proceedings of the 26th Annual Conference of the Southeastern Association of Game and Fish Commissioners, p. 519-529.

3. Anderson, W. W. 1958. Larval development, growth, and spawning of striped mullet (*Mugil cephalus*) along the South Atlantic Coast of the United States. U.S. Fish and Wildlife Service, Fishery Bulletin, Vol. 58, p. 501-519.

4. Arnold, C. R., W. H. Bailey, T. D. Williams, A. Johnson, and J. L. Lasswell. 1977. Laboratory spawning and larval rearing of red drum and southern flounder. Proceedings of the 31st Annual Conference of the Southeastern Association of Fish and Wildlife Agencies, p. 437-440.

5. Ball, R. L., and R. V. Kilambi. 1972. The feeding ecology of the black and white crappies in Beaver Reservoir, Arkansas, and its effect on the relative abundance of the crappie species. Proceedings of the 26th Annual Conference of the Southeastern Association of Game and Fish Commissioners, p. 577-590.

6. Bayliff, W. H. 1980. Synopsis of biological data on the northern bluefin tuna, *Thunnus thynnus* (Linnaeus 1758), in the Pacific Ocean, p. 261-293. *In* W. H. Bayliff (ed.), Synopses of biological data on eight species of scombrids. Inter-American Tropical Tuna Commission, Special Report, No. 2.

7. Bearden, C. M. 1963. A contribution to the biology of the king whitings, genus *Menticirrhus*, of South Carolina. Bears Bluff Laboratories, Contribution, No. 38, p. 1-27.

8. Beardsley, G. L. 1971. Contribution to the population dynamics of Atlantic albacore with comments on potential yields. U.S. National Marine

317

Fisheries Service, Fishery Bulletin, Vol. 69, p. 845-857.

9. Berrien, P., and D. Finan. 1977. Biological and fisheries data on king mackerel, *Scomberomorus cavalla* (Cuvier). U.S. National Marine Fisheries Service, Northeast Fisheries Center, Sandy Hook Laboratory, Technical Series Report, No. 8. 40 p.

10. Berrien, P., and D. Finan. 1978. Biological and fisheries data on Spanish mackerel, *Scomberomorus maculatus*, (Mitchill). U.S. National Marine Fisheries Service, Northeast Fisheries Center, Sandy Hook Laboratory, Technical Series Report, No. 9. 52 p.

11. Berry, F., and E. S. Iversen. 1967. Pompano: Biology, fisheries and farming potential. Proceedings of the 19th Annual Session, Gulf and Caribbean Fisheries Institute, p. 116-128.

12. Bigelow, H. B., and W. C. Schroeder. 1948. Fishes of the western North Atlantic, Part 1. Sears Foundation for Marine Research, Yale University, Memoir, No. 1. 576 p.

*13. Bigelow, H. B., and W. C. Schroeder. 1953. Fishes of the Gulf of Maine. U.S. Fish and Wildlife Service, Fishery Bulletin, Vol. 74. 577 p.

*14. Bigelow, H. B., and W. C. Schroeder. 1953. Fishes of the western North Atlantic, Part 2. Sears Foundation for Marine Research, Yale University, Memoir, No. 1. 588 p.

*15. Bigelow, H. B., and W. C. Schroeder. 1966. Fishes of the western North Atlantic, Part 3. Sears Foundation for Marine Research, Yale University, Memoir, No. 1. 630 p.

*16. Bigelow, H. B., and W. C. Schroeder. 1966. Fishes of the western North Atlantic, Part 5. Sears Foundation for Marine Research, Yale University, Memoir, No. 1. 647 p.

*17. Böhlke, J. E., and C. C. G. Chaplin. 1968. Fishes of the Bahamas and adjacent tropical waters. Livingston, Wynnewood, Pa. 771 p.

18. Bortone, S. A. 1971. Studies on the biology of the sand perch, *Diplectrum formosum*, (Perciformes:Serranidae). Florida Department of Natural Resources, Technical Series, No. 65. 27 p.

19. Briggs, P. T. 1969. The sport fisheries for tautog in the inshore waters of eastern Long Island. New York Fish and Game Journal, Vol. 16, p. 238-254.

20. Burch, R. K. 1979. The greater amberjack, *Seriola dumerili*: Its biology and fishery off southeastern Florida. M.S. thesis, University of Miami, Coral Gables, Fla. 112 p.

21. Burnett-Herkes, J. 1975. Contribution to the biology of the red hind, *Epinephelus guttatus*, a commercially important serranid fish from the tropical western Atlantic. Ph.D. thesis, University of Miami, Coral Gables, Fla. 154 p.

22. Caldwell D. K. 1957. The biology and systematics of the pinfish, *Lagodon rhomboides* (Linnaeus). Bulletin of the Florida State Museum, Vol. 2, No. 6, p. 77-173.

23. Caldwell, D. K., H. T. Odum, T. R. Hellier, Jr., and F. H. Berry. 1957. Populations of spotted sunfish and Florida largemouth bass in a constant-temperature spring. Transactions of the American Fisheries Society, Vol. 85, p. 120-134.

*24. Calhoun, A. 1966. Inland fisheries management. California Department of Fish and Game, Sacramento. 546 p.

25. Calkins, T. P. 1980. Synopsis of biological data on the bigeye tuna, *Thunnus obesus* (Lowe, 1839), in the

Pacific Ocean, p. 213-259. In W. H. Bayliff (ed.), Synopses of biological data on eight species of scombrids. Inter-American Tropical Tuna Commission, Special Report, No. 2.

26. Carlander, K. D. 1969. Handbook of freshwater fishery biology, Vol. 1. Iowa State University Press, Ames. 752 p.

27. Carlander, K. D. 1977. Handbook of freshwater fishery biology, Vol. 2. Iowa State University Press, Ames. 431 p.

28. Casterlin, M. E., and W. W. Reynolds. 1979. Diel activity patterns of the smooth dogfish shark, Mustelus canis. Bulletin of Marine Science, Vol. 29, p. 440-442.

29. Chapman, R. W. 1978. Observations of spawning behavior in Atlantic spadefish, Chaetodipterus faber. Copeia 1978, p. 336.

30. Chew, R. L. 1974. Early life history of the Florida largemouth bass. Florida Game and Fresh Water Fish Commission, Fishery Publication, No. 7. 76 p.

31. Cole, J. S. 1980. Synopsis of biological data on the yellowfin tuna, Thunnus albacares (Bonnaterre, 1788), in the Pacific Ocean, p. 71-150. In W. H. Bayliff (ed.), Synopses of biological data on eight species of scombrids. Inter-American Tropical Tuna Commission, Special Report, No. 2.

*32. Collette, B. B., and C. E. Nauen. 1983. FAO species catalogue, Vol. 2. Scombrids of the world, an annotated and illustrated catalogue of tunas, mackerels, bonitos and related species known to date. FAO Fisheries Synopsis, No. 125, Vol. 2. 137 p.

33. Cooper, R. A., 1967. Age and growth of tautog, Tautoga onitis (Linnaeus), from Rhode Island. Transactions of the American Fisheries Society, Vol. 96, p. 134-142.

*34. Cross, F. B. 1967. Handbook of fishes of Kansas. University of Kansas, Museum of Natural History, Public Education Series, No. 3. 189 p.

35. Crossman, E. J. 1962. The redfin pickerel, Esox a. americanus in North Carolina. Copeia 1962, p. 114-123.

36. Dahlberg, M. D. 1975. Guide to the coastal fishes of Georgia and nearby states. University of Georgia Press, Athens. 186 p.

37. Darcy, G. H. 1983. Synopsis of biological data on the grunts, Haemulon aurolineatum, and H. plumieri (Pisces: Haemulidae). NOAA Technical Report NMFS Circular, No. 448; and, FAO Fisheries Synopsis, No. 133. 37 p.

38. Darcy, G. H. 1983. Synopsis of biological data on the pigfish, Orthopristis chrysoptera (Pisces: Haemulidae). NOAA Technical Report NMFS Circular, No. 449; and, FAO Fisheries Synopsis, No. 134. 23 p.

39. Davis, J. C. 1976. Biology of the hogfish, Lachnolaimus maximus (Walbaum), in the Florida Keys. M.S. thesis, University of Miami, Coral Gables, Fla. 86 p.

40. Davis, J. R. 1971. The spawning behavior, fecundity rates, and food habits of the redbreast sunfish in southeastern North Carolina. Proceedings of the 25th Annual Conference of the Southeastern Association of Game and Fish Commissioners, p. 556-560.

41. deSylva, D. P. 1970. Systematics and life history of the great barracuda, Sphyraena barracuda (Walbaum). University of Miami, Studies in Tropical Oceanography, No. 1. 179 p.

42. Dovel, W. L., J. A. Mihursky, and A. J. McErlean. 1969. Life history aspects of the hogchoker, *Trinectes maculatus* in the Patuxent River Estuary, Maryland. Chesapeake Science, Vol. 10, p. 104-119.

43. DuPaul, W. D., and J. D. McEachran. 1973. Age and growth of the butterfish, *Peprilus triacanthus*, in the lower York River. Chesapeake Science, Vol. 14, p. 205-207.

*44. Eddy, S. 1957. How to know the freshwater fishes. William C. Brown Co., Dubuque, Iowa. 253 p.

45. Fahay, M. P. 1978. Biological and fisheries data on American eel, *Anguilla rostrata* (LeSueur). U.S. National Marine Fisheries Service, Northeast Fisheries Center, Sandy Hook Laboratory, Technical Series Report, No. 17. 82 p.

46. FAO species identification sheets for fishery purposes. 1978. Food and Agriculture Organization of the United Nations, Rome. 7 Vols.

47. Finucane, J. H. 1969. Ecology of the pompano (*Trachinotus carolinus*) and the permit (*T. falcatus*) in Florida. Transactions of the American Fisheries Society, Vol. 98, p. 478-486.

48. Foreman, T. J. 1980. Synopsis of biological data on the albacore tuna, *Thunnus alalunga* (Bonnaterre, 1788), p. 17-70. *In* W. H. Bayliff (ed.), Synopses of biological data on eight species of scombrids. Inter-American Tropical Tuna Commission, Special Report, No. 2.

49. Forsbergh, E. D. 1980. Synopsis of biological data on the skipjack tuna, *Katsuwonus pelamis* (Linnaeus 1758), in the Pacific Ocean, p. 295-360. *In* W. H. Bayliff (ed.), Synopses of biological data on eight species of scombrids. Inter-American Tropical Tuna Commission, Special Report, No. 2.

50. Francis, M. P. 1981. Von Bertalanffy growth rates in species of *Mustelus* (Elasmobranchii: Triakidae). Copeia 1981, p. 189-192.

51. Frankensteen, E. D. 1976. Genus *Alosa* in a channelized and an unchannelized creek of the Tar River Basin, North Carolina. M.S. thesis, East Carolina University, Greenville, N.C. 123 p.

52. Freeman, B. L., and S. C. Turner. 1977. Biological and fisheries data on tilefish, *Lopholatilus chamaeleonticeps* Goode and Bean. U.S. National Marine Fisheries Service, Northeast Fisheries Center, Sandy Hook Laboratory, Technical Series Report, No. 5. 41 p.

53. Germann, J. F., L. E. McSwain, D. R. Holder, and C. D. Swanson. 1974. Life history of warmouth in the Suwannee River and Okefenokee Swamp, Georgia. Proceedings of the 28th Annual Conference of the Southeastern Association of Game and Fish Commissioners, p. 259-278.

54. Ginsburg, I. 1952. Flounders of the genus *Paralichthys* and related genera in American waters. U.S. Fish and Wildlife Service, Fishery Bulletin, Vol. 52, p. 267-351.

55. Gray, G. A., and H. E. Winn. 1961. Reproductive ecology and sound production of the toadfish, *Opsanus tau*. Ecology, Vol. 42, p. 274-278.

56. Grimes, C. B. 1976. Certain aspects of the life history of the vermilion snapper *Rhomboplites aurorubens* (Cuvier) from North and South Carlina waters. Ph.D. thesis, University of North Carolina, Chapel Hill. 240 p.

57. Grimes, C. B., C. S. Manooch, III, G. R. Huntsman, and R. L. Dixon. 1977. Red snappers of the Carolina coast. U.S. National Marine Fisher-

ies Service, Marine Fisheries Review, Vol. 39, No. 1, p. 12-15.

58. Gudger, E. W. 1910. Habits and life history of the toadfish (*Opsanus tau*). Bulletin of the U.S. Bureau of Fisheries, Vol. 28, Pt. 2, p. 1071-1109.

59. Gulf of Mexico and South Atlantic Fishery Management Councils. 1982. Fishery management plan, final environmental impact statement, regulatory impact review for the coastal migratory pelagic resources (mackerels). Gulf of Mexico Fishery Management Council, Tampa, Fla. 250 p.

60. Hackney, P. A., W. M. Tatum, and S. L. Spencer. 1967. Life history study of the river redhorse, *Moxostoma carinatum* (Cope), in the Cahaba River, Alabama, with notes on the management of the species as a sport fish. Proceedings of the 21st Annual Conference of the Southeastern Association of Game and Fish Commissioners, p. 324-332.

61. Hall, G. E. 1971. Reservoir fisheries and limnology. American Fisheries Society, Special Publication, No. 8. 511 p.

62. Hansen, D. J. 1969. Food, growth, migration, reproduction, and abundance of pinfish, *Lagodon rhomboides*, and Atlantic croaker, *Micropogon undulatus* near Pensacola, Florida, 1963-65. U.S. National Marine Fisheries Service, Fishery Bulletin, Vol. 68, p. 135-146.

63. Heacox, C. E. 1974. The compleat brown trout. Winchester Press, New York. 182 p.

64. Hildebrand, S. F., and W. C. Schroeder. 1928. Fishes of the Chesapeake Bay. Bulletin of the U.S. Bureau of Fisheries, Vol. 53, No. 1. 388 p.

*65. Hoese, H. D., and R. H. Moore. 1977. Fishes of the Gulf of Mexico, Texas, Louisiana, and adjacent waters. Texas A & M University Press, College Station. 327 p.

66. Hogarth, W. T. 1976. Life history aspects of the wahoo, *Acanthocybium solandri* (Cuvier and Valenciennes), from the coast of North Carolina. Ph.D. thesis, North Carolina State University, Raleigh. 107 p.

67. Horvath, M. L. 1982. Age, growth, and mortality of the knobbed porgy, *Calamus nodosus*, of the South Atlantic Bight, with notes on reproduction and possible gear selectivity of the recreational fishery. M.S. thesis, Rutgers University, New Brunswick, N.J. 70 p.

*68. Hubbs, C. L., and K. F. Lagler. 1964. Fishes of the Great Lakes region. University of Michigan Press, Ann Arbor. 213 p.

*69. International Game Fish Association. 1984. World record game fish. International Game Fish Association, Fort Lauderdale, Fla. 319 p.

70. Johnson, A. G. 1983. Age and growth of yellowtail snapper from South Florida. Transactions of the American Fisheries Society, Vol. 112, p. 173-177.

71. Johnson, D. G. 1978. Development of fishes of the Mid-Atlantic Bight, an atlas of egg, larval and juvenile stages. Vol. 4, Carangidae through Ephippidae. U.S. Fish and Wildlife Service, Biological Services Program, FWS/OBS-78/12. 314 p.

72. Kelley, J. R., Jr. 1968. Growth of blue catfish *Ictalurus furcatus* (LeSueur) in the Tombigbee River of Alabama. Proceedings of the 22nd Annual Conference of the Southeastern Association of Game and Fish Commissioners, p. 248-253.

73. Kelley, J. R., Jr., and D. C. Carver. 1965. Age and growth of blue catfish,

Ictalurus furcatus (LeSueur), in the Recent Delta of the Mississippi River. Proceedings of the 19th Annual Conference of the Southeastern Association of Game and Fish Commissioners, p. 296-299.

74. Kendall, A. W. 1977. Biological and fisheries data on black sea bass, *Centropristis striata* (Linnaeus). U.S. National Marine Fisheries Service, Northeast Fisheries Center, Sandy Hook Laboratory, Technical Series Report, No. 7. 29 p.

75. Kendall, R. L. 1978. Selected coolwater fishes of North America. American Fisheries Society, Special Publication, No. 11. 438 p.

76. Koski, R. T. 1978. Age, growth, and maturity of the hogchoker, *Trinectes maculatus*, in the Hudson River, New York. Transactions of the American Fisheries Society, Vol. 107, p. 449-453.

*77. Lagler, K. F. 1956. Freshwater fishery biology. William C. Brown Co., Dubuque, Iowa. 421 p.

78. Lee, D. S., C. R. Gilbert, C. H. Hocutt, R. E. Jenkins, D. E. McAllister, and J. R. Stauffer, Jr. 1980. Atlas of North American freshwater fishes. North Carolina State Museum of Natural History, Raleigh. 854 p.

79. Lee, G. 1937. Oral gestation in the marine catfish, *Galeichthys felis*. Copeia 1937, p. 49-56.

80. Link, G. W. 1980. Age, growth, reproduction, feeding and ecological observations on the three species of *Centropristis*. Ph.D. thesis, University of North Carolina, Chapel Hill. 277 p.

81. McBride, F. T., R. I. Jones, and F. A. Harris. 1980. Growth rates and food habits of Roanoke bass in the Eno and Tar Rivers, North Carolina. Proceedings of the 34th Annual Conference of the Southeastern Association of Fish and Wildlife Agencies, p. 341-348.

82. Manooch, C. S., III. 1975. A study of the taxonomy, exploitation, life history, ecology and tagging of the red porgy, *Pagrus pagrus* Linnaeus, off North Carolina and South Carolina. Ph.D. thesis, North Carolina State University, Raleigh. 271 p.

83. Manooch, C. S., III, and C. A. Barans. 1982. Distribution, abundance, and age and growth of the tomtate, *Haemulon aurolineatum*, along the southeastern United States coast. U.S. National Marine Fisheries Service, Fishery Bulletin, Vol. 80, p. 1-19.

84. Manooch, C. S., III, and M. Haimovici. 1978. Age and growth of the gag, *Mycteroperca microlepis*, and size-age composition of the recreational catch off the southeastern United States. Transactions of the American Fisheries Society, Vol. 107, p. 234-240.

85. Manooch, C. S., III, and M. Haimovici. In press. Foods of greater amberjack, *Seriola dumerili*, and almaco jack, *Seriola rivoliana* (Pisces: Carangidae), from the South Atlantic Bight. Journal of the Elisha Mitchell Scientific Society.

86. Manooch, C. S., III, and W. W. Hassler. 1978. Synopsis of biological data on the red porgy, *Pagrus pagrus* (Linnaeus). NOAA Technical Report NMFS Circular, No. 412; and, FAO Fisheries Synopsis, No. 116. 19 p.

87. Manooch, C. S., III, and W. T. Hogarth. 1983. Stomach contents and giant trematodes from wahoo, *Acanthocybium solanderi*, collected along the south Atlantic and Gulf coasts of the United States. Bulletin of Marine Science, Vol. 33, p. 227-238.

88. Manooch, C. S., III, and D. L. Mason. 1984. Age, growth, and mortality of lane snapper collected off South Florida. Northeast Gulf Science, Vol. 7, p. 109-115.

89. Manooch, C. S., III, and D. L. Mason. 1983. Comparative food studies of yellowfin tuna, *Thunnus albacares*, and blackfin tuna, *Thunnus atlanticus*, (Pisces: Scombridae) from the southeastern and Gulf coasts of the United States. Brimleyana, No. 9, p. 33-52.

90. Manooch, C. S., III, and D. L. Mason. Unpublished manuscript. Age and growth of warsaw grouper. Located at: U.S. National Marine Fisheries Service, Southeast Fisheries Center, Beaufort Laboratory, Beaufort, N.C. 28516. 11 p.

91. Manooch, C. S., III, D. L. Mason, and R. S. Nelson. 1983. Food and gastrointestinal parasites of dolphin, *Coryphaena hippurus*, collected along the southeastern and Gulf coasts of the United States. NOAA Technical Memorandum, NMFS-SEFC-124. 36 p.

92. Manooch, C. S., III, D. L. Mason, and R. S. Nelson. Unpublished manuscript. Foods of the little tunny, *Euthynnus alletteratus*, collected along the southeastern and Gulf coasts of the United States. Located at: U.S. National Marine Fisheries Service, Southeast Fisheries Center, Beaufort Laboratory, Beaufort, N.C. 28516. 30 p.

93. Manooch, C. S., III, and R. H. Matheson, III. 1983. Age, growth and mortality of gray snapper collected from Florida waters. Proceedings of the 35th Annual Conference of the Southeastern Association of Fish and Wildlife Agencies, p. 333-346.

94. Mansueti, R. J. 1961. Movements, reproduction, and mortality of the white perch, *Roccus americanus*, in the Patuxent Estuary, Maryland. Chesapeake Science, Vol. 2, p. 142-205.

95. Mansueti, R. J., and R. Pauly. 1956. Age and growth of the northern hogchoker, *Trinectes maculatus maculatus*, in the Patuxent River, Maryland. Copeia 1956, p. 60-62.

96. Marshall, A. R. 1958. A survey of the snook fishery of Florida with studies of the biology of the principal species *Centropomus undecimalis* (Bloch). Florida Department of Natural Resources, Technical Series, No. 22, p. 1-37.

97. Matheson, R. H., III. 1981. Age, growth, and mortality of two groupers, *Epinephelus drummondhayi* Goode and Bean and *Epinephelus niveatus* (Valenciennes), from North Carolina and South Carolina. M.S. thesis, North Carolina State University, Raleigh. 67 p.

98. Matheson, R. H., III, G. R. Huntsman, and C. S. Manooch, III. In press. Life history aspects of the scamp, *Mycteroperca phenax*, collected off North Carolina and South Carolina. Bulletin of Marine Science.

99. Matthews, F. D., D. M. Dankaer, L. W. Knapp, and B. B. Collette. 1977. Food of western North Atlantic tunas (*Thunnus*) and lancetfishes (*Alepisaurus*). NOAA Technical Report NMFS Special Scientific Report—Fisheries, No. 706, p. 1-19.

100. Mayhew, J. K. 1969. Age and growth of flathead catfish in the Des Moines River, Iowa. Transactions of the American Fisheries Society, Vol. 98, p. 118-121.

101. Mercer, L. P. 1978. The reproductive biology and population dynamics of the black sea bass, *Centropristis striata*. Ph.D. thesis, College of William and Mary, Williamsburg, Va. 195 p.

102. Merriner, J. V. 1973. Assessment of the weakfish resource, a suggested management plan, and aspects of life history in North Carolina. Ph.D. thesis, North Carolina State University, Raleigh. 201 p.

103. Merriner, J. V., and W. A. Foster. 1974. Life history aspects of the tripletail, *Lobotes surinamensis* (Chordata-Pisces-Lobotidae), in North Carolina waters. Journal of the Elisha Mitchell Scientific Society, Vol. 90, p. 121-124.

104. Meyer, W. H. 1962. Life history of three species of redhorse (*Moxostoma*) in the Des Moines River, Iowa. Transactions of the American Fisheries Society, Vol. 91, p. 412-419.

105. Moe, M. A., Jr. 1969. Biology of the red grouper *Epinephelus morio* (Valenciennes) from the eastern Gulf of Mexico. Florida Department of Natural Resources, Professional Papers Series, No. 10. 95 p.

106. Morse, W. W. 1978. Biological and fisheries data on scup, *Stenotomus chrysops* (Linnaeus). U.S. National Marine Fisheries Service, Northeast Fisheries Center, Sandy Hook Laboratory, Technical Series Report, No. 14. 41 p.

107. Morse, W. W. 1980. Maturity, spawning, and fecundity of Atlantic croaker, *Micropogonias undulatus*, occurring north of Cape Hatteras, North Carolina. U.S. National Marine Fisheries Service, Fishery Bulletin, Vol. 78, p. 190-195.

108. Moyle, P. B. 1976. Inland fishes of California. University of California Press, Berkeley. 405 p.

109. Munro, J. L., V. C. Gaut, R. Thompson, and P. H. Reeson. 1973. The spawning seasons of Caribbean reef fishes. Journal of Fish Biology, Vol. 5, p. 69-84.

110. Murawski, S. A., D. G. Frank, and S. Chang. 1977. Biological and fisheries data on butterfish, *Peprilus triacanthus* (Peck). U.S. National Marine Fisheries Service, Northeast Fisheries Center, Sandy Hook laboratory, Technical Series Report, No. 6. 38 p.

111. Murawski, S. A., and A. L. Pacheco. 1977. Biological and fisheries data on Atlantic sturgeon, *Acipenser oxyrhynchus* (Mitchell). U.S. National Marine Fisheries Service, Northeast Fisheries Center, Sandy Hook Laboratory, Technical Series Report, No. 10. 69 p.

112. Nelson, R. S., and C. S. Manooch, III. 1982. Growth and mortality of red snapper in the west-central Atlantic and northern Gulf of Mexico. Transactions of the American Fisheries Society, Vol. 111, p. 465-475.

113. Olson, R. J. 1980. Synopsis of biological data on the southern bluefin, *Thunnus maccoyii* (Castelnau, 1872), p. 151-212. *In* W. H. Bayliff (ed.), Synopses of biological data on eight species of scombrids. Inter-American Tropical Tuna Commission, Special Report, No. 2.

114. Oviatt, C. A., and P. M. Kremer. 1977. Predation on the ctenophore, *Mnemiopsis leidyi*, by butterfish, *Peprilus triacanthus*, in Narragansett Bay, Rhode Island. Chesapeake Science, Vol. 18, p. 236-240.

115. Palko, B. J., G. L. Beardsley, and W. J. Richards. 1981. Synopsis of the biology of the swordfish, *Xiphias gladius* Linnaeus. NOAA Technical Report NMFS Circular, No. 441; and, FAO Fisheries Synopsis, No. 127. 21 p.

116. Palko, B. J., G. L. Beardsley, and W. J. Richards. 1982. Synopsis of the biological data on dolphin-fishes, *Coryphaena hippurus* Linnaeus and *Coryphaena equiselis* Linnaeus.

NOAA Technical Report NMFS Circular, No. 443; and, FAO Fisheries Synopsis, No. 130. 28 p.

117. Pate, P. P., Jr. 1972. Life history aspects of the hickory shad, *Alosa mediocris* (Mitchell), in the Neuse River, North Carolina. M.S. thesis, North Carolina State University, Raleigh. 66 p.

118. Pierce, R. A., and J. Davis. 1972. Age, growth, and mortality of the white perch, *Morone americana*, in the James and York Rivers, Virginia. Chesapeake Science, Vol. 13, p. 272-281.

119. Powell, A. B. 1974. Biology of the summer flounder, *Paralichthys dentatus*, in Pamlico Sound, and adjacent waters, with note comments on *P. lethostigma* and *P. albigutta*. M.S. thesis, University of North Carolina, Chapel Hill. 145 p.

120. Powles, H. 1980. Descriptions of larval silver perch, *Bairdiella chrysoura*, banded drum, *Larimus fasciatus*, and star drum, *Stellifer lanceolatus* (Sciaenidae). U.S. National Marine Fisheries Service, Fishery Bulletin, Vol. 78, p. 119-136.

121. Randall, J. E. 1967. Food habits of reef fishes of the West Indies. University of Miami, Studies in Tropical Oceanography, No. 5, p. 665-847.

*122. Randall, J. E. 1968. Caribbean reef fishes. T.F.H. Publications, Jersey City, N.J. 318 p.

123. Reed, R. J. 1971. Biology of the fallfish, *Semotilus corporalis* (Pisces, Cyprinidae). Transactions of the American Fisheries Society, Vol. 100, p. 717-725.

124. Reintjes, J. W. 1969. Synopsis of biological data on the Atlantic menhaden, *Brevoortia tyrannus*. U.S. Fish and Wildlife Service, Circular, No. 320; and, FAO Species Synopsis, No. 42. 30 p.

125. Richards, C. E., and M. Castagna. 1976. Distribution, growth, and predation of juvenile white mullet (*Mugil curema*) in oceanside waters of Virginia's eastern shore. Chesapeake Science, Vol. 17, p. 308-309.

126. Roberts, S. C. 1978. Biological and fisheries data on northern searobin, *Prionotus carolinus* (Linnaeus). U.S. National Marine Fisheries Service, Northeast Fisheries Center, Sandy Hook Laboratory, Technical Series Report, No. 13. 53 p.

*127. Robins, C. R., R. M. Bailey, C. E. Bond, J. R. Brooker, E. A. Lachner, R. N. Lea, and W. B. Scott. 1980. A list of common and scientific names of fishes from the United States and Canada. 4th ed. American Fisheries Society, Special Publication, No. 12. 174 p.

128. Ross, J. L. 1978. Life history aspects of the gray *Caulolatilus microps* (Goode and Bean, 1878). M.S. thesis, College of William and Mary, Williamsburg, Va. 120 p.

129. Ross, M. R., and R. J. Reed. 1978. The reproductive behavior of the fallfish, *Semotilus corporalis*. Copeia 1978, p. 215-221.

130. Sandow, J. T., D. R. Holder, and L. E. McSwain. 1974. Life history of the redbreast sunfish in the Satilla River, Georgia. Proceedings of the 28th Annual Conference of the Southeastern Association of Game and Fish Commissoners, p. 279-295.

131. Schaefer, R. K. 1965. Age and growth of the northern kingfish in New York waters. New York Fish and Game Journal, Vol. 12, p. 191-216.

*132. Schwartz, F. J. 1975. Sharks of North Carolina and adjacent waters. North Carolina Department of Natural and Economic Resources, Division of Marine Fisheries, Information Series. 59 p.

*133. Scott, W. B., and E. J. Crossman. 1973. Freshwater fishes of Canada. Bulletin of the Fisheries Research Board of Canada, No. 184. 866 p.

134. Sekavec, G. B. 1974. Summer foods, length-weight relationship, and condition factor of juvenile ladyfish, *Elops saurus* Linnaeus, from Louisiana coastal streams. Transactions of the American Fisheries Society, Vol. 103, p. 472-476.

135. Setzler, E. M., W. R. Boynton, K. V. Wood, H. H. Zion, L. Lubbers, N. K. Mountford, P. Frere, L. Tucker, and J. A. Mihursky. 1980. Synopsis of biological data on striped bass, *Morone saxatilis* (Walbaum). NOAA Technical Report NMFS Circular, No. 433; and, FAO Fisheries Synopsis, No. 121. 69 p.

136. Shafland, P. L., and D. H. Koehl. 1979. Laboratory rearing of the common snook. Proceedings of the 33rd Annual Conference of the Southeastern Association of Fish and Wildlife Agencies, p. 425-431.

137. Shomura, R. S., and F. Williams. 1974. Proceedings of the International Billfish Symposium, Kailua-Kona, Hawaii, 9-12 August 1972, Part 2. Review and contributed papers. NOAA Technical Report NMFS Special Scientific Report—Fisheries, No. 675. 335 p.

138. Shomura, R. S., and F. Williams. 1975. Proceedings of the International Billfish Symposium, Kailua-Kona, Hawaii, 9-12 August 1972, Part 3. Species synopses. NOAA Technical Report NMFS Special Scientific Report—Fisheries, No. 675. 159 p.

139. Sibunka, J. D., and A. L. Pacheco. 1981. Biological and fisheries data on northern puffer, *Sphoeroides maculatus* (Bloch and Schneider). U.S. National Marine Fisheries Service, Northeast Fisheries Center, Sandy Hook Laboratory, Technical Series Report, No. 26. 56 p.

140. Silva, E. I. L., and S. S. De Silva. 1981. Aspects of the biology of grey mullet, *Mugil cephalus* L., adult populations of a coastal lagoon in Sri Lanka. Journal of Fish Biology, Vol. 19, p. 1-10.

141. Silverman, M. J. 1979. Biological and fisheries data on black drum, *Pogonias cromis* (Linnaeus). U.S. National Marine Fisheries Service, Northeast Fisheries Center, Sandy Hook Laboratory, Technical Series Report, No. 22. 35 p.

142. Simmons, E. G., and J. P. Breuer. 1980. A study of redfish, *Sciaenops ocellatus* Linnaeus and black drum, *Pogonias cromis* Linnaeus. Proceedings of the 31st Meeting of the Gulf States Marine Fisheries Commission, Paper No. 5, p. 184-211.

143. Smith, D. G. 1980. Early larvae of the tarpon, *Megalops atlanticus* Valenciennes (Pisces: Elopidae) with notes on spawning in the Gulf of Mexico and the Yucatan Channel. Bulletin of Marine Science, Vol. 30, p. 136-141.

144. Smith, J. W. 1980. The life history of the cownose ray, *Rhinoptera bonasus* (Mitchell) in lower Chesapeake Bay, with notes on the management of the species. M.S. thesis, College of William and Mary, Williamsburg, Va. 151 p.

145. Smith, R. W., and F. C. Daiber. 1977. Biology of the summer flounder *Paralichthys dentatus* in Delaware Bay. U.S. National Marine Fisheries Service, Fishery Bulletin, Vol. 75, p. 823-830.

146. Smith, W. B. 1969. A preliminary report on the biology of the Roanoke bass, *Ambloplites cavifrons* Cope, in North Carolina. Proceedings of the 23rd Annual Conference of the South-

eastern Association of Game and Fish Commissioners, p. 491-500.

147. Smith, W. B. 1971. The biology of the Roanoke bass, *Ambloplites cavifrons* Cope, in North Carolina. Proceedings of the 25th Annual Conference of the Southeastern Association of Game and Fish Commissioners, p. 561-570.

148. South Atlantic Fishery Management Council. 1981. Source document for the fishery management plan for the snapper-grouper complex of the South Atlantic region. South Atlantic Fishery Management Council, Charleston, S.C. [223 p.]

149. Starck, W. A., II, and R. E. Schroeder. 1971. Investigations on the gray snapper, *Lutjanus griseus*. University of Miami, Studies in Tropical Oceanography, Vol. 10. 224 p.

150. Stickney, R. R., G. L. Taylor, and D. B. White. 1975. Food habits of five species of young southeastern United States estuarine Scianenidae. Chesapeake Science, Vol. 16, p. 104-114.

151. Stokes, G. M. 1977. Life history studies of southern flounder (*Paralichthys lethostigma*) and Gulf flounder (*P. albigutta*) in the Aransas Bay area of Texas. Texas Parks and Wildlife Department, Technical Series, No. 25, p. 1-37.

152. Street, M. W. 1970. Some aspects of the life histories of hickory shad, *Alosa mediocris* (Mitchill) and blueback herring, *Alosa aestivalis* (Mitchill) in the Altamaha River, Georgia. M.S. thesis, University of Georgia, Athens. 86 p.

153. Tabb, D. C. 1961. A contribution to the biology of the spotted seatrout, *Cynoscion nebulosus* (Cuvier) of east central Florida. Florida Board of Conservation, Marine Research Laboratory, Technical Series, No. 35. 22 p.

154. Tardif, C., and C. S. Manooch, III. Unpublished manuscript. Age, growth, and length-weight relationship of the spottail pinfish, *Diplodus holbrooki*, in the South Atlantic Bight. Located at: U.S. National Marine Fisheries Service, Southeast Fisheries Center, Beaufort Laboratory, Beaufort, N.C. 28516. 8 p.

155. Tatum, W. M., and P. A. Hackney. 1969. Age and growth of river redhorse, *Moxostoma carinatum* (Cope) from the Cahaba River, Alabama. Proceedings of the 23rd Annual Conference of the Southeastern Association of Game and Fish Commissioners, p. 255-261.

*156. Trautman, M. B. 1957. The fishes of Ohio. Ohio State University Press, Columbus. 683 p.

157. Turner, P. R. 1980. Procedures for age determination and growth rate calculations of flathead catfish. Proceedings of the 34th Annual Conference of the Southeastern Association of Fish and Wildlife Agencies, p. 253-262.

158. Turner, P. R., and R. C. Summerfelt. 1970. Food habits of adult flathead catfish, *Pylodictis olivaris* (Rafinesque), in Oklahoma reservoirs. Proceedings of the 24th Annual Conference of the Southeastern Association of Game and Fish Commissioners, p. 387-400.

159. van der Elst, R. P. 1981. Use of the bill during feeding in the black marlin (*Makaira indica*). Copeia 1981, p. 215.

160. Volpe, A. V. 1959. Aspects of the biology of the common snook, *Centropomus undecimalis* (Bloch) of southwest Florida. Florida Board of Conservation, Marine Research Laboratory, Technical Series, No. 31, p. 1-37.

161. Walburg, C. H., and P. R. Nichols. 1967. Biology and management of the American shad and status of the fisheries, Atlantic coast of the United States, 1960. U.S. Fish and Wildlife Service, Special Scientific Report —Fisheries, No. 550. 105 p.

162. Walls, J. G. 1975. Fishes of the northern Gulf of Mexico. T. F. H. Publications, Neptune, N.J. 432 p.

163. Waltz, C. W., W. A. Roumillat, and C. A. Wenner. 1981. Biology of the whitebone porgy, *Calamus leucosteus* in the South Atlantic Bight. South Carolina Wildlife and Marine Resources Department, Charleston. 44 p.

164. Wilber, R. L. 1969. The redear sunfish in Florida. Florida Game and Fresh Water Fish Commission, Fishery Bulletin, No. 5. 64 p.

165. Wilk,, S. J. 1977. Biological and fisheries data on bluefish, *Pomatomus saltatrix* (Linnaeus). U.S. National Marine Fisheries Service, Northeast Fisheries Center, Sandy Hook Laboratory, Technical Series Report, No. 11. 56 p.

166. Wilk, S. J. 1979. Biological and fisheries data on weakfish, *Cynoscion regalis* (Bloch and Schneider). U.S. National Marine Fisheries Service, Northeast Fisheries Center, Sandy Hook Laboratory, Technical Series Report, No. 21. 49 p.

167. Wise, J. P. 1961. Synopsis of biological data on cod *Gadus morhua* Linnaeus 1758. FAO Fisheries Biology Synopsis, No. 21. 58 p.

168. Yoshida, H. O. 1979. Synopsis of biological data on tunas of the genus *Euthynnus*. NOAA Technical Report NMFS Circular, No. 429; and, FAO Fisheries Synopsis, No. 122. 57 p.

169. Yoshida, H. O. 1980. Synopsis of biological data on bonitos of the genus *Sarda*. NOAA Technical Report NMFS Circular, No. 432; and, FAO Fisheries Synopsis, No. 118. 50 p.

PARTS OF A HYPOTHETICAL FISH

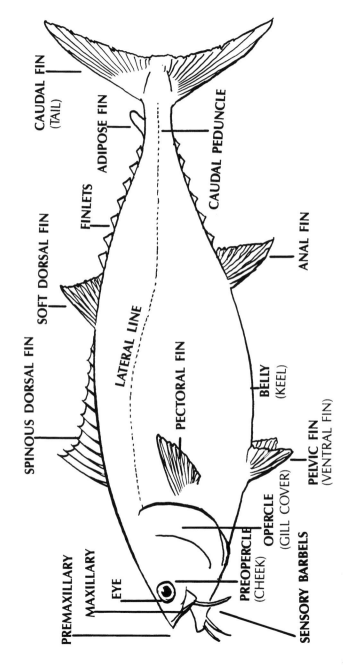

CAUDAL FIN (TAIL)

ADIPOSE FIN

CAUDAL PEDUNCLE

FINLETS

ANAL FIN

SOFT DORSAL FIN

SPINOUS DORSAL FIN

LATERAL LINE

PECTORAL FIN

BELLY (KEEL)

PELVIC FIN (VENTRAL FIN)

PREMAXILLARY

MAXILLARY

EYE

PREOPERCLE (CHEEK)

OPERCLE (GILL COVER)

SENSORY BARBELS

329

GLOSSARY

Adhesive—Sticky.

Adipose Fin—A relatively small fleshy fin on the back of some fishes between the dorsal and caudal fins.

Adipose Membrane—A membrane covering the surface of the eyeball except for a vertical slit.

Air Bladder—A gas-filled sac in the body cavity below the vertebrae (swim bladder).

Ammocoetes—The larvae of any of various lampreys.

Anadromous—Fishes living in the sea and entering fresh water to spawn.

Anal Fin—The fin on the median ventral line between the anus (vent) and the tail.

Anal Spines—Stiff, pointed processes located on the anterior portion of the anal fin.

Anatomical—Pertaining to the anatomy or structure of the body.

Aquatic—Of, or pertaining to water.

Barbels—Slender, tactile (sensory), whiskerlike projections extending from the head of some fishes.

Benthic—Bottom dwelling.

Blind Side—The side in flatfishes without eyes.

Brackish—Slightly salty.

Carnivores—Flesh eaters.

Cartilage—A translucent, elastic connective tissue usually forming part or all of the skeleton.

Catadromous—Fish living in fresh water but spawning in the sea.

Caudal Fin—The tail fin.

Caudal Peduncle—The slender portion of a fish's body just in front of the tail fin.

Caudal Saddle—A mark or blotch of color saddling the caudal peduncle of some fishes.

Charter Boats—Boats for hire that usually carry six or fewer passengers and charge by the trip.

Ciguatera—Poisoning caused by eating fish with flesh toxic to man.

Circumtropical—Encompassing the tropical regions of the world.

Claspers—A pair of male reproductive organs on the front of the pelvic fins of sharks, rays, and skates.

Cosmopolitan—Pertaining to many parts of the world.

Creel—The catch, or take of fish; a basket for holding fish.

Crepuscular—Active at twilight.

Ctenoid Scale—Bony scale with tiny spines on the exposed surface.

Cycloid Scale—Bony scale with a smooth surface.

Demersal—Bottom dwelling.

Denticle—A small tooth, or toothlike part.

Dentition—The type, arrangement, and number of teeth of an animal.

Detritus—Finely divided material suspended in the water that usually settles to the bottom; organic detritus from the decomposition of organisms.

Digenetic Trematodes—Internal parasitic worms that have two or more hosts.

Disk Width—The distance from the tip of one extented pectoral fin to the other on skates and rays.

Dorsal Fin—The median fin on the back of fishes. It may be divided into spiny-rayed and soft-rayed parts.

Elasmobranchs—Group of fishes—including skates, sharks, and rays—that have cartilaginous skeletons and five to seven pairs of gill openings.

Elvers—Young eels, especially those migrating upstream from the ocean.

Embryo—A young animal in the early stages of growth before birth or hatching.

Endemic—Belonging or native to a particular place.

Encapsulated—Surrounded; enclosed in or formed in a capsule.

Estuary—An area where salt water is measurably diluted by fresh water; usually the lower course of a river where its current is met and influenced by tides.

Euryhaline—Able to live in waters having a wide range of salinity.

Eyed Side—The side in flatfishes that has eyes.

Fathometer—An electronic instrument used to indicate water depth, profile of the bottom, and concentrations of fish.

Fecundity—The number of eggs produced by a mature female.

Fetus—An unborn or unhatched young vertebrate, especially one in the later stages of development.

Filamentous—Composed of filaments or threads.

Finlets—A series of small, usually separate fin rays situated behind the main dorsal or anal fin.

Fishing Machine—A fishing device consisting of lift nets or scoops attached to poles and turned by the currents of a river. Two parallel-positioned wooden boats serve to float the gear and also to store the captured fish.

Fork Length—The measurement from the tip of a fish's snout to the fork in the tail.

Fusiform—Shaped like a spindle; tapered at both ends.

Fyke Net—A fixed conical, cylindrical net distended by a series of hoops covered by web netting and having one or more internal, funnel-shaped throats. The net has one or two wings or walls of netting that direct migrating fish into the main net.

Ganoid Scale—A diamond-shaped scale having an enamel-like surface and not overlapping to any extent.

Gelatinous—Having the nature of jelly; thick and viscous.

Generic—Pertaining to genus, or the first of two scientific names of a fish.

Genetic—Dealing with resemblances and differences of related organisms; pertaining to the science of heredity.

Gestation—The time from conception to birth.

Gig—To spear; an instrument for spearing.

Gill Arches—The bony supports to which the gills are attached.

Gill Net—An upright floating or anchored fence of netting in which the fish become entangled as they swim into it.

Gill Rakers—A series of bony projections attached to the inside of the gill arches, used to strain food from the water.

Gravid—Pregnant.

Habitat—The type of place where a given animal or plant normally lives or grows.

Handline—A single line with one or more baited hooks held or attended by one person. In some cases the line is attached to a pole.

Head Boats—Boats for hire that charge on a per passenger basis, thus by the head. The boats are capable of carrying from about 10 to over 100 anglers.

Hoop Net—Like a fyke net but without wing nets.

Hybrid—The offspring of two animals or plants of different species, races, breeds, varieties, or other genetically dissimilar forms.

Incisors—Front teeth flattened to form a cutting edge.

Incubation—The act of causing development of unborn young; time from fertilization to hatching.

Inferior—Below and often somewhat behind another structure.

Intergrade—To merge gradually one kind with another through a continuous series.

Intermuscular Bones—Small bones lying between muscles of some fishes.

Isthmus—Fleshy area extending forward on the throat between the gills.

Keel—See Lateral Keel.

Lamphredin—Enzyme secreted by lampreys.
Larva—The early form of a fish that at hatching is fundamentally unlike its parent.
Lateral—Pertaining to the side.
Lateral Keel—A ridge situated on the side.
Lateral Line—A longitudinal line on each side of a fish's body, composed of pores opening into sensory organs.
Leptocephalus—The small-headed, transparent, ribbonlike pelagic first larva of various eels and some other fishes.
Longevity—Length or duration of life.
Longline—An extremely long, horizontal line with a series of baited hooks on short, separate, but attached, lines. The gear may be anchored and fished on the bottom or surface, or left floating and fished on the surface.
Loran—A device by which a navigator can locate his position by determining the time displacement between radio signals from two known stations.

Mandible—Lower jaw.
Maturity—The age (size) when a fish is able to reproduce.
Molars—Grinding teeth usually situated toward the back of the mouth.

Natal—Pertaining to a fish's birth; usually in reference to its place of birth.
Nocturnal—Active at night.
Nonstriated—Not marked with furrows, stripes, or streaks.
Nuchal—Relating to, or lying in, the region of the back of the neck (nape).
Nursery—Any place where something is bred, nourished, or fostered.

Ocellus—A spot of color encircled by a band of another color.
Oligotrophic—Deficient or low in plant nutrients; relatively sterile.
Olivaceous—A deep shade of green; olive.
Omnivorous—Eating all kinds of foods indiscriminately.
Opercular Flap—A fleshy extension of the rear edge of the gill cover.
Operculum—The gill cover (opercle).
Opportunistic—Nonselective in feeding.
Organic—Characteristic of, pertaining to, or derived from living organisms.
Oshushi—Raw fish usually served on small rice patties.
Otoliths—The bones found in the inner ear of fishes.
Outcropping—The part of a rock formation that appears at the surface of the ground, or bottom of the sea.
Outriggers—Two long, whiplike poles mounted on boats and used to troll baits for billfish.
Ova—Eggs.
Ovary—The female reproductive gland that produces eggs.

Oviparous—Producing eggs that are matured or hatched after being expelled from the body.

Ovoviviparous—Producing eggs that develop within the maternal body and hatch within, or immediately after extrusion from the parent.

Pairing—Behavior of two courting fish just prior to spawning.

Pectoral Fins—The paired fins attached to the shoulder girdle, immediately behind the gill opening.

Peduncle—See Caudal Peduncle.

Pelagic—Living or growing in the region of free water in seas and inland lakes.

Pelvic Fins—The paired hind fins (ventral fins).

Peritoneum—The membrane lining of the body cavity.

Pharyngeals—Grinding teeth in the throat of some fishes.

Phototrophic Negative—Orientation away from light; an organism that avoids light.

Planer—A small hydrodynamically designed piece of metal that when trolled behind a boat, pulls the line and bait deep below the surface and is triggered to rise to the surface when a fish strikes.

Plankton—The small animals and plants that float or drift in the water, usually on or near the surface.

Pod—A small group of several fish.

Polygamy—The practice or condition of having more than one female mate.

Population—The whole number of a species inhabiting or occupying a specific geographical locality.

Potamodrous—Migrating in fresh water; making short spawning runs in fresh water.

Pound Net—A fixed entrapment fishing gear consisting of a large enclosure (pound or pocket), and a smaller one from the entrance to which a straight wall of netting extends shoreward.

Ppt—Parts per thousand.

Predator—An animal that captures or feeds on another.

Preopercular Margin—Posterior edge of the preopercle bone.

Preoperculum—Bone before or in front of the opercle.

Profile—The side view or outline, such as the profile or relief of the ocean floor.

Protogynous Hermaphrodite—A fish that changes sex from female to male with age (size).

Protractile—Capable of being extended forward.

Protuberance—A rounded projection.

Redd—A spawning site constructed on the bottom by certain freshwater fishes, especially trouts and salmons.

Riffles—Areas in relatively shallow, fast-flowing rivers and streams where the contour of the bottom causes visible disturbances in the water.

Roe—Eggs.

Salinity—The quality or state of being saline; salt content of the water, often measured in parts per thousand (0/00).

Sargassum—Any of several brown algae that are widely distributed in the warmer waters; the floating common gulfweed.

Sashimi—A dish of raw fish.

Scute—An external horny or bony plate or scale.

Sea Wrack—Seaweeds, especially of the larger kinds, cast up on the beach.

Seine—A fine-mesh net having the top edge lined with floats and the bottom edge with sinkers so that it hangs vertically in the water. The net is used to surround fish and is pulled by hand, vehicles on the shore, or boats.

Semianadromous—Partially anadromous.

Semibuoyant—Partially floating, such as a fish egg that will remain suspended with the aid of water currents.

Serrated—Having sharp teeth.

Sexual Dimorphism—Body form or shape related to sex or sexual development.

Spear—Another name for a billfish's bill.

Spiracle—Airhole; a breathing hole.

Stock—A reproductively distinct population of fish; to move from one place to another, as when introducing a species to a body of water where it does not naturally occur.

Substrate—The base on which organisms live; underlying surface.

Subterminal—Situated or occurring near but not precisely at an end.

Suctorial—Adapted for sucking.

Synchronous Hermaphrodite—Both sexes functioning in the same fish at the same time.

Tailrace—The channel, race, or flume leading away from below a dam.

Terminal—At the end or tip.

Territorial—Associated with or restricted to a particular territory or district; defending a certain portion of habitat.

Terrestrial—Of or pertaining to the earth.

Tetrodotoxin—A poison found in certain members of the fish family Tetraodontidae.

Total Length—The measurement from the tip of a fish's snout to the tip of the tail.

Toxin—A poison.

Trammel Net—Like a gill net but consisting of three panels of netting instead of one.

Translucent—Transmitting light diffusely or imperfectly.

Transverse—To cross.

Traps—Wire or wooden rectangular or square cages, usually placed on the bottom and baited to catch fish.

Trawl—A large, small-mesh, funnel-shaped net that is towed by a boat at the surface or on the bottom. Rectangular boards, floats, and sinkers keep the mouth of the net open.

Trotline—A long line fixed on both ends and having numerous shorter perpendicular branched lines placed at intervals with baited hooks attached.

Turbid—Opaque or muddy with particles of extraneous matter; not clear or transparent.

Uric Acid—A compound that is present in urine.

Vent—Anus; the posterior external opening of the intestine.

Ventral Fins—The pelvic fins.

Viscera—The soft internal organs in the cavities of an animal's body.

Viviparous—Producing living young instead of eggs from within the body in the manner of nearly all mammals, many reptiles, and a few fishes.

Weir—A fence or enclosure set to capture fish.

Xanthid—A yellow phase.

2007 IGFA ALL-TACKLE WORLD RECORDS

FRESH WATER

Species	Weight (lb-oz)	Place (yr)
Bass, Largemouth	22-4	Montgomery Lake, GA (1932)
Bass, Redeye	8-3	Flint River, GA (?)
Bass, Rock	3-0	York River, Ontario, Canada (1974)
Bass, Rock	3-0	Lake Erie, PA (1998)
Bass, Smallmouth	11-15	Dale Hollow Lake, TN (1955)
Bass, Spotted	10-4	Pine Flat Lake, CA (2001)
Bass, Striped (landlocked)	67-8	O'Neill Forebay, Los Banos, CA (1992)
Bass, White	6-13	Lake Orange, Orange, VA (1989)
Bluegill	4-12	Ketona Lake, AL (1950)
Bowfin	21-8	Forest Lake, Florence, SC (1980)
Bullhead, Black	7-7	Mill Pond, Long Island, NY (1993)
Bullhead, Brown	6-5	Lake Mahopac, NY (2002)
Bullhead, Yellow	4-15	Ogeechee River, GA (2003)
Carp,Common	75-11	Lac de St. Cassien, France (1987)
Catfish, Blue	124-0	Mississippi River, Alton, IL (2005)
Catfish, Channel	58-0	Santee-Cooper Res., SC (1964)
Catfish, Flathead	123-0	Elk City Res., Independence, KS (1998)
Catfish, White	19-5	Oakdale, CA (2005)
Crappie, Black	5-0	Private Lake, MO (2006)
Crappie, White	5-3	Enid Dam, MS (1957)
Fallfish	3-8	Lake Winnipesaukee, NH (1991)
Flier	1-4	Little River, Spring Lake, NC (1988)
Flier	1-4	Lowndes County, GA (1996)
Gar, Alligator	279-0	Rio Grande, TX (1951)
Gar, Florida	10-0	Florida Everglades, FL (2002)
Gar, Longnose	50-5	Trinity River, TX (1954)
Gar, Shortnose	5-12	Rend Lake, IL (1995)
Gar, Spotted	9-12	Lake Mexia, Mexia, TX (1994)
Muskellunge	67-8	Haywood, WS (1949)
Perch, White	3-1	Forest Hill Park, NJ (1989)
Perch, Yellow	4-3	Bordentown, NJ (1865?)
Pickerel, Chain	9-6	Homerville, GA (1961)
Pickerel, Redfin	2-4	Gall Berry Swamp, NC (1997)
Pike, Northern	55-1	Lake of Grefeern, W.Germany (1986)
Pumpkinseed	1-6	Mexico, NY (1985)

Species	Weight (lb-oz)	Place (yr)
Redhorse, River	8-11	Trent River, Ontario, Canada (1997)
Redhorse, Silver	11-7	Plumb Creek, WS (1985)
Salmon, Atlantic	79-2	Tana River, Norway (1928)
Sauger	8-12	Lake Sakakawea, N.D. (1971)
Shad, American	11-4	Connecticut River, MA (1986)
Shad, Gizzard	4-6	Lake Michigan, IN (1996)
Shad, Hickory	2-8	James River, Richmond, VA (2006)
Sturgeon, White	468-0	Benicia, CA (1983)
Sunfish, Green	2-2	Stockton Lake, MO (1971)
Sunfish, Longear	1-12	Elephant Butte Lake, NM (1985)
Sunfish, Redbreast	1-12	Suwannee River, FL (1984)
Sunfish, Redear	5-7	Diversion Canal, SC (1998)
Trout, Brook	14-8	Nipigon River, Ontario, Canada (1916)
Trout, Brown	40-4	Little Red River, AR (1992)
Trout, Rainbow	42-2	Bell Island, AK (1970)
Walleye	25-0	Old Hickory Lake, TN (1960)
Warmouth	2-7	Guess Lake, Holt, FL (1985)

SALT WATER

Allbacore	88-2	Gran Canaria, Canary Is., Spain (1977)
Amberjack, Greater	155-12	Bermuda (1992)
Barracuda, Great	85-0	Christmas Is., Repub. of Kiribati (1992)
Bass, Black Sea	10-4	Virginia Beach, VA 2000)
Bluefish	31-12	Hatteras, NC (1972)
Bonefish	19-0	Zululand, Republic South Africa (1962)
Bonito, Atlantic	18-4	Faial Island, Azores (1953)
Catfish, Hardhead	3-5	Sebastian, FL (1993)
Cobia	135-9	Shark Bay, W.A., Australia (1985)
Cod, Atlantic	98-12	Isle of Shoals, NH (1969)
Croaker, Atlantic	5-8	Dauphin Island, AL (2000)
Dogfish, Smooth	26-12	Galveston, TX (1998)
Dolphin	87-0	Papagallo Gulf, Costa Rica (1976)
Drum, Black	113-1	Lawes, DE (1975)
Drum, Red	94-2	Avon, NC (1984)
Eel, American	9-4	Cape May, NJ (1995)
Eel, Conger	15-0	Cape May Harbor, NJ (2002)

Species	Weight (lb-oz)	Place (yr)
Flounder, Gulf	6-4	Dauphin Island, AL (1996)
Flounder, Southern	20-9	Nassau Sound, FL (1983)
Flounder, Summer	22-7	Montauk, NY (1975)
Grouper, Black	124-0	Gulf of Mexico, TX (2003)
Grouper, Gag	80-6	Destin, FL (1993)
Grouper, Red	42-4	St. Augustine, FL (1997)
Grouper, Snowy	37-9	Virginia Beach, VA (2006)
Grouper, Warsaw	436-12	Gulf of Mexico, FL (1985)
Grouper, Yellowedge	41-1	Gulf of Mexico, Destin, FL (1998)
Grunt, Tomtate	1-4	Hatteras, NC (2006)
Grunt, White	6-8	North Brunswick, GA (1989)
Halibut, Atlantic	418-13	Vannaya Troms, Norway (2004)
Hind, Red	8-7	East Flower Gardens Bank, FL (2004)
Hind, Speckled	52-8	Destin, FL (1994)
Hogfish	21-6	Frying Pan Tower, NC (2005)
Jack, Almaco	78-0	Argus Bank, Bermuda (1990)
Jack, Crevalle	58-6	Barra do Kwanza, Angola (2000)
Kingfish, Gulf	3-0	Salvo, NC (1999)
Kingfish, Northern	2-7	Salvo, NC (2000)
Kingfish, Southern	2-13	Virginia Beach, VA (2002)
Ladyfish	8-0	Sepatiba Bay, Brazil (2006)
Mackerel, King	93-0	San Juan, Puerto Rico (1999)
Mackerel, Spanish	13-0	Ocracoke Inlet, NC (1987)
Marlin, Blue (Atlantic)	1402-2	Vitoria, Brazil (1992)
Marlin, White	181-14	Vitoria, Brazil (1979)
Permit	60-0	Ilha do Mel, Paranagua, Brazil (2002)
Pinfish	3-5	Horn Island, MS (1992)
Pollock	50-0	Salstraumen, Norway (1995)
Pompano, African	50-8	Daytona Beach, FL (1990)
Pompano, Florida	8-4	Port St. Joe Bay, FL (1999)
Porgy, Knobbed	5-12	Gulf of Mexico, TX (2000)
Porgy, Red	17-0	Gibraltar (1997)
Porgy, Whitebone	3-5	Orange Beach, AL (2003)
Sailfish (Atlantic)	141-1	Luanda, Angola (1994)
Scamp	29-10	Dauphin Island, AL (2000)
Scup	4-9	Nantucket Sound, MA (1992)
Seatrout, Spotted	17-7	Ft. Pierce, FL (1995)

Species	Weight (lb-oz)	Place (yr)
Shark, Blacktip	270-9	Malindi Bay, Kenya (1984)
Shark, Blue	528-0	Montauk Point, NY (2001)
Shark, Great Hammerhead	1280-0	Boca Grande, FL (2006)
Shark, Porbeagle	507-0	Pentland Firth, Scotland (1993)
Shark, Sand Tiger	350-2	Charleston Jetty, SC (1993)
Shark, Scalloped Hammerhead	353-0	Key West, FL (2004)
Shark, Shortfin Mako	1221-0	Chatham, MA (2001)
Shark, Silky	762-12	Port Stephen's, Australia (1994)
Shark, Spinner	197-12	Malindi, Kenya (1999)
Shark, Thresher	767-3	Bay of Islands, New Zealand (1983)
Shark, Tiger	1785-11	Ulladulla, Australia (2004)
Shark, Tiger	1780-0	Cherry Grove, SC (1964)
Shark, White	2664-0	Ceduna, South Australia (1959)
Sheepshead	21-4	New Orleans, LA (1982)
Snapper, Cubera	121-8	Cameron, LA (1982)
Snapper, Gray	17-0	Port Canaveral, FL (1992)
Snapper, Lane	8-3	Horseshoe Rigs, MS (2001)
Snapper, Red	50-4	Gulf of Mexico, LA (1996)
Snapper, Silk	18-5	Venice, FL (1986)
Snapper, Vermilion	7-3	Gulf of Mexico, Mobile, AL (1987)
Snapper, Yellowtail	11-0	Challenger Bank, Bermuda (2004)
Snook, Common	53-10	Parismina Ranch, Costa Rica (1978)
Spadefish, Atlantic	14-0	Chesapeake Bay, VA (1986)
Spearfish, Longbill	127-13	Gran Canaria, Spain (1999)
Spot	1-6	Virginia Beach, VA (2004)
Spot	1-7	Hampton Roads Bridge, VA (2004)
Swordfish	1182-0	Iquique, Chile (1953)
Tarpon	286-9	Rubane, Guinea-Bissau (2003)
Tautog	25-0	Ocean City, NJ (1998)
Tilefish, Blueline	17-7	Norfolk Canyon, VA (2006)
Tilefish (Great Northern)	56-5	Canyons, NY (2005)
Toadfish, Oyster	4-15	Ocracoke, NC (1994)
Triggerfish, Gray	13-9	Murrells Inlet, SC (1989)
Tripletail	42-5	Zululand, Republic South Africa (1989)
Tuna, Bigeye (Atlantic)	392-6	Gran Canaria, Spain (1996)
Tuna, Blackfin	49-6	Marathon, FL (2006)
Tuna, Bluefin	1496-0	Aulds Cove, N.S., Canada (1979)
Tuna, Skipjack	45-4	Baja California, Mexico (1996)
Tuna, Yellowfin	388-12	Isla San Benedicto, Mexico (1977)
Tunny, Little	35-2	Cape de Garde, Algeria (1988)
Wahoo	184-0	Cabo San Lucas, Mexico (2005)
Weakfish	19-2	Jones Beach Inlet, NY (1984)
Weakfish	19-2	Delaware Bay, DE (1989)

INDEX TO RECIPES

INDEX TO SCIENTIFIC NAMES

A number in bold type indicates a color plate.

348

INDEX TO COMMON NAMES

A number in bold type indicates a color plate.

353

357